FROM THE COCKPIT

Bruce McLaren

FROM THE COCKPIT

FREDERICK MULLER LIMITED
LONDON

Originally published in 1964 by Frederick Muller Limited
This reprint published in October 2016

ISBN 978-1-910505-14-4

Published by Evro Publishing
Westrow House, Holwell, Sherborne, Dorset DT9 5LF

Printed and bound in China
by 1010 Printing International Ltd

www.evropublishing.com

To Pop

PREFACE

By Amanda McLaren

THIS BOOK WAS ORIGINALLY published in 1964. In it, my father describes his time as a young boy battling a crippling disease, through his early career and the formation of Bruce McLaren Motor Racing, to the death of his team mate, Timmy Mayer, in 1964. It was this tragic accident that prompted my father to write an epitaph for Timmy that later became his own.

'To do something well is so worthwhile that to die trying to do it better cannot be foolhardy. It would be a waste of life to do nothing with one's ability for I feel that life is measured in achievement, not in years alone.'

'Achievement' has become synonymous with McLaren.

In the 12 years after leaving New Zealand, my father's achievements included being the youngest driver to win a Grand Prix, winning the 24 Hours of Le Mans, only the second driver in history to win a Grand Prix in their own car, and domination of the mighty Canadian-American Challenge Cup series (Can-Am).

After my father's death in 1970, the team perpetuated his memory with victories at the Indianapolis 500 and two coveted F1 championships. Following the merger with Project 4, the team is now one of the most successful F1 teams in history.

It was also my father's dream to produce road cars. He designed, built and drove the prototype M6BGT but unfortunately this project did not come to fruition. Now, almost 50 years after his death, McLaren Automotive is fulfilling that dream with a range of high-performance supercars and sports cars.

As Brand Ambassador for McLaren Automotive, I am endorsing the relationship between my father's achievements and the current cars of which I am convinced he would be extremely proud.

My mother was fully supportive of the reprinting of this book but sadly did not live to see this happen. Throughout her life she remained a stalwart supporter of the racing team and of McLaren Automotive. I dedicate this reprint of my father's book, the story of their adventures and the triumphs and tragedies of motor racing in the 1960s, to both my parents.

CONTENTS

ILLUSTRATIONS

The following supplied photographs for reproduction in this book and are acknowledged with grateful thanks:

Michael R. Hewett; Robert de Hoé; Bryon Kallend; Barry McKay; Dr. Benno Müller; Planet News; *Auckland Star*; B. C. Stevens; H. N. Vachon; Franco Villani; Studio Wörner.

Introduction

IT WAS AS though I had been dreaming, except that it seemed a bit harder to wake up. I opened my eyes a couple of times. At least I thought I did. But I didn't see anything. Then I was suddenly wide awake. There were other people in the room, all sitting on beds and peering at me. Some with bandaged heads, others with arms or legs in plaster. I'm in hospital, I thought, but I didn't feel excited or alarmed. I closed my eyes again and wondered why I was there.

Thoughts filtered down like letters being dropped in a post-box and I tried to assemble them. I was dreaming again about riding in the back of an ambulance. Someone with a big smile was assuring me I was all right. I made a conscious effort, opened my eyes again and found I was still in the hospital bed. I must have had an accident.

Then I remembered. I had been in the German Grand Prix on the Nürburgring. The top half of me looked all right. Arms were intact. Head undamaged. What about my legs? I ran my hands underneath the blankets and felt. Thighs, knees, calves, feet—all OK. I lay back feeling happier.

It must have been on the third lap. I remembered Graham Hill waving me by, just after the pits. His BRM was in some sort of trouble. What then? I recalled diving down through the woods with John Surtees' Ferrari and Jimmy Clark's Lotus not far ahead.

But this bed was lovely and comfortable. It was all rather strange. I felt fine, really. The people sitting on the other beds were smiling now and talking to each other in German.

Then it struck me. I was in the little hospital in Adenau, where I had once visited Peter Arundell when his Lotus had left the road on the 'Ring.

I tried to pick up the threads again. . . . I was motoring down through the woods, over the bridge, up towards the Flugplatz, over the hump, still chasing the red Ferrari and green Lotus. Could I catch them in a lap? It was worth a try . . . but what had happened after that?

I had obviously had a crash. But had I put all these other people in hospital? I resolved to ask the first person who came in.

People are always telling us motor racing is dangerous. "One of these days you'll be walking around with your head under your arm," a friend once joked.

Most racing drivers have some sort of accident during their career and deep in my heart I knew there was no reason why I should be an exception. I think this might have been why I wasn't alarmed at finding myself in hospital. I had probably been subconsciously prepared for this moment for the previous five years.

I had been very lucky and was well aware of the fact. Ten years earlier, almost to the month, I had been gunning my little Ulster Austin up a loose metal hill-climb in New Zealand in my first-ever try at competition driving. Ten years of motor racing and although I'd had my share of narrow escapes I'd never actually been involved in a major crash. Until now.

Accidents had always been things that happened to other people. I'd had plenty of "moments" and phenomenal near-misses but this was the first time the Reaper and I had crossed scythes, so to speak.

I had once promised myself I would give up motor racing if I had a major crash. Well, this was it. I wasn't quite sure what had happened, but knew I must have gone off the road in a fairly big way.

I lay back and considered what motor racing had done for me in the ten years from being a secretly scared sixteen-year-old in an Austin Seven to a twenty-six-year-old "veteran" in the current European formula-one school.

It took me only a few seconds to talk myself out of retiring from what, to me, is the greatest sport in the world. Then, as the German doctor administered another sedative I relaxed to ponder on the career I had briefly considered ending.

ONE

"Dicing" in a Bathchair

IT IS SAID that racing drivers are born not made, but I guess I happened along somewhere in between these two categories.

My father runs a service station and garage business in New Zealand and from a tender age I was involved with cars. I might have been too young to drive, or even see over the steering wheel for that matter, but I was quite capable of tumbling off running boards, jamming my fingers in doors and carrying out some unwarranted underside checking to the detriment of clean clothes.

My grandfather started one of the early bus and truck businesses in Auckland before the first war and since then there has always been a McLaren connected with motor transport. In those days an operator had to be his own designer, engineer and mechanic, as well as a businessman.

My father and his three brothers were motor-cycle addicts and between them almost dominated the sport locally. Races and hill-climbs were the main events in which they specialized and at times they would scoop the field, taking first four places and making the whole thing a bit of a McLaren monopoly. Pop was the oldest, and usually had the best-prepared bike; as a result he often led home the McLaren quartet.

I arrived on the McLaren motoring scene on August 30th,

1937, and as I was only a bouncing two-year-old when the second war called a halt to motor-sport, remember nothing of the McLaren brothers' two-wheel exploits. I do have vague recollections of Pop competing in a trial on a Royal Enfield soon after the war, but he must have decided motor-cycle racing was a young man's game and turned his attention to cars.

After saying good-bye to pram and pushchair and venturing into the uncertain world of self-propulsion on my own two legs, my next goal was a tricycle. In 1936 Pop had given up his position on the transport side of the Caltex Oil Company and bought a service station in Remuera, a pleasant, scenic suburb of Auckland.

During the war the most regular and persistent customer at McLaren's Service Station was, needless to say, yours truly on the smartest trike in Auckland. This fine machine required a service at least once a day and something close to a major overhaul every other day. Perhaps foreseeing a life bound up with things mechanical, I apparently insisted on doing all the maintenance myself, usually grabbing just the spanner a mechanic's greasy hand was groping for, from underneath a lorry, while he held up a sump with the other. The day the trike was sold must have been a cause for secret celebration by the Staff.

The first car I can remember was Pop's Singer Le Mans, a four-seater version which didn't look as good as the two-seater with the slab tank on the back, but enabled Pop to transport the growing McLaren family around in reasonable comfort, while still retaining an air of sportiness.

I came midway along my particular branch of the family tree, my sister Patricia being seven years older than I and Janice ten years younger.

Janice was just a baby in the Singer's day and Pop realized that soon he would have to start looking for something a little larger and perhaps slightly more like a family carriage than a racing car.

He soon found the answer in a 1935 SS I, a fine-looking car with a long cream bonnet, flared brown wings and huge head-lamps. Wonderful! It was huge compared with the Singer but the previous owner had looked after it and the appearance belied its twelve years. I had heard Pop excitedly describing the car to Mother when he first discovered it and was worried at the thought of the "bucket" seats. According to my limited vocabulary at the time, we seemed about to be transported in a row of kitchen pails!

Competitive motoring was just getting under way again after the war and Pop probably had an ulterior motive in buying the 2½-litre SS, as it was a potential winner in sprints and hill-climbs. He had joined the Auckland Car Club and before long was entering the SS in the odd event. It didn't have the accelera-tion of the Ford V8 saloons, then all the rage, but its top speed of close to 90 mph was above most of the V8s, which usually faded out at much over 80 mph. In beach racing, where the straights were a mile each way, the top speed of the SS used to pay off, but unfortunately races with half-mile straights proved more popular and the V8 specials came out on top.

But motor-bikes, not cars, first caught my fancy. Pop was a referee at the local speedway, where they ran races for midget-cars of the type on which Jack Brabham cut his racing teeth. I enjoyed watching the cars, but really sat up and took notice when the speedway bikes came out to race on the cinders. This was a real man's sport, I decided. On the way home in the car I pictured myself digging a steelshod boot into the cinders. Bruce McLaren was about to launch himself on to the speed-way. Or so he thought.

All these dreams of glory at nine-and-a-half tumbled sharply when I felt pain in my left hip and developed a bit of a limp. This caused consternation at home as it happened in the middle of a polio epidemic. Naturally everyone, including the doctor, thought I had caught the germ, so I was bundled into bed at home and given anti-polio treatment. This went on for several days, but I wasn't responding and it began to look as though it wasn't polio after all, so I was sent to the local hospital and X-rayed.

Soon the specialists decided I had contracted Perthes Disease. They said it could have happened after a heavy fall which affected lubrication of the hip joint. This ball-and-socket joint, like any other bearing, will seize up if it is allowed to run dry and the only answer was to have plenty of rest. They said I would be laid up for several months, but these dragged on into two years.

I was kept in hospital a month and when the specialists were satisfied that rest would be the best cure was transferred to the Wilson Home for Crippled Children on the other side of Auckland harbour.

On arrival at the Wilson Home I was put in a Bradshaw frame, my legs encased in a thick elastic plaster with weights dangling from the end. As I was putting no pressure on my hip, there was no real pain and I soon became used to enforced idleness.

There were four or five other boys about my age with similar complaints and we were all given a sort of elongated bathchair which carried the Bradshaw frames and allowed us to be wheeled around. We soon discovered we could just reach the big rear wheels and were off in an awkward convoy on a tour of the hospital and grounds. All unofficial, of course. I discovered my chair had larger front castors than the others and handled fairly well. The outcome was inevitable.

One night we felt bored, so someone (guess who?) suggested a race round the corridors. It was a great success and the first of many secret, after-dark sprints.

We had some exciting crashes at times and although nothing drastic ever happened, the bumps and scrapes were not quite the type of therapy the specialists intended. We always made sure the nurses were well out of the way before we started, but when they discovered a couple of bent frames and bruised patients at breakfast time, they could hardly be expected to believe "both vehicles were stationary at the kerb when the accident occurred!"

One morning we decided to try something new, so we hitched three or four bathchairs into a train and crept out into the grounds. Naturally there were ramps instead of steps and these were ideal for a bit of extra acceleration.

We pushed off down the first slope and were soon gathering speed. We were going very fast off the second ramp when the horrible thought struck me that there was a slow right-hander at the end of the drive on which we were all bearing down. There was no question of slowing our ungainly entourage, or making the corner in any respectable fashion, so we had our accident in a straight line.

It was a colossal pile-up with bathchairs going in all directions, but I had the biggest crunch of all. My Bradshaw frame whistled off the chair and launched me feet first into a flower bed. Panic reigned as we struggled to get my frame back on the chair, the flower bed restored to near-normal and ourselves indoors before the matron arrived. I don't think anyone ever found out about that little dawn escapade.

But from that day the McLaren name dropped out of the race results, as my chair had mysteriously developed decidedly odd handling characteristics bordering on the unmanageable and when even the nurses couldn't manœuvre it, I was given as replacement a standard model on small castors.

I spent my tenth and eleventh birthdays at the Wilson Home, then came the big day when I was allowed to get up. The doctor told me to stand, not to try and walk, but just try and stand normally. My legs had been hanging in the air for a couple of years and I suppose I must have forgotten how to stand on my own. I levered myself up until I figured I was standing quite naturally.

The doctor looked serious and had a technical discussion with the nurses. This unnerved me a little and I looked down to make sure my feet were pointing the right way The main trouble turned out to be that I was holding my legs straight. I'd forgotten that when you stand up, your knees are slightly bent and no one had thought to remind me. I relaxed the muscles and everyone, myself included, breathed a sigh of relief. But it seemed the weights on my left leg had not been completely successful and the leg was a little shorter than the right, which meant I would always have a slight limp.

All the same it was good to be up again and I was as eager to learn about crutches as I had been to "drive" the wheelchair nearly two years earlier. Getting better meant the wheelchair races were over, but I found I could cover far more ground on the crutches than when propelling myself in the wheelchair. After a few months pounding about the hospital grounds on crutches I developed shoulders like a prize-fighter.

At the end of 1949 the doctors told me I could go home. This was terrific news, although it was a big break to leave behind all the friends I had made during the three years. The staff were great and they are still doing a wonderful job with those who need their help. I'll always be grateful to them.

Soon after returning home I graduated from crutches to a couple of sticks. This gave me a bit more mobility, but they said I had to spend a year at home before I could lead a normal boy's outdoor life.

During the previous two years I'd done a lot of reading. The full education course at the Wilson Home had kept me up-to-date with school studies, so Mum and Pop decided I should have a year of correspondence lessons to keep me in trim, before I could go to the local technical college. My enforced rest had given me a greater interest in schoolwork, especially if it had anything to do with mathematics or mechanics. Not many twelve-year-olds *like* school, but without distractions such as rugby and swimming, I found myself absorbed in studies.

Thanks to Pop these included an insight into an internal

combustion engine and how it worked. Shortly before I left the Wilson Home, Pop had brought along a brochure on the new Jaguar XK120 sports car, which had just been announced as the fastest production car in the world and was creating a sensation. He was keen to buy one and had collected the brochure to try and convince himself he could afford it. Eventually he dropped the idea, but I kept the brochure with its magnificent cutaway drawing of the 3·4-litre engine.

I pored over this cutaway and for a long time it meant nothing more to me than an intricate mass of cogs and shafts, but after reading the specification sheet and putting two and two together I began to realize how an engine worked.

This fascinated me and I began to think that maybe I was cut out to be a mechanic, not a speedway rider. I was also engrossed in building model aeroplanes and powering them with a baby 1 cc high-speed diesel engine. I stripped this tiny unit down so often that I wore it out.

I was enrolled for an engineering course at an Auckland college and the "quite normal" report after my aptitude test at the beginning of 1951 must have shaken many people, who remembered those diabolical "William" type reports from any primary school. I was even starting off in the "A" class, which I'd regarded as a seat of much higher learning than I would ever reach.

They'll never keep me there, I thought nervously . . . surely they'll find out their mistake and drop me back to a nice easy life in the "B" class. But when the half-term test showed me second in class, it looked as though I was stuck with all the boffins and I decided to become a civil engineer. I'd thrown away the sticks for good and was making many new friends at college. Ahead lay the chance of a good career. Life was really looking up.

TWO

Climbing My First Hill

MOTOR RACING WAS beginning to liven up in New Zealand and there were a fair number of speed events during the year, either on some of the local hills or a disused airfield at Seagrove, where the car club had formed a two-mile circuit from runways and access roads.

These Seagrove races became popular by local standards and there were often crowds of two or three hundred to watch the "star" of those days, George Smith with his Ford V8 special. George and his special had headed the New Zealand Championship for as long as I could remember. Ron Roycroft was another favourite. Then in his early thirties, he was turning on polished performances with a superb old Grand Prix Bugatti. The rest of the fields were made up by specials of various shapes and sizes powered by Ford Ten and Austin Seven engines, which, along with the Ford V8s, formed the basis for most of the racing machinery at that time.

Racing at Seagrove was usually run by the Auckland Car Club or the Northern Sports Car Club. On ACC days Pop was often on the organizing side, occasionally having a run in the SS. But it wasn't an ideal tool for these races and Pop must have become a little tired of being beaten by the V8s with their impressive acceleration. I don't suppose racing the family car was such a good idea either—it was a long walk home from Seagrove!

So Pop began quietly searching for something at the right price, solely for competition. He eventually hunted down an Ulster Austin, one of the open competition versions of the evergreen Seven, which was very popular at Brooklands and other circuits in the early 1930s.

For a real "racer" it sounded a bargain at £110, but when we went round with one of the mechanics from our workshop to collect it, the reason for the price became obvious.

That Ulster didn't look much like a racing car to me. It sat there with no bonnet and the engine consisted of a lot of bits and pieces in boxes. But Pop apparently decided the Ulster could be rebuilt, so we loaded the boxes on the back of the workshop truck and towed the rest. I sat on the tray of the truck among the boxes of engine bits and eyed the dilapidated Ulster on the end of the rope with deep suspicion. Racing car indeed! Little did I realize this same Ulster was to give me my start in motor racing and years of enjoyment in local events.

It took Pop a year to collect the necessary bits to get the Ulster mobile again and all his spare time went into rebuilding it. I was usually hovering around, watching Pop's every move. Watching and I hoped learning. The future had taken another turn and, although there was still a two-year wait before I could get a driving licence, I made up my mind to be a racing driver.

Meanwhile my means of transport was a pushbike, with all the "go faster" modifications. The handlebars turned down, mudguards removed and everything not absolutely necessary to operating the cycle stripped in the interests of a better power-to-weight ratio. Each morning I set off for college pedalling furiously, with the aim of lowering my previous best time. This satisfied my appetite for speed until I could get behind the wheel of a racing car.

Thrashing around on my bike and swimming were the only sports in which I could take part, as the doctors had warned against anything like football. Cricket was permitted, though it never appealed to me, but the biggest blow was the veto on rugby. This meant good-bye to an ambition that dated back to my primary school days, when I was captain of the football team; like most youngsters in New Zealand, I'd had visions of becoming an "All Black".

All this was forgotten, however, in the excitement as the finishing touches were put to the Ulster and Pop prepared to start the engine for the first time. After seeing the engine gradually assembled from those worrying boxes of bits and pieces, it was thrilling to hear it cough into life and set up a healthy bark as Pop tuned the carburettor. I felt as proud as if I had done all the work myself.

Pop set off on his first trial run and I waited anxiously at the end of the drive for his first impressions. When he eventually brought the smoking Ulster to a halt he was pale and shaken. It was the most diabolical racing car he could imagine. Sure, it went all right, but it wouldn't stop, it wouldn't steer and, as for the handling . . . words failed him! The prospect of racing the Ulster appalled him and he was all for selling the car forthwith.

After all the hours of work put into the little Ulster, it seemed a shame to drop it like that. Besides, it interfered with my plans to become a racing motorist. After lengthy pleading from various suitable angles, Pop finally relented and told me that I could have the car, providing I looked after it myself. So now I had a racing car of my own. Undaunted by the fact that it was a somewhat lethal machine, my main problem was that I still had more than a year to wait for my fifteenth birthday and a driving licence.

Necessity being the proud mother of McLaren invention, I soon had a small circuit marked out in our back garden. Fortunately there was a fairly large area of lawn, a wide gravel path and a couple of sturdy fruit trees at the bottom as turning points. Without knowing it, I had planned a miniature replica of the Brands Hatch racing circuit in England. They have a noise problem at Brands Hatch, with the nearest neighbour half-a-mile away, so you can imagine what our neighbours thought about the initial activities of the B. McLaren racing school, driver and pupil B. McLaren, age thirteen and a half!

Billy Fowlds, a director of the local Austin distributors, lived next door and the fact that I was playing around with an Austin may have stayed his complaints, but I noticed the trees along his garden fence were growing larger than ever. He must have been using them to try and cut out some of the noise.

Belting round my little circuit, tearing up the lawn and barking the apple trees, didn't bring much support from the kitchen window, but it taught me the basic principles of car control. I found I could get it to start, stop and point in the right direction with a fair amount of certainty before anything terrible happened and gradually became bolder with a confidence bred of ignorance. When I think back, I must have been hurtling round those apple trees at an alarming rate.

One day I overcooked it. The gravel patch at the end of the circuit formed a tight right-hand turn between the house and the three-car garage. I came on to this gravel so fast that even I knew I wasn't going to make it. I shut my eyes, held my breath and went straight ahead along the side of the house, missing everything by a coat of paint and coming to a shaken halt. My first reaction was relief at my masterly evasion of an early demise, but when I realized what I must have done to avoid the side of the house I was thrilled. I'd held an opposite lock slide— and told everyone about it for days.

With her only son churning up the family lawn in a stripped-down, noisy racing car (Heaven help what the neighbours thought) and her kitchen table taken over from time to time for cleaning and polishing the engine's internals, Mother must have regretted the day when I tired of my model aeroplanes and the little 1 cc engine.

Inevitably I began to tire of the miniature Brands Hatch and hankered for drives on the public roads. As I wanted my licence immediately I was fifteen, I decided a spot of unofficial practice might come in useful, so started to carry out a few early-morning sorties while the roads were empty and the law (I hoped) slumbered. Pop turned a blind eye to these dawn forays, but made it clear that if I were caught it would be my own look-out.

One early morning I had to call him out for mechanical, rather than legal aid. I'd risen at some ridiculously early hour and found the car difficult to start. An under-bonnet check showed both fuel and ignition systems operational, but the engine still refused to fire. So I rolled the car down the drive and hopped in to let it trundle off down the road. I was nearly at the bottom of the hill before it fired, then everything happened at once. It went charging up the other side, locked solid and skidded to a halt. I had no idea what had happened, but fearing the worst I enlisted Pop's aid to tow the Ulster home with the workshop truck.

It turned out that I'd over-richened the mixture in my attempts to start the car and the neat petrol had washed all the lubricating oil off the cylinder walls. When the engine fired there was no film of oil between the piston and the wall and the engine seized. Pop wasn't amused. He told me that if I insisted on these early-morning excursions, I should restrict my test area to within pushing distance of home.

Fortunately the engine was not badly damaged, the pistons having just been nipped in the bores. Following Pop's instructions I took off the head—my first major mechanical job—squirted oil down the cylinder bores and the pistons freed themselves, seemingly none the worse.

I was surprised and delighted when the engine fired, after I had bolted it back together.

My fifteenth birthday was a long time coming, but when it arrived I hastily booked a driving test. I didn't suppose a noisy little Ulster Austin with virtually no brakes, questionable steering and highly suspect suspension would impress the Traffic Inspector, so I borrowed a friend's 1949 side-valve Morris Minor. I was nervous at first—isn't everyone?—but after driving him round the block a couple of times, doing a few turns and a reverse and answering the stock questions from the road code, he gave me a column of ticks and I had my licence. At last. Now I was ready for business.

With a brand-new licence and tweaked-up racer, I was anxious to start dicing as soon as I could, but there didn't seem many events on the calendar suitable for a complete novice.

Pop solved the problem by "finding" an ideal hill-climb venue. We had a summer house at Muriwai Beach, some 25 miles from Auckland, and Pop had been collecting road metal from the local quarry to lay a drive for the house. The quarry was at the bottom of a hill about five-eighths of a mile long and between truck loads of shingle it must have dawned on him that the road was tailor-made for competition. Being a local resident as well as Chairman of the Auckland Car Club, he soon obtained permission for the ACC to use the hill and I looked forward to the first event and my motor-racing debut. I'd taken it for granted Pop would let me compete!

Unfortunately the first hill-climb coincided with one of Pop's rare visits to hospital, but my entry was accepted and I was in the paddock polishing the little Ulster and making all those nervous last-minute modifications that seem so important.

Not being able to give me a last-minute lecture, Pop settled for a few well-chosen words from his hospital bed, the general message being that if I so much as scraped a guard, the Ulster and I would part company for good.

This probably did me the world of good, as I was so busy being scared of bending my car and having it taken from me, that I forgot to be nervous about my debut. I took things reasonably steadily, with Pop's lecture in mind, as the tail of the little Ulster slid on the loose metal corners and reached the top in one piece. When all the runs were over, I learned with amazement that I had made fastest time in the 750 cc class. A first at my first attempt. I was thrilled. Second in the class was Phil Kerr, one of my closest friends ever since. Phil had an Austin Nippy and this started a friendly rivalry that was to last for several years.

It is interesting to recall that our times, something over 70 sec, were almost double the 37 sec it took me four years later in a centre-seat Cooper-Climax sports car, when setting a Muriwai course record. On later attempts Phil and I were able to take our Austins to the top in around 45 sec, which seems to show we both had a few rough edges on that first climb.

But such an early success was a wonderful tonic and we both earned our restricted competition licences that day. First stop on the way home was at the hospital to tell Pop the news and reassure him that the Ulster was still in one piece. I also wanted to reassure myself that its ownership was now on a permanent basis.

I wouldn't like to say that a hot Austin Seven is a short-trip ticket to a Formula One racing car, but that Ulster taught me a lot.

Not only did I learn at a comparatively safe speed what happens to a car when it begins to slide and how to tackle it when it does, but also the importance of careful maintenance and preparation. Painstaking work in the garage before a race can mean the difference between winning and failing to finish.

The Ulster was subjected to "the treatment" during the three years I used it and, by the time we parted company, it was barely recognizable as the car I had been given, while its performance was so far removed that it might have been a different car.

Pop and his workshop foreman Harold Bardsley were expert tutors, who taught me more about the practical side of automobile engineering than I could have found in a dozen textbooks. Both, to my mind, are typical of the breed of mechanic for which New Zealand is famous. I think it stems from the war years, when there was such a shortage of spares that improvisation was accepted as normal workshop practice. If a particular part wasn't available, the next best thing was found and modified to suit, or a new part was made, starting from scratch with raw materials. Unwittingly they became skilled engineers with a pride of workmanship, which in many parts of the world is only to be found among the enthusiasts who work for racing teams.

One of my first lessons was to tackle one job at a time, do it thoroughly and be satisfied with the result before passing on to the next. This was Pop's doctrine and it has always stood me in good stead.

When Pop came out of hospital, he suggested that we should modify the front end by giving the wheels more castor action. This helped it travel in a straight line, which it had previously been reluctant to do, and also improved the handling through corners. Pop would always advise, but he left the practical work to me. For the first year the car seemed to get progressively worse, but I was learning by my mistakes and soon felt I had the measure of the car's shortcomings and could do something about them.

I became increasingly ambitious with my modifications, but when I suggested replacing the large single Zenith carburettor with twin SUs, Pop put his foot down. However, the Zenith wasn't performing as well as it might have done and it was affecting my times, so with the help of Harold, the workshop foreman, I discovered the secrets of the welding torch and lathe and quietly went about building up my own manifolds for the twin carburettors. These worked extremely well when fitted and after that Pop became more co-operative when I came up with the odd inspired thought.

I don't think the Ulster even contested two successive events in exactly the same form; I was always trying out different modifications. There was always something going on or coming off in the workshop and the only time the car seemed to be roadworthy was immediately before, during or after an event.

I traced the car's oversteering traits to the fact that the rear springs flattened on the outside when taking a corner—a fault commonly known as rear-axle steer. We compensated for this by completely flattening the rear springs. We then had trouble with the spokes pulling out of the 19-in wheels—it was disconcerting to hear the "ping, ping, ping" as spokes broke under the tension of a full-blooded slide. This trouble was overcome by fitting 16-in disc wheels at the rear and 17-in wheels with stronger spokes at the front.

The front spring had been reverse-curved, which helped to make the car very low-slung indeed, but then the steering kingpins started to chew themselves out after about 150 miles. I wanted to convert the car to independent front suspension, but Pop convinced me a really good beam axle lay-out was better than an indifferent independent set-up.

We decided to fit an axle from an Austin Big Seven, which had kingpins twice the size of the earlier types and we fitted Girling front brakes.

It turned out to be a complicated conversion, as the Austin tie-rod would not fit on its normal position, but we managed to overcome this by mounting it ahead instead of behind the axle and linked it up with forward-facing steering arms. I just guessed at the Ackermann steering angle and it worked out fine.

For the first year or so Pop entered the car for both of us, saying he thought he'd better keep a check on my times. This suited me fine, as I could keep track of my progress by following up Pop's hints and trying a few of my own. The Ulster gave me my first win in a race, as distinct from a sprint or hill-climb. This meeting was held on a beach and I soon discovered the little Austin was in its element on sand. Pop tried the car on the beach, but brought it back to the pits looking a trifle grey. Apparently he preferred a car with brakes! I had become so used to the anchorless state of the Ulster, that I probably would have found myself in trouble with a braking system in it. Ettore Bugatti once said something about brakes not being essential, as they slowed a car down, and I subscribed to this.

During the three years the Ulster and I battled together, it never once failed to finish a hill-climb or win its class. I was immensely pleased with my little "bomb", although the owners of some of the more exotic (and slower) machinery were probably not quite so impressed.

Phil Kerr had changed his Nippy for a Ford Ten special and was providing stiff opposition, but one day at a Muriwai hill-climb when he was having troubles with his car, I offered him a drive in the Ulster. By this time I had chopped my original 72-sec run down to a more respectable 47 sec, but imagine how my ego deflated when Phil tore off on his first run in my car to clock a cool 45 sec. That brought me down to earth with a bang and thoughts of collecting butterflies or dried leaves, or some other gentler pursuit, must have gone through my head before I made my run. Things were more settled in the McLaren mind when the timekeepers confirmed that I had also managed the climb in 45 seconds. Phew!

For Phil to have put up the time he did confirmed what many people were saying—that he was among the most promising of New Zealand's up-and-coming drivers. It would have been interesting to see how far Phil would have gone on the track, had he not decided to accept a behind-the-scenes job as Jack Brabham's manager.

Phil and I went around a lot together in 1954 and 1955, by which time I was at university and Phil on his way to becoming an accountant. They were good times for both of us and for anyone who was involved with motor sport in New Zealand. Thanks to a group of forward-thinking enthusiasts, something was being done on an international scale and the big-time

European drivers were starting to come over and show us how a racing car should be handled.

At last the gap between racing in Europe and New Zealand was being bridged—we now had a date on the international calendar, were in touch with the latest developments and stood to learn much from direct contact with overseas motor racing.

THREE

The New Zealand "Circus"

NEW ZEALAND'S TRANSITION to big-time motor racing started in 1953, when a group of the more enthusiastic members of the Auckland Car Club formed an association to promote a race on international lines. It became known as the Auckland International Grand Prix Association and later the New Zealand International Grand Prix (Inc.).

Reg Grierson was one of the prime early movers. He had raced one of the supercharged "Rubber Duck" Austins—the single-seater derivative of the Ulster—which had a top speed of about 110 mph and looked extremely dangerous but Reg's quarter-century of racing experience doubtless helped him to tame it. There were always plenty of thrills when he and the Rubber Duck were racing.

Ross Jensen, a future New Zealand champion driver, was another original member of the NZIGP, as were Pop, Ian Chalmers and Ivan Parton. They all had competitive experience, but lacked the organizational finesse to launch an international race. The aim was to promote a Formula Libre race, which would be open to almost anything on wheels. Their ambitious plan was to invite some of the best European drivers at a time when they would otherwise be out of work during their winter and confront them with local drivers in a widely-varied collection of racing machinery.

If the race were to be a success, it obviously had to be done properly, so Dean Delamont, competitions chief of Britain's Royal Automobile Club, was invited to supervise and offer helpful suggestions.

Shaken by the haphazard way in which enthusiastic Aucklanders went about their motor racing, he caused a stir by suggesting they should throw away all their clapped-out specials and invest in Cooper 500s or something similar.

The hottest thing on the New Zealand scene at that time was George Smith's V8 special which was good for around 125 mph, although Ron Roycroft had just forsaken his Bugatti for a P3 Alfa Romeo which looked like being the fastest car in the country. Clapped-out specials, indeed! Dean Delamont's suggestion received a hot reception at the time, but he was perfectly right.

Motor racing in Europe had progressed from its post-war era of "hairy" specials and was getting established with factory F1 (Formula One) cars forming the basis of the main entry lists. Clearly these were the ones we wanted, but as Dean pointed out it was hard enough to stage a good F1 race in England and New Zealand would be best advised to start with F3 cars.

These 500s were losing popularity in Europe, mainly due to Cooper domination of the class, so there were many race-worthy cars on the market. Some found their way to New Zealand, but were no match for the performance of the big specials, or the spectacle the latter provided.

The NZIGP staged the first Grand Prix on a disused airfield at Ardmore, some 20 miles south of Auckland, in January 1954. Like most airfield circuits it was almost dead flat, but it certainly drew the crowds and continued to do so up to 1962, when the ninth Grand Prix marked the end of Ardmore as a motor-racing circuit. The NZIGP did well to keep the race there so long, as the airport had been re-opened and was operational over the final few years.

How the organization matured in those eight years. I'll never forget the chaos of that first international meeting. Time-keeping and lap scoring fell to pieces during the race and there were so many protests and counter-protests that it took six months of arbitration, with countless letters between London and New Zealand, to sort out the shambles and arrive at a final result.

The trouble started when Horace Gould, who brought out a Cooper-Bristol, claimed he had won the race after completing 101 laps and that he had refrained from passing Australian Stan Jones—who had been declared the winner—on the final lap because he knew Jones was a lap behind.

The stewards upheld the protest, but only moved Gould from fourth place to second. This brought a counter-protest from Ken Wharton, who had been placed second in the 16-cylinder BRM, and Tony Gaze, who had been classified third with his HWM. Ironically, Gould had to give moral support to this claim, as he agreed he could only have been first or fourth.

Eventually the stewards reverted to their original placings, giving victory to Jones in the Maybach Special, a remarkable car with a 4-litre straight-eight engine taken from an abandoned Maybach scout car found in the Western Desert.

The shambles over the results was only one of the sore points. Although an estimated 60,000 people saw the race—one in every ten of the population of Auckland province—many had slipped in without paying. Some of the amenities were primitive and spectator control often purely nominal. Phil and I were crowd marshals at one point, but you can imagine what happened when a pair of teenagers tried to tell a crowd of boisterous racegoers what to do. We took the easy way out and sat down to watch the race, while the crowd behind happily sorted themselves out.

Seventh place was taken by Ross Jensen in a car which was later to give me my first "real" motor race. It was one of the first production Austin Healey 100s, one of three entered in the Grand Prix by various distributors with a certain amount of backing from the works in England. The agents for Auckland, Wellington and Christchurch had each been given one and provided their own drivers. Ross represented Auckland and his was the first sports car home.

The entrants had been a little over-ambitious, as they fondly hoped their cars would trounce the foreign opposition, but all the same it was good to see the new sports cars dicing among the single-seaters and not being disgraced. The Austin Healeys were well prepared and modified with bigger carburettors, metal tonneau covers and Alfin brake drums.

The Auckland car was looked after by Seabrook Fowlds Ltd. As Billy Fowlds was our long-suffering neighbour, who had to put up with the rowdy Ulster over the garden wall, we felt we had quite a stake in Ross and were delighted at his placing.

A few months later we really did have a stake in the car. The story went round that the agents, after entering Ross in four or five races, were becoming embarrassed by preparation of the car taking up too much of their time. They told Pop they had been watching the progress of the Ulster with interest and thought the Healey might make a suitable replacement. Would we be interested? Pop, who had never been really happy with the Ulster, thought this a wonderful idea, figuring that he could race the Healey, while I continued flogging round in the Ulster.

But we didn't know the other reason for the Healey being put on the market. Ross was impatiently waiting to take delivery of the special competition version of the Healey—the 100S. Ross had a garage business about a couple of miles from ours and this marked the beginning of a most gentlemanly type of rivalry.

Pop decided to enter himself in the Healey for the 1955 Grand Prix and for the next few months wrapped himself up in the car, having time for little else. When he finished, it was quite a sports car. After running it for about 1,000 miles, he completely stripped it down and embarked on a big souping-up session. Everything that moved was polished and balanced. Chrysler pistons were fitted, along with Buick cam followers and pushrod gear and Chrysler exhaust valves. The ports were opened out and highly polished and a special twin-pipe exhaust system made up and fitted.

A full-length undertray was made and the cast-iron brake drums were re-fitted with plenty of cooling holes and big scoops on the back plates to draw in the air; they proved to be superb brakes with the aid of Mintex M20 linings. Finally the spring rates were changed to improve the Healey's handling and Pop could hardly wait to try it out at Ardmore. It performed to expectations and for the next three years was a class-winner at nearly every event in which we entered it—even beating the 100S Healey five times at sprints!

The Grand Prix proved something of an anti-climax. Pop did not feel at his best on the day, but was running well and nicely placed when the teeth stripped off second gear and he retired. Perhaps it was a blessing in disguise, as it may have saved the car from going up in flames. We were planning to refuel during the race, pouring in the fuel at the rate of eight gallons every four to five seconds from large churns, but when we tried a quick fill-up a few days after the race we found the tank would take only a gallon every ten seconds. In other words it would have been a case of one in the tank and seven on the ground, splashing around the hot exhaust . . . it hardly bore thinking about!

In the meantime we had tweaked the Ulster to the stage where it was a little fireball, but Pop had decided that there was no point in driving it on the roads and letting it go off tune, so the Ulster sat on a trailer while I rode my pushbike once again.

The practical mechanics I had absorbed in our garage came

in useful when the cylinder head of the Ulster cracked at a beach race. Being unable to pluck another cylinder head out of the air, I decided to build one, using the head of a 1936 Austin Ruby saloon. I filled all the combustion chambers with bronze, then re-cut them with rotary files keeping as closely as I could to the specifications laid down by Sir Harry Ricardo, the famous engine designer. To my everlasting amazement and pride the Ulster went better than ever and was timed at 87 mph, regularly turning in times under 20 sec for the standing quarter-mile.

My first circuit race in the Ulster was on Ohakea airfield. The grid start must have been unique, as there were some 40 cars on the first row and another 30 in the second. Admittedly the track was about 200 yards wide at this point, but we were all aimed at the first corner where the circuit narrowed ominously. I thoroughly enjoyed the race and, after a great dice with a Singer Nine, finished third on handicap.

In August 1955, I made the big decision to sell the Ulster. We had battled together for three years and it had taught me all I knew, but I was tired of being without road transport. Pop didn't seem to mind, so I discovered a smart Ford Ten Special which filled the bill for road and competition work. I sold the Ulster for £280 and with a borrowed £30 clinched the deal on the Ford at £310.

But the Ford and I never clicked. I'd had a lot of fun in the Ulster and knew it inside out. I didn't feel the same way with the Ford and never had much success with it, entering auto-cross and gymkhana events rather than races.

My racing future was beginning to look a little gloomy, but in November a misfortune for Pop brought a big opportunity. Pop was in hospital for a couple of weeks and returned home to break the news that the doctor had advised him against driving in the Grand Prix, which was two months away.

Pop wracked his brains for a suitable substitute and I don't think my name was very high on his list. But everyone who counted themselves as racing drivers of any calibre was fixed up at that late stage and although Pop was apprehensive about putting me into an important race with people like Brabham and Moss, he finally relented.

Even then he didn't say I was in, not in so many words. He told me I could reckon on a good chance of starting and after that I put up such a good public relations barrage and worked so hard on the Healey, that I don't suppose he had the heart to stop me. With Pop's final agreement and signature on the bottom of the entry form came the usual strict instructions not to make a fool of myself and remember I was very much a new boy in select company.

By this time the NZIGP boys had begun to get the race on a sound footing and they decided to run a special race for sports cars before the Grand Prix. With production models and home-built specials mixing it with genuine Grand Prix cars, the previous race had been a bit of a nightmare. It was obvious that another Grand Prix run that way could cause an almighty shunt.

Even so, I was far from having the fastest car in the race. The opposition included Moss (Porsche) and a D-type Jaguar among others and I felt relieved the race was being run on a handicap basis.

I was really enjoying practising in what was to me a real racing car, when the gearbox started to clatter and I spent one of my first all-nighters putting in new parts. Phil was also having gearbox dramas with his fast little Buckler special so neither of us got much sleep.

I wasn't all that confident on the starting grid, but after the first few laps found myself lying third on handicap. Then a gasket blew and after losing a lot of water the engine seized momentarily when I was in the middle of a full-blooded drift. I thought the steering had gone, so pulled into the pits for Pop to check the front end. He said the steering was all right and the trouble was probably a blown gasket. I told him I couldn't see how that would affect the car the way it did, so he sent me out again, warning me not to ruin the engine.

I soon discovered he was right and after another couple of laps with the engine sounding decidedly rough, pulled in and called it a day. Phil didn't finish either and we both felt so utterly exhausted that we slept soundly through the Grand Prix that followed.

Pop must have been reasonably impressed with my race performance, as he entered me in the Healey for a hill-climb soon afterwards. It was a qualifying event for the New Zealand championship, run purely on a capacity-class basis, with racing cars, sports cars and saloons battling together for placings. The Healey performed well on hills and I managed second fastest class time behind a P3 Alfa Romeo racing car.

By March 1956, Pop was starting to get fit again and, although still officially convalescing, entered us both for a race at Ohakea, saying that whoever turned in the fastest practice lap should have the drive. Actually there were two races for which we were eligible—one for sports cars, the other an all-comers' Formula Libre event. The chances of having two races on one day sounded too good to miss, so I tried really hard in practice and collected the staggering time of 1 min 40 sec—seven seconds faster than Pop! After that he decided to stick to the role of entrant and proud father and drive himself only occasionally.

Australian Tommy Sulman was the star attraction at Ohakea that day with his Aston Martin DB3S sports car and really impressed me by coming over and lending a hand after I had crept to the pits with a wheel flapping, when a steering arm broke during the sports car race. Earlier I had thoroughly enjoyed myself following Tommy's Aston Martin round to finish fifth behind him in the Formula Libre race.

After Ohakea we went to a number of hill-climbs and sprints, with the Hautapu sprint as the most important. A year earlier at Hautapu Pop had bettered our arch-rival Ross

Jensen's time with the 100S, on its New Zealand debut. The Austin agents, Seabrook Fowlds Ltd., had been so sure the new car would win that R. B. Seabrook presented a special trophy for the fastest sports car over 1500 cc. There must have been some red faces in Auckland that night!

Ross's 100S was once again the main opposition to our 100-4, and I had to pull out all the stops to safeguard family honour.

It worked out that year that I could usually pip Ross in sprints, but on hills, where driving was more important he could always get to the top just that fraction quicker.

Encouraged by the way the car was going in short events, Pop decided we should do the complete "circus" of the 1957 races in New Zealand, starting with the Ardmore sports car race preceding the Grand Prix on January 12th, then moving south to Levin, Christchurch, Dunedin, Invercargill and finally back to Christchurch. Naturally I thought this a splendid idea.

But what was a fabulous tour started on a sad note at Ardmore. Ken Wharton, leading us all in his 3-litre Monza Ferrari sports car, was fatally injured when it crashed and somersaulted several times, hurling him out. The accident happened right in front of the main stands and the large crowd was stunned. But no one could have received a greater shock than my mother. Ken's Ferrari was carrying the number 64. Mine was 46—and when the Ferrari ended upside down, mother thought for a few terrifying seconds that it was the Healey. To make matters worse, Ken invariably wore a yellow jersey when he was racing and that day I was wearing one, too. I've never worn a yellow jersey since.

Bob Gibbons went on to win the race with his D-type Jaguar and I finished fifth behind Brabham's centre-seater Cooper, a Maserati-looking sports car called an Ausca, and Ross in the 100S; on handicap I was elevated to second place behind Gibbons.

At Levin we picked up a third place behind a Lotus and a Jaguar XK140 and then we took the ferry down to Christchurch and the Lady Wigram Trophy meeting.

Here we were entered for the preliminary sports car race and the main event, but things didn't work out that way. I made a good start in the sports car race and headed the field for the first half lap, until Brabham buzzed by me in the Cooper. One or two others swallowed me up and I found myself embroiled in quite a dice with Ronnie Moore, the speedway rider, in his centre-seater Cooper 1100.

This was great fun until I realized the Healey had fluttered on to three cylinders. I streaked into the pits, shouting that I thought a plug had cooked. Pop didn't think so, but he changed plugs and sent me out again. It was no better and next lap I was back at the pits suggesting that the valve clearances could be faulty. Once again Pop didn't agree with my diagnosis—come to think of it, he didn't seem to agree with much I suggested that season and he was usually right!—but he checked the clearances to show there were no hard feelings and off I set again. It had to be right this time. But it was hopeless and I dejectedly pulled in for good.

Later we stripped the engine and found a hole in the top of one of the pistons, about the size of an orange. A valve head had snapped off and thrashed around the combustion chamber until it hammered its way through the piston and dropped into the sump. Fortunately it hadn't damaged the crankshaft on its way down and we were able to repair the engine in time for the Dunedin meeting the following weekend.

Meanwhile I was left without a mount for the main race at Wigram, so we optimistically mentioned to Brabham that he had a spare Cooper in the paddock. Jack displayed remarkable lack of interest—and who could blame him?

I was entered in the Formula Libre event for New Zealand drivers only on the wharf circuit at Dunedin and lined up on the grid with an assortment ranging from F3 Coopers with

500 cc motor-cycle engines to Duncan Rutherford's 4·7-litre Lycoming aero-engined special.

Alex Stringer, who had won the race the year before in a Porsche, repeated the performance in a Cooper 1100 sports car, with Dick Campbell's baby F3 Cooper second. I was having a battle royal for third place with the Lycoming special, but got by and succeeded in building a big lead which came in useful when I was black-flagged going into the last lap. Officials had spotted one of my back wheels wobbling, so I eased up, but still finished third.

At Invercargill, our next event, we noticed something mysteriously wrong with the engine. The Healey performed well in short sprints and hill-climbs, but had a reputation for being fast and unreliable. I don't think this could have stemmed from over-tuning, because at the beginning of the season we had specially tuned the car for a record attempt. The compression ratio had been increased from our usual 10·5 : 1 to 11·2: 1, and we were using a methanol and nitro-benzine mix for fuel.

We had joined forces with Ross Jensen for that effort and over the measured kilometre he recorded 130 mph, while I was just 1 mph slower. It had proved perfectly reliable then, so it was puzzling why it should play up when "de-tuned".

At Invercargill, on the Ryall Bush circuit with its long straights, the Healey went like a rocket, indicating over 130 mph at times, then a little misfire would creep in at peak revs. This proved a teaser and we tried everything in the book to find the reason. We had the head off, fitted new valve springs, cleaned everything up, but still the trouble persisted.

We hadn't found a cure for the misfire by the time we got back to Christchurch and were beginning to think it must have something to do with ignition. Then it happened! Pop had removed one of the plug leads and was watching the spark jumping as the engine turned gently over at 2,000 rpm, when with a clatter and shower of oil a connecting rod poked through the side of the block. I never knew Pop had such a devastating command of the English language. He was covered in oil and the look of utter bewilderment on his face was so funny that we all burst out laughing.

It took Pop a while to see the joke, but in the end he condescended to grin.

That meant the end of the engine and as we shovelled the bits together, loaded the car on the trailer and began the long haul back to Auckland, we realized that the future of our modest racing activities looked black. It was costing a lot of money and with my engineering studies at university reaching an important stage, there seemed no alternative but to forget about motor racing and start on mathematics. That's exactly what happened . . . for about a month. Then Buzz Perkins, secretary of the NZIGP, upset my scholastic applecart with a proposition that was to lead to the turning-point in my career.

Buzz was a regular petrol customer at our garage and one day told us that Brabham had left his centre-seater Cooper sports car behind with instructions for it to be sold. Buzz thought we would be ideal buyers. This was fantastic. All ideas of an engineering degree flew out the window and I offered to sell the Ford, my bike and just about everything I owned, reasoning that if Pop would part with the Healey we could just make it.

I've never been quite sure how we clinched that deal, but on signing the ownership papers we entered the Cooper in the Horahora hill-climb—the very next day.

This was a championship event and although it rained heavily, making the course fairly tricky, I thoroughly enjoyed myself and won the 1½-litre class. It was a dream to drive. I'd never experienced such responsiveness to the controls and right from the start felt at home in the driving seat.

Next on the competition calendar was a race meeting at Levin, but attending this would mean missing an important university test. When I asked for permission to sit the test later, my professor told me he thought I was spending far too much time racing at the expense of my studies. He was right, of course, but I knew which were my chosen priorities, so we loaded the Cooper on the trailer and headed for Levin.

I won three races there, then brought the Cooper back to Auckland to strip down and rebuild. Levin was the beginning of a successful season with the Cooper, which went on to break records at every hill on which it competed.

It was good to be at the wheel of a really competitive car and Phil and I began to have grandiose ideas of races further afield. Our main ambition was to enter the car for the international sports car race at Sebring the following March and to this end we kept pestering Buzz Perkins. I think we would have probably won his support, but for two McLaren-shaking pieces of news that broke almost simultaneously.

Through the year I had been keeping in close touch with Jack Brabham by letter and he had suggested that he could arrange for a 1·7-litre single-seater F1 Cooper to be shipped out for me to use in the next Grand Prix. This was staggering, but something even better was to follow. The long-suffering Buzz, fighting off yet another of our pleas about Sebring, let it slip that if I played my cards right he might be able to do something even better for me. It turned out that the NZIGP had decided to sponsor a New Zealand driver for a year of top-class racing in Europe and I was on the short list of candidates!

Obviously if I had a single-seater Cooper laid on, my chances of being chosen as the "Driver to Europe" would be vastly improved, so we accepted Jack's offer. This meant parting with the sports Cooper and, despite the stakes involved, I must confess it was some time before I convinced myself we were doing the right thing.

Eventually it was sold to Merv Neil, who had a successful run with it. While I waited for the single-seater to arrive, I busied myself with my two final university exams. These over, I settled down to contemplate the effect the aforementioned racing car would have on my career.

FOUR

Into a Cooper Cockpit

PEOPLE IN NEW ZEALAND tend to regard racing drivers with a special sort of awe—I'm not sure whether it is respect or sympathy—and if they happen to be overseas drivers, the awe develops into hero-worship. I suppose that is how I regarded Jack Brabham in the years when I was racing the Ulster and the Healey, but after phone calls and incessant letters to Jack in England, while I had the Cooper sports car, I began to think of him as a decent bloke, always willing to help.

Jack's early New Zealand visits in the Cooper-Bristol days made him a popular figure to New Zealand crowds and when he began to make a name for himself in European motor racing, most enthusiasts began to regard him almost as a "local boy making good", despite the fact that a large amount of ocean separated the Brabham family from our house.

In 1956 Jack had some trouble with his Cooper-Bristol and he was working on it at Geoff Wiles' garage down the road. Hearing that he needed some steel plate, I scrabbled round our garage hunting out all the pieces I could find and hurried down in hopes of seeing Jack at work. Conversation was brief. Jack was up to his ears in work and clearly the last thing he wanted was a lad like me peering over his shoulder. He grunted

"No thanks", and I trudged back home with my armload of steel.

The following year I came to know him a bit better and found him one of the easiest overseas drivers to approach from a youngster's point of view. When he wasn't in a flap, he didn't mind a juvenile audience.

When we persuaded Jack to tell us about racing overseas, we heard stories of wild days barrelling along in columns of dust on Australia's back roads in the gruelling Redex Trials. Of the time the front suspension was torn out of his Holden and the sump smashed in the middle of a desert. He trudged miles to a gold-mining camp to borrow a truck and some welding equipment. The sump was removed and repaired and the damaged suspension knocked into running order. Borrowed oil made the engine a runner and they returned the empty gas bottles to their puzzled owner, who could not quite figure out the trial anyway.

The 250F Maserati days had not yet begun in New Zealand in 1956 and Jack painted hair-raising pictures of Fangio's 250F passing him at Rouen, with wheels pounding at all angles as the master forged away. Fangio . . . Phil and I had avidly read Continental race reports, usually six weeks' old by the time they arrived in New Zealand, and marvelled at his prowess, but we had never previously heard him talked of as "one of the boys".

Towards the end of 1957 when the exams were over, I didn't feel like waiting impatiently until the single-seater arrived—by then I had found it was to be the car Roy Salvadori had driven for the factory that year—so I set about tuning and polishing up an 8CLT Maserati that had been stored for some time by Freddie Zambucka, an old motor-cycle mate of Pop's.

Freddie had been one of the top drivers in New Zealand when he raced his De Soto special in the Seagrove and Muriwai days. He was a big man, renowned for his good humour, and left a gap in Auckland motoring circles when he died suddenly

of a heart attack. Zambucka had imported an 8CM Maserati
to New Zealand and raced it with reasonable success, before
selling it to Tom Clark. He then bought two 8CLT Maseratis
which had been built and prepared for Indianapolis, but never
actually raced there. Included in this deal was a 6C Maserati.

The big supercharged 3-litre 8CLTs—actually two 4CLT
1½-litre engines joined together with a carburettor and blower
to each half—were built to special order and had reputedly
been clocked at 200 mph in the hands of some brave Italian
before they left for America. Although they never approached
the performance of the faithful old Offenhauser, they seemed
admirably suited to Formula Libre racing in New Zealand. The
6C later changed hands and was popularly known as the
Lollipop Special, as it was painted red outside and gold inside
and—sacrilege—fitted with a hopped-up Ford V8 engine.

The Maseratis, painted gleaming black with a silver stripe
down the centre, were always kept immaculate. Reg Parnell and
Peter Whitehead used to think it a shame that the Italian cars
were not painted red, but I disagreed. The New Zealand racing
colours are actually green with a silver stripe, but black and
silver are the colours worn by New Zealand sportsmen abroad
and they have been generally adopted by the motor-racing
fraternity.

Frank Shuter, a leading South Island driver who had already
bought and raced a 6CM Maserati, bought the two 8CLTs from
the Zambucka estate. One, I was to clean up for an attempt at
the New Zealand land speed record. The Maseratis had been
stored a long time, but not much work was needed to make one
a runner. We fired it up in the quiet of Upland Road and the
noise on that summer afternoon was deafening.

It was one of the first single-seaters I had driven and
certainly a monster on which to cut my teeth. The long gear-
lever sprouted up in the centre of the cockpit and was cranked
to the left. The blown 3-litre engine had miles of power in a
straight line, but was a bit unpredictable around corners. It had

At seventeen months Bruce McLaren is already attracted to cars . . .

. . . and at sixteen he is racing an Ulster Austin with friend and mechanic Warwick Davis

McLaren crossing the line in the Ulster at Muriwai after his first experience of loose metal hill-climbing

With the Ulster Austin at Ohakea airfield for his first circuit race

four speeds, all distinctly crash, but would spin wheels at anything up to 140 mph.

However, Coopers were still uppermost in my mind and I was eager to meet Derek Edwards, the mechanic who was looking after Englishman Dick Gibson's brand-new F2 Cooper. I learned that the Cooper had just arrived in Auckland and couldn't wait to see it.

Derek wasn't too sure about me. "A fresh-faced kid like that, driving a works car!" He couldn't believe it.

I was entranced by my first view of the Cooper. I climbed in. The front wheels seemed close and gave me the feeling that it would be very stable. It had more instruments than the sports car—even a wood-rimmed steering wheel. Little did I realize how many hours I would later be spending in a Cooper cockpit.

After this, time hung heavy until just before Christmas when a lorry pulled into the garage to unload the two Coopers, a 1960 cc F1 car for Jack and a 1750 cc F2 car for myself. They were beautifully prepared and I was most impressed. The gear-levers, screens, exhausts, and mirrors had been greased and packed separately, along with anything else that seemed likely to suffer on the journey out. Phil and I got to work assembling the cars and cleaning them up. Phil did most of the polishing —I think I spent more time just sitting in the cockpit dreaming.

Jack soon arrived from England and we loaded the Coopers on trailers to take out to Ardmore. We had built a trailer during the winter which ended up a big flashy thing like Boadicea's chariot. The Cooper felt tiny after the sports car and especially after the Maserati! The gear-change worried me a bit, but otherwise it was splendid. The engine was smooth, with plenty of power.

Jack led me around for a few laps and I had a marvellous time following his lines and hanging the tail out when "teacher" did. Then I was waved on and Jack sat on my tail and followed me. When we pulled in at the pits, I was told off

4

for hanging the tail out too far—a case, I thought, of the pot calling the kettle black, but I tried hard afterwards to motor in a neater fashion.

The family was in another phase of Jaguar motoring. Pop's 2·4 arrived in Wellington late in 1956 and in 1957 we did the full New Zealand season with it.

Spare moments in 1957 were usually spent with Phil and Colin Beanland, helping Merv Mayo build his Buckler special. Phil was secretary to a company that imported tuning equipment for racing enthusiasts and built Buckler chassis's under licence in New Zealand, so Merv did fairly well in acquiring parts. The special was a sports car built round a Buckler chassis with an Elva-headed Ford 1172 cc engine. It was the best of the Ford specials available and could give an 1100 single-cam Climax sports car a run for its money.

Sports cars of any vintage are not easy to come by in New Zealand and Colin's Prefect, fitted with an Elva head, was regarded as a legitimate competition tool. I first met Colin when we were working on Phil's Buckler, and we began a friendship that was to stand me in good stead. When the Cooper arrived, Colin was taken on as mechanic and, as his father was managing director of one of the largest wholesale motor spares firms in Auckland and he could virtually quote the part number and availability of any part required, he was appointed chief of the bits-and-pieces department. Many overseas drivers must have blessed the Beanland presence when they required bearings, bushes or other parts at some crucial moment.

As it turned out, the "Driver to Europe" short-list that Buzz Perkins had in the Grand Prix office included the names of Phil and Merv, as well as mine, and we stood equal chances of getting the coveted trip. When I was eventually picked to go, Colin came with me as racing mechanic. We have all progressed since then. Merv is now a top engineer, partner with his father in their precision engineering and well-drilling firm; Colin has a motor accessory shop in Auckland, and Phil made a trip to

England on his own and stayed to become Jack Brabham's company secretary.

I'm sure I had covered half the 1958 GP distance in my sleep before I woke on the morning of January 12th, helped load the Coopers and set off for Ardmore. My Cooper was in the second heat, with Jack in the 1960 cc Cooper, Roy Salvadori (Syracuse-Connaught) and Ross Jensen in Stirling Moss's old 250F Maserati. So far as I was concerned—a warning from Jack and Pop helped—this heat was strictly to warm up for the main race, but I managed to finish second.

The Cooper was running beautifully and I couldn't have felt better. I was hoping the powers that mattered in the NZIGP Association were favourably impressed.

Colin and I had given the Cooper its umpteenth polish, lifted it on the jack, started up and were warming up the engine and transmission when the gearbox gave a horrible "clunk". I didn't make a habit of swearing, but a few well-chosen adjectives were in order at that moment—just 23 minutes before the start of the race.

Jack thought I was joking when I rushed over to tell him. He should have been able to tell by the look on my face that I wasn't. The gearbox was obviously out of commission for the rest of the day, so the only answer was a quick replacement. Jack came back a few minutes later lugging a new gearbox he had brought out for Dick Gibson. I don't think Dick realizes even now what happened to it.

A swarm of spanners round the gearbox removed it in great haste while the cars were forming up on the grid. I was well aware of the vacant space on the front row, so were the organizers and crowd. Starting time came and went and still we were battling under the Cooper, while the cars sat on the grid with drivers looking impatiently for the starter.

Suddenly came a report that there was some oil on the track. No one was quite sure where, but an official car set out to look for it . . . then they found some oil . . . and a little bit more . . .

and then, of course, they had to let the cement dry.

There may have been some oil on the circuit, but looking back I think the organizers were being helpful to the local boy, although he didn't have time to appreciate the gesture while sweating away three inches from the underside of a Cooper gearbox.

When the flag eventually fell, the final bolts were being done up. The oil was splashed in while I hastily donned helmet and goggles, then I was off half a lap behind the field, but definitely in the race. By the eighth lap I had passed ten of the specials and oldsters at the tail of the field and was climbing out of eighth place when the engine started missing. I whistled into the pits to change the plugs. This took seven minutes and by that time I was at the back of the field again. I kept plugging on and was starting to enjoy myself when the gear-lever jerked coming out of College Corner and I was temporarily in neutral. Pulling away from the hairpin the same thing happened, so I made another stop.

One look was enough. My helmet, goggles and gloves were tossed on the pit counter. The bolts holding the bell housing had worked loose, the oil was somewhere on the circuit and all the gears were red hot. The distorted gears made an indecent racket as we pushed the car on to the trailer. I sat glumly in the pit with the family, watching Jack show Ross the way home in the final laps and thought of my European chances going steadily down the drain.

At the presentation of trophies that night, it was announced that I had been chosen as the first "Driver to Europe". All at once my ambitions had been fulfilled and, as the crowd clamoured for a speech, I vaguely remember standing, muttering something about doing my best for the country, that I was very grateful, stuttered something else, and sitting down very embarrassed.

March 15th was sailing date, which meant I could race the Cooper at all the other New Zealand meetings before shipping

it. Next race on the calendar was Levin, 400 miles south of
Auckland. It was a tight one-mile circuit built by Ron Frost,
who also raced a 1500 cc single-cam Cooper. Ron is a short
Englishman with a small moustache and an accent that makes
every one of his vast repertoire of stories side-splitting. In New
Zealand all English people have accents, almost in the manner
of a Frenchman speaking English. To a New Zealander all
Englishmen are "pommies" and their accents pick them out
in a crowd, just as my New Zealand twang branded me a
Colonial when I stepped off the plane at London Airport.

Uncrowned king of the Levin circuit was Syd Jensen, who
raced an immaculate 500 cc F3 Cooper and as a former motor-
cyclist of long experience—he had raced in England and on the
Isle of Man with the two-wheelers—he knew the tricks that
made the double-knocker Norton really go. Syd and his father
were also stalwarts of the local club and a Levin race was nearly
always won by "Frosty" or Syd.

There was a "New Zealanders only" race before the main
event and I managed to win this. Before we lined up on the
grid for the big race, I told Jack and Archie Scott-Brown, who
was racing his Lister-Jaguar, about the starting procedure. The
idea was to ignore the starter and watch Syd Jensen who always seemed to get away well. When he moved everyone
moved and we always made good starts there.

Archie was a great favourite in New Zealand. He arrived
late in Auckland for the GP and was not on the expected plane.
There was a parade of competing cars and drivers through the
main street and the green-and-gold Lister-Jag was to be one of
the main eye-catchers. Archie was missing when the other cars
were being loaded, so Reg Grierson decided they would put
the Lister on a flat-deck truck and explain it away to him when
he arrived. Half a dozen people were pushing the big Lister
on to the truck when a diminutive figure wearing a sports
jacket pushed through the onlookers and offered to lend a hand.
That was Archie.

The way he could throw the Lister round, despite the physical disability of his unformed right arm always amazed me.

Brabham seemed a certainty to win at Levin, which was a real Cooper circuit until Archie confounded everyone, Jack included, by keeping the Lister right on the tail of the 1960 cc Cooper. Archie passed me with little bother just before the straight and I sat behind him as long as I could, watching the Lister swinging from lock to lock to lock as Archie played continual correction to keep the car pointing the right way through the tricky bits, then crabbing away from the corner under acceleration. I took a third behind Jack and Archie.

The overnight ferry from Wellington to Christchurch's port of Lyttelton becomes a seagoing Steering Wheel Club as drivers, mechanics and hangers-on gather in the saloon to swap yarns. During these sessions we would try and get overseas drivers to unwind with lurid motor-racing tales, both sporting and social.

Wigram has never been kind to me. The first year we raced the Austin Healey there I dropped out with a holed piston; the next year with the 1750 cc Cooper the crown-wheel and pinion gave up; the third year the head gasket went on the 2-litre Cooper, but I managed to finish third behind Ron Flockhart's BRM and Jack's Cooper. In 1960 I blew a works 2·5 motor all over the track in practice, as I watched helplessly in the mirrors. I was accelerating between the hairpin and a fairly quick left-hander when everything locked in a billow of white smoke and bits of engine were bouncing along the track behind me, just like a Brockbank cartoon.

An Auckland student mate of mine, Malcolm Gill, lent me his Lycoming Special for the race and I thundered round behind 5 litres of air-cooled aeroplane engine. The car was designed and built in Auckland by Ralph Watson and featured independent suspension all round.

At the following meeting it had rained hard for days and the track was virtually under water. Ponds on the back straight set several cars into high-speed spins on to the wet grass and it took me almost half a mile of muddy grass before I caught my spin. The 1962 race was run under respectable conditions, but again a spin put me out of the running. So Wigram is justifiably not among my favourite circuits.

Stuart Lewis Evans and Roy Salvadori both had their Connaughts at Wigram in 1958, Stuart with the weird-looking "toothpaste tube" and Roy with the more conventional-bodied car. I really liked Roy. He is the epitome of smoothness and calmness, though his nickname "smoothadori" did not stem from his prowess in a racing car. The average New Zealand racing driver has six big races a year if he is lucky and regards a spin as a black mark and a shunt of any magnitude as a hint that he should retire. I suppose this was my outlook in the early years and I remember Roy walking back to the pits after nearly writing off the Connaught and himself as well, saying with disarming nonchalance, "I've bent it."

I was using a little side-valve Morris Minor as a runabout in Auckland and had lent the car to Jack over the race period. When we were taking Roy to the airport after the GP, he turned to Jack and said quietly, "Do you really think you ought to take a young fellow like this to Europe and turn him into another motor-racing layabout?"

Archie won at Wigram in the Lister and I retired miserably with a broken crown-wheel and pinion. Dick Gibson's Cooper did not last much longer than mine, but the evening paper was full of the Gibson race saga, with a mention that Scott-Brown had won. A girl reporter had spent the race in Gibson's pit!

Pop must have started to think I was losing my touch on the wharf circuit at Dunedin the next week-end and I was beginning to have doubts myself after two shunts in two laps of practice.

On my second practice lap I went too quickly into the "esses". I made the first half, but ploughed straight ahead into a bank of sand going out. I limped back to the pits and we took the body off to extricate the sand. This done, I dashed out again, only to meet a chap in a Citroen Special on his first tour. He was going far slower and I shunted him square in the tail. The nose of the Cooper was square, too, when we pushed the cars apart and the radiator broken. Pop wasn't impressed, but we beat out the nose and soldered the radiator and I finished second behind Ross in the 250F and ahead of Archie in the Lister.

The Southland Sports Car Club had built themselves an ambitious 1·5-mile circuit in the sand dunes near Oreti, where beach racing had been held previously. The circuit was not unlike Zandvoort, according to visitors, but the surface of smooth riverbed shingle was very slippery. I tried Michelin Xs on the back of the Cooper and, although understeering a bit, it held the road better. This must have been one of the few times Michelin Xs have been used successfully on a Formula car. Ross was going well in the 250F and won after both Jack and Archie made excursions into the sand. Jack had flown hurriedly out from Australia for the race and left his racing shoes at home. He drove in ordinary shoes, but caught the web of the right one under the brake pedal going into a corner and spun—or so he said. I finished second.

We had entered the Cooper in a hill-climb near Timaru, where the shingle surface was very loose, so we locked the differential by filling it with plumber's lead. This gave a better grip—good enough to break a half-shaft at the second start— but I could not get near the times Maurie Stanton was setting with his ungainly-looking rear-engined Stanton Special. It was a cleverly -designed car, powered by a supercharged air-cooled Gypsy Moth aeroplane engine and had independent suspension all round with olio struts at the rear.

This special held all the New Zealand sprint records, had covered a standing quarter-mile in 12·42 sec and Maurie was the fastest man in New Zealand, having recorded 173·8 mph over a measured kilometre near Christchurch.

The evening after the hill-climb I went to a dance in Timaru and was immediately attracted by a very pretty blonde girl called Patricia and, as the songs say, this was the start of something big. I didn't realize it at the time, but Pat was to become my wife four years later, although a lot of turbulent water was to flow under my bridge before thoughts of matrimony began to catch up with me.

There was one last race at Ardmore on March 1st, which resulted in another win for Ross in the 250F. He was really sparkling after a season which won him the New Zealand Gold Star award as top driver. I had a brief tussle with him, which ended when I stopped to replace a plug lead. I drove hard after the stop and eventually was placed fifth.

Details of the "Driver to Europe" scheme had now been arranged and Buzz Perkins had written to most of the race organizers in Europe, telling them a raw colonial would soon be arriving on their doorsteps and would they please look after him.

Colin was going to England and Jack's suggestion that he should work for me as racing mechanic was enthusiastically received by both of us, although Colin was worried that his lack of qualifications would be a handicap. This was amply compensated by his being a hard worker and learning quickly. The Grand Prix Association thought the arrangement excellent.

Buzz arranged bookings by air to Sydney and from there on the *Orantes*. He arranged a bank account of about £500 for us in England, with a promise of more to come later. Department stores around Auckland had donated shirts, overalls, jackets and ties. Our smart black blazers with "NZIGP Driver to Europe" in silver letters under a fern leaf on the pocket looked really smart.

The publicity began to snowball as departure day drew near, and on March 15th we were swept out to the airport to be bundled on the plane amid a swarm of photographers, reporters friends and both our mothers, who cheered us by making a bad attempt to cover up the fact that they were crying.

As the plane taxied down the runway, I felt miserable.

The hostess had seen it all before and took us into the cabin of the plane to introduce us to the crew, who described the complicated mass of gauges and switches on the control panels. On every air trip to or from New Zealand since then I have visited the crew and have come to know most of the pilots on TEAL fairly well. On homeward trips, I invariably watch the North Auckland coastline coming into view, standing up front beside the crew.

Travelling on this scale was new to me. I had never been out of New Zealand and regarded Colin as an experienced traveller because he had once visited Sydney. Colin was twenty-two and I was twenty—a young twenty at that.

We were met at Sydney airport by Noel Naylor, a liaison arranged by Geoff Wiles, a NZIGP member and old friend of the family in Auckland. Noel took us round Sydney showing us through the National Park and visiting Wollongong and Botany Bay.

The Cooper had been shipped from Auckland to Sydney, so Noel took us down to the wharves to supervise the loading of the car on to the *Orantes*. Seeing cars loaded on boats scares me. Each time my heart stops beating while the car is swaying in the sling.

The next day we embarked, took a brief glance at the tiny four-berth cabin and hurried back on deck to watch the ship leave port. After the ballyhoo at Auckland, Colin and I felt flat as the *Orantes* pulled away from the wharf. Hundreds of people waving up at hundreds more waving down and trying vainly to catch paper streamers. Everyone waving at someone else. Except us.

The ship was loading cargo in Melbourne for three days, which gave us a chance to explore the town. We were invited to dinner with Lex Davison and slept the night at his fabulous home "Killara Park". Lex is a wealthy man who has been motor racing for longer than he cares to remember. He graduated through the old specials to P3 Alfa Romeos, Super-Squalo Ferraris, Coopers and now he races a 2·6 lowline Cooper and one of the big factory Aston Martin DBR1/300 GP cars. When we visited him his garage housed a 1914 GP Delage with desmodromic valves, a 1933 Alta sports car, an 1100 cc supercharged Cooper-Vincent, a big Ford-Customline, a Ranchwagon and a couple of boats!

Back on board we were soon in the swing of shipboard life, synchronizing dressing in the tiny cabin so that one person at a time went out properly dressed, instead of four people leaving together fastening the final buttons. We were both seasick and refused to leave our bunks, fully expecting to hear Gabriel's final trumpet call and determined to be in the correct dying position when it came.

The weather soon improved and we spent most of our time sunbathing or lying in the swimming pool. Among the mail we had received in Melbourne was a letter from Pop saying Buzz had arranged a race in a works F2 Cooper at Aintree on April 15th. As the *Orantes* would not arrive in time, Buzz had booked an air passage for me from Aden.

With permission granted to climb into the hold, I spent an hour with the Cooper, taking off the brake and clutch pedals and collecting my St Christopher medal and my helmet and goggles, all of which I would be needing at Aintree. Roy and Jack, the Cooper drivers at this time, both had considerably longer legs than I and my tailor-made pedals might save time in England.

We docked at Aden on March 10th. I was treated royally by the Shell Company representatives. Their public relations officer, Mr Pepper, had booked me in at the Crescent Hotel—the best in Aden—and in the next few days took me everywhere there was to go. This was the first "foreign" soil on which I had spent any time and I was frightened by a shifty-looking character with swivel eyes and a grubby suit, who haunted the hotel lobby. I felt sure he was a spy.

The Shell agents in Aden were Besse and Company and I was taken out to Tony Besse's Hollywood-style home. Mrs Besse lent me her XK140 Jaguar for the afternoon, on condition that I tuned it, so after a carburettor check Mr Pepper and I motored out to Little Aden, about 25 miles from the city, where the big BP refinery is situated. I spent the next morning driving around in an Austin Healey that belonged to another of the Besse brothers and swam all afternoon in the near-tepid sea. Luncheons, dinners, introductions and swimming turned the four-day wait into a luxury holiday and I was almost sorry to board the plane the next morning.

By the time the plane circled down through the cloud to land at London Airport, I had convinced myself I was looking forward to England, so buttoned up my new blazer and stepped into the sub-zero English summer. I had arrived—and was scared stiff.

FIVE

First Races in Europe

EVERYTHING WAS VASTLY different to the pictures I had conjured up, with so many people going everywhere so quickly. Long rows of houses followed each other down narrow streets in the suburbs. Sports cars were everywhere. If someone had an MG TC in Auckland, I usually knew him by name. The owner was an enthusiast and the car usually had a competition history. It was obviously very different in England.

Jack drove me to his Dorking home, where I met his wife, Betty, and his parents, who were over from Australia. Early next morning Jack and I drove to Surbiton, through the town and down Ewell Road to the Cooper works. The factory was a modern brick building with an unusual curved frontage, large windows and the name COOPER in large letters across the top. John Cooper, his jet-black hair sleeked down, pipe clamped firmly between his teeth and wearing a brown overall, was introduced. "Pleased to meet you, boy," he said from behind the pipe. "Come in and have a look round."

All around the workshop were Coopers in various stages of assembly and I asked where my car was. "Your car, boy?" said the pipe. "In that tube rack, I reckon." I couldn't see any car in the pile of chassis tubes, but it slowly dawned on me. I felt very small.

I cheered up when John pointed out a freshly-painted chassis as mine. He took me round to meet the rest of the boys. His mechanic Bill James and Mike "Noddy" Grohman were preparing the works car for Monaco. Dougie Johnson became a close friend in the early days and was a big help when Colin and I were assembling the Cooper. On discovering I was a New Zealander he announced to the shop, "Here's another one—lock up your tools, or you'll lose 'em." I soon learnt that to be called "another bloody colonial" wasn't half as bad as it sounded.

My tools were still on the water, so I had to badger some spanners from Dougie to fit my special pedals. The drive at Aintree was uppermost in my mind and I was worried about it. It had been arranged with John Cooper that I should drive the Cooper with which Jack had won a Goodwood race the week before, but Charles Cooper, John's father, was not in favour of providing anyone who walked into the shop with a works racing car, and seemed about to scuttle my plans. John suggested I find some overalls and start cleaning the Cooper, while he went upstairs to attend to the domestic difficulties.

The prototype coil-spring F2 Cooper had not been touched since Jack's Goodwood win. I was only too glad to get my hands dirty—at least it wasn't something strange and new.

Fortunately things went smoothly in the top office, Cooper Senior's only stipulation being that I should insure the car, which I did for £50. As the starting money had been fixed at £60, I was making a profit before the race even started. Things were not so bad after all.

From the outside, a drearier place than Aintree couldn't be imagined. High, dirty brick walls didn't improve the picture, but we were soon in the paddock and I was marvelling at the grand transporters fielded by even the smallest équipes—I later learnt from tedious experience that the transporters were handy shelters from the rain.

Racing cars require the same treatment the world over and I occupied myself topping up the Cooper with water, fuel and oil, checking the tyres and warming it up. I felt like a fish out of water coming from circuits where I knew everyone to Aintree where I didn't know a soul. Every second male sported a handlebar moustache and everyone seemed to have an Oxford accent. If you wanted to find anyone, the best bet was the bar. This shook me. Surely there was a race on and work to be done?

I didn't drink, but was intrigued by the licensed bars in the paddock, where liquor is forbidden in New Zealand. Sly boozing there is usually done from bottles behind car boots in the car park.

I liked the circuit, apart from Waterways, the long, fast right-hander with a solid brick wall all the way round the outside. Airfield racing in New Zealand had spoiled me and I was used to wide-open spaces, with plenty of room for painless correction of mistakes. During the race the carburation played up— the 1500 Climax had 42 mm Webers fitted and wouldn't accelerate cleanly. With every lap I reminded myself that after a lot of dreaming I was actually racing in England. The race results made me think I had been dreaming too much in the race itself, as I had finished ninth in the F2 section. I knew about Tony Brooks and Stuart Lewis Evans and didn't mind being beaten by them, but I went looking for Jack to find who the other names were—Russell, Burgess, Marsh, etc.

I hadn't exactly rocketed to the top with my first belated effort and a further blow was to come when I called on a particular oil Company's competitions manager to organize a fuel contract. The New Zealand office had told me I wouldn't have much trouble securing a fat retainer, but the gentleman in London thought otherwise. He informed me I was only one of hundreds who arrived in the spring and suggested I should do a year of club racing, then see him again. I was shattered.

At eight o'clock on the Monday morning after the race, I was waiting at the factory gate, eager to start building "my"

Cooper. Dougie Johnson and I set to work bending water pipes, fitting brackets and assembling the suspension.

That morning a letter from the BRDC (the British Racing Drivers' Club) made me feel much happier. My entry had been accepted for the International Daily Express Trophy meeting at Silverstone on May 3rd, providing I performed to the satisfaction of the observers in practice. Even better, I was to get £75 for my services. Jack had been at work on the entry apparently. I now had a car and an entry, but also another worry, as my Coventry-Climax engine had not arrived and I gathered that if one dropped on the Cooper doorstep I would be trampled in the rush of other drivers to collect it.

Colin had arrived with the rest of my luggage and our tools. There were four Coopers being built in the factory by ''amateurs'' at the time—Syd Jensen, Allan Mackay, myself and one other. We must have covered miles during the assembly, running up to the spares department with a cardboard box, coming down to screw on the bits, then back up the stairs for another helping. It was almost a case of locking scarce parts in the toolbox overnight. Allan Mackay was a great winter sports enthusiast and returning from a week-end's skiing was puzzled to find his car was not as far advanced as he could have sworn it was when he left. Ours, on the other hand, were nearly complete, apart from the engines.

Colin and I returned from lunch one afternoon to find a little two-stroke Villiers motor-cycle engine sitting in the chassis, much to the shop's amusement.

Colin bought a Mark I Zephyr from New Zealander Ray Thackwell, who had been racing a F2 Cooper with the world champion speedway rider and compatriot Ronnie Moore. The boys had formed the "Kiwi Equipe" and toured the smaller meetings with their Coopers. Colin and I moved into the Royal Oak Hotel, adjoining the Cooper premises. Nothing could have been handier. They did not usually take boarders and once again we were grateful for Brabham's persuasive

The McLaren stable: left, the Ford Pilot, used for trials and rallies as well as family shopping; centre, the much-raced Austin Healey and, right, the Ulster Austin

McLaren is welcomed home by "Pop", mother, and sister Janice after his second season on the European circuit

Rowing and water ski-ing provide pleasant relaxation for a racing driver. Above, with coach "Rub" Ferron in New Zealand; below, "cornering" at Lakeside in Australia

powers. The saloon bar of the Oak was also the unofficial Cooper Clubhouse.

It appeared the only way to get an engine was to collect one off the production line at the factory, so we followed John to Coventry in our Zephyr, fully extended to a proud 92 mph trying to keep up with the flying Cooper.

On leaving New Zealand we were issued with impressive International Driving licences, with sections in nearly every language in the world. New Zealand "old lags" in England soon put us wise and we found an international licence had little effect on official wrath, after being stopped for doing 31 mph with a trailer. Producing a New Zealand licence and pleading ignorance of "foreign" road rules usually averted a summons and brought only a paternal warning.

At the Climax works we met technical chiefs Wally Hassan and Harry Spears, and were taken to see my engine on the brake.

Seeing the engine vibrating and bellowing on the brake scared me. When the big needle flickered up to 5000 revs, I thought I had better leave before our little group was felled with flying con rods.

With our new motor proudly installed, the Cooper was one of the quickest assembly jobs to come out of the works. By the end of the first week Cooper Senior had softened towards us, when he saw that we meant business and I think he probably had a hand in the early delivery of the engine.

We finished the Cooper at nine o'clock on Thursday night and the following morning were at Silverstone getting ready for practice. The engine was still tight and at times a little disappointing. I ran the car up and down the club straight, to loosen things up, fearing that I would be branded as one of those obnoxious people who keep trying to break the lap record around the paddock.

After a good start in the race I had a terrific dice with Jim Russell, Ivor Bueb and Ian Burgess. I had no idea I was third

5

until the race finished. This Cooper was a great improvement on the car I had driven at Aintree and I was very pleased. The circuit was impressively fast and called for concentration, but I was proud of my best lap of 99·4 mph, not far short of the "ton".

The next week-end I was at Silverstone again and won a club race, to the disgust of the other drivers, who objected to "factory" participation at their meeting. I should have referred them to the oil company competition manager.

Colin and I had been working on the Cooper from dawn to dark every day, so a letter from home asking if we had visited Buckingham Palace or the Strand received a dusty answer. While the works F1 team were on the Continent, Colin and I had moved into their shed and now had the use of welding equipment and other F1 facilities.

With a race at Brands Hatch in the offing, I took the car down on a "Cooper" School day. Ian Burgess, the teacher, took me for a lap in the school's Cooper sports car. Then I brought out my F2 car and, after nine laps, had managed 58·6 sec and broken the lap record. But perhaps I was trying a bit too hard and suddenly it was "grass, track, grass, track" as I spun at Kidney Bend.

"Big Ginger" Devlin from Coopers, who had been standing with Colin, said, "That mate of yours will either be bloody good, or he'll kill himself." Colin said nothing. The same thing had occurred to him.

I was on the front row of the grid at Brands and led off the line with 5500 rpm on the clock and not too much wheelspin, when Ken Tyrrell went sizzling past in Alan Brown's blue Cooper.

I didn't even know him and was perturbed that he should be going so much faster. I pulled up beside him at Clearways and he left me standing. I later found he was using second and third gears and high revs, while I had been using third and fourth. Ken owns a big timber business near Guildford and runs a team of works-supported Cooper Formula Three cars as a hobby.

I managed to sneak by this puzzlingly quick car at the hairpin a couple of laps later and won the heat from Wicken's Cooper. In the second heat I piled on a few extra revs and headed Tyrrell into Paddock Bend and held the lead to the finish. Ronnie Moore was placed third behind Wicken and Syd Jensen was seventh, handicapped by an obsolete set of tyres.

Australians and New Zealanders are fanatical gamblers, but at home they stick to horses. I was amazed to learn there were bookies complete with bags and blackboards, laying the odds on the field at the back of the stands. They must have been happy after the race, as I was a rank outsider whom no one had fancied much and the bookies had cleaned up.

Crystal Palace on Whit Monday was next on the list, but the concrete walls curbed my enthusiasm and I was fourth fastest in practice, equal with Syd Jensen at 1 min 3·8 sec. We spent most of Sunday afternoon changing tyres, putting more braking on the front and increasing the rear toe-in to promote understeer.

Monday morning was a shocker, raining hard and the track covered with water. At anything above 50 mph the car just sat up on the pools and sailed straight ahead like a hydroplane without a rudder. Dicey wasn't the word. One of the walls altered my line in one corner and also increased the carefully-set rear toe-in by bending a wishbone. This, I thought, had really cooked my chances, and to make matters worse the engine started to boil on the starting line. The temperature stayed reasonably respectable in the race, however, and I began to enjoy dicing with Syd for seventh place.

I was well back on the grid for the final, but it had stopped raining and I shocked Colin and myself by lying 4th on the first lap. Poor Colin had missed me and thought I had spun, as he ignored the leaders to scan the group towards the tail of the field. The bent rear end made it just right for right-hand corners, with exactly the desired amount of oversteer, although it was a little peculiar on left-handers and the straight. Burgess, Tommy Bridger, Wicken, Bueb and myself had a terrific battle. Wicken blew up and Burgess led Bridger home, with me third. Our race average was two miles an hour higher than Brabham's previous lap record!

For the next meeting at Brands Hatch, Ian Burgess and I fitted double wishbones at the back of our Coopers, following the F1 lead. But they were no improvement, in fact the cars handled worse than before and we were both disgusted, especially when Jack told us Trintignant's old Cooper had been handling better than the new double-wishbone works cars at Monaco. Burgess' mechanics worked most of Saturday night, converting his rear suspension back to normal, but I didn't feel like burning that much midnight oil with a race the next day.

Ian made a terrific start in the first heat, as did Syd Jensen in his Cooper, but Lewis Evans overwhelmed the pair of them to win. The second heat looked like a New Zealand benefit for a while. On the first lap Lewis Evans and Henry Taylor led Ronnie Moore (Cooper), Syd (Cooper), myself and Burgess. The "down under" gang finished third, fifth and sixth after a spirited dice. The wheel-to-wheel scraps we had in the F2 days were exciting affairs then, but I shudder to think what they would have been like with some of the present Formula Two boys mixing it in as well.

I had never been to the Continent and the prospect of a race on the banked Montlhéry circuit, just outside Paris, was exciting. Ian Burgess was driving Tommy Atkins' F2 Cooper and I was grateful of Tommy's offer to take my car in the transporter, under the guidance of chief mechanic Harry Pearce. There was a spare seat in the cab, so Colin accompanied Harry and Peter, while I went in Ian Burgess' Anglia with his charming wife, Solvei and Charles Cooper.

The Montlhéry banked oval has staged several speed records and endurance attempts. In the F2 Coopers we were in low gear three times on each lap, yet still averaged 100 mph.

Only one end of the banking was used and a large road section was incorporated. As it was my first experience on this type of circuit, I received plenty of advice. People told me to hold the car high on the banking and dive off the end, but I preferred to let the car find its own line and banking height, so that it wasn't affected by either up or down thrust.

I finally rejected the advice of the "keep it high" school when I was shown the missing bricks at the top of the banking and the concrete plaque at the bottom, where someone had gone into orbit. I was to be reminded of this incident and poisoned against banked circuits a few months later at Avus.

As the circuit was about 15 miles from Paris, we booked at an hotel there and commuted to the track. I toured "Gay Paree" and gaped in the approved tourist manner. The jam of Citroens, Simcas and Renaults battling around the Arc de Triomphe was thrilling and inevitably we found ourselves at the top of the Eiffel Tower.

In practice we were pulling a 3·7 back-end ratio, but our times were rather miserable compared with other Cooper drivers using the same ratio. Fastest in practice was Frenchman Guelfi in Alan Brown's Cooper. The race day was a scorcher with hardly any wind and it looked grim for Ian and me, who were two of the few without oil coolers.

An overnight ratio change made all the difference and Ian and I led the pack for about six laps. I was slipstreaming Ian on the fast bits trying to save my engine, but when I saw Guelfi starting to close on us, I took over the lead and drew out three seconds on the Frenchman, before I had to make a dead stop to avoid a Lotus at the hairpin. Guelfi ducked through on the inside. The air temperature on the banking was very high, so was the oil temperature, and the oil pressure was 30 lb lower than normal.

I caught Guelfi again and we were racing side by side around the banking, but fortunately he braked early for the 150 mph right-hander which Ian and I had found we could take flat and I led for another six laps, until the oil pump ate something it didn't like, and the "clonk" as it burped dropped my engine 400 revs and I had to wave Guelfi and Henry Taylor by to finish third.

That night I had my introduction to champagne at a riotous dinner in a little hotel off the Pont d'Orleans, which ended in pandemonium when Harry Pearce jammed me in a dustbin outside.

Our mechanical misfortunes for the week-end had not ended with the race, however, as the top-moulded radiator hose split on the Anglia as we were rushing across France to catch the ferry. We found a tiny French garage and borrowed a vintage acetylene rig, battling for hours to make a Heath Robinson repair which got us back to England.

After Montlhéry my engine was taken back to Coventry, where they found the oil pumps had seized, one big-end bearing gone and another on the way. With Rheims coming up, we persuaded Climax to fit a set of the super-scarce 11 : 1 pistons; back at the factory I had spent four days fitting a set of disc brakes and a larger radiator for better cooling on the fast circuit. We had also fitted higher "glass house" screens to aid the streamlining and improved the double-wishbone suspension.

Ross and Hazel Jensen had just arrived in England with Buzz Perkins, so there was a New Zealand contingent in the pits at Rheims. I walked down to watch the F1 cars going through the Grand Curve—the long, fast right-hander after the pits. Fangio was barrelling through on full noise with the 250F Maserati. He tweaked the tail out coming under the Dunlop Bridge and held the drift all the way through the curve. Mike Hawthorn was another spectacular performer in the Ferrari, but though he wasn't lifting his foot through the curve—and only a brave few were game to keep it down all the way—he was working hard at the wheel and did not seem as neat as

Fangio. This was the curve where Musso was killed during the race in the works Ferrari.

Rheims was a new experience. There was no question of taking the cars to the circuit in the transporter; we simply climbed in and went barking through the traffic in the Coopers! It seemed strange to be encouraged by the gendarmes, who waved us through the race queues. Our race ended in a faster queue with Jean Behra's Ferrari at the head. Henry Taylor and I had a terrific slipstreaming dice in our Coopers and eventually placed sixth and seventh. With only two really slow corners, the rest of the circuit was flat out in the F2 cars and the answer was to tuck into the slipstream of a faster car and sit inches from his exhaust, being towed.

I often think the enthusiasm of racing people for Rheims is not for the excitement of the circuit—featureless in flat corn-fields—but the nocturnal antics at Brigitte's Bar. This tiny bar in a back street is packed every night after practice, with a grand finale on race night.

After Mike Hawthorn's win, Brigitte's was clearly the place to go. Colin and I arrived early and wandered into the little garden, admiring the French girls. Peter Collins and Louise turned up, followed by a noisy mob centred round the irrepressible Mike. Stuart Lewis Evans, Salvadori, Ross and Hazel Jensen, and Buzz and his wife had also arrived to see the fun, which soon started.

A marble bust of a dowdy old gentleman stood on a four-foot pedastal at one end of the little garden, in the centre of which was a mosaic dance floor. Trees grew around the borders of the garden with a fishpond in one corner. An ideal setting for the shambles which was to follow.

Mike and Peter dragged the statue on to the dance floor and painted it with lipstick, a cigarette was fed between the marble lips and a Russian flag materialized to be draped around it. The party was getting under way. It was decided to dress the statue more respectably, so John Cooper was divested of his coat and trousers, while the flag was removed from the statue and draped around his torso. To much clapping and cheering John set off on a complicated Russian dance, in which he was soon joined by a neat French girl.

Then a tree-climbing competition caught on and Mike, leaning against a trunk, looked up thinking it had started to rain. The audience nearly went hysterical as someone announced from his perch that at last he had peed on Hawthorn from a great height.

Mike was the next performer, wrestling with a huge earthenware plant pot in the centre of the floor. Inevitably it overturned and Mike stood surveying a pile of earth with a French beret on his blond hair and a large broom in his hands.

"Oh no," said John, "this is it." Mike needed no encouragement and with a swing that would have done credit to Sammy Snead he showered an innocent group of drinkers with earth. Soon the air was thick with flying earth and the pile had disappeared from the floor. While everyone was spitting earth and rubbing it from hair and eyes, Mike was into the next act, coupling up a hose. "Don't worry, it'll get the dirt off," he yelled and proceeded to sluice the garden and everyone in it.

The atmosphere quietened when Mike went indoors for a drink, but Britt Pearce, his mechanic sprawled asleep in a chair, was regarded as fair game in the absence of the boss. So Britt and the chair were slowly submerged in the fishpond. Mike came crashing out of the bar to find the culprit and, as I happened to be standing beside the pool, he grabbed me and would have tossed me into the pool with Britt, had I not wriggled free.

The party finished in chaos as Britt, now fully awake, stormed into the bar and started throwing chairs round until Mike calmed him down and we all went home.

Our little group of New Zealanders were overawed. Nothing like this ever happened at home. Perhaps it happened after every championship race?

SIX

Hawthorn's World Title

THE 1958 GERMAN GP, to be run as a combined F1 and F2 event on the Nürburgring, was a race on which I had set my heart. Entries were extremely tight, as Schmitz the organizer had fixed the overall list at 18 cars and there were at least 20 people trying for a start in both sections. John Cooper was in trouble over his own entries and had little time to worry about mine. He could secure only Salvadori's entry in the F1 car and Brabham was the only team entry accepted for the F2 section. Buzz Perkins tried an approach from the NZIGP, but did not even get a reply.

By late July I was getting despondent. The Nürburgring was the one track that had captured my imagination and it looked as though I was going to miss it. John Cooper persuaded me to go along with the team, if only as a spectator, and Tommy Atkins offered space for my Cooper in his transporter, which was taking Burgess' car. In desperation I sent Schmitz a cable, requesting a place as first reserve, and was thrilled to learn that I would be on the reserve list and almost assured of a start. John Cooper was morbidly optimistic, "Someone will shunt in practice for sure."

I had just taken a third at Snetterton (Bueb won in his Lister Jaguar) and the car was running well, but as a precautionary measure we decided to drop the sump for a check. To our horror we found three of the main bearing caps were cracked and we were due to leave for the 'Ring in less than a week.

We phoned Climax's, who sent a set of new, stronger un-machined caps, which had to be fitted, then line bored. Colin and I stripped the engine and took the crankcase and bearing caps to Prince Engineering in Kingston. The helpful foreman was worried about the job: an aluminium crankcase of this type was not difficult to line bore starting from scratch, but on this occasion a lot of setting up was required, as metal had to be removed only from the caps, not the block. When they finished we re-fitted the crank, but found it wouldn't turn, so had to take the whole thing back and beg the foreman to try again. This time I suggested that they bore out to the top limit suggested by the bearing manufacturers and not worry if a little metal was removed from the block. When we refitted the shaft it spun in the bearings to our great relief. While the head was off we also ground the valves and fitted new springs.

Ian Burgess and I drove over to the 'Ring in his long-suffering Anglia, arriving at the little village of Adenau just outside the circuit on the Wednesday afternoon. I had spent hours studying maps of the circuit and couldn't wait to get to grips with it. According to my map there seemed only six obviously tricky corners and I fondly imagined I would soon pick up the rest. I hadn't taken into account that the circuit runs round a choice section of the Eifel Mountains and included many vertical hazards not indicated on my map. These made a simple curve, hidden by a hump on the approach, a trap that had to be carefully memorized to avoid breasting the rise at 100 mph getting ready for a right-hand sweep, when the track dropped away to the left.

We pumped the Anglia's tyres up hard and headed for the 'Ring, joining the circuit at the entrance near the Adenau Bridge. As the Anglia ground over the hill leading away from the bridge, I saw the circuit winding up through the forest and, with a sinking feeling in my stomach, realized I had been taking it too cheaply. Ian was hurling the poor little Anglia into the corners. "It's the only way to learn," he said with a hint more of glee than apology as I braced myself in the seat.

A signboard indicated a hairpin which Ian approached as though he wasn't aware of the fact. This was my first introduction to the famous Karussel. Ian knew the circuit like the back of his hand. Just as it seemed we must depart through the high hedge, he swung left, dropping over the lip into the banking of the Karussel at 50 mph, and we bounced round like the ball in a roulette wheel. A mild application of "G" force had me pinned in the Anglia seat and as I was bracing myself for being slung over the hedge instead of through it, we were off the banking and motoring level again.

My first fears of meeting someone coming the other way while we were using the whole road sideways were dispelled when I learned that, even though it is a toll road open to the public for two shillings a lap, all traffic has to travel in a clockwise direction. I had many frights on that first lap, with Ian winding up the Anglia and approaching blind bends at a suicidal rate, only to have them open out in front of us as kinks in the forest.

The dips and rises on the main straight made the overhead bridge at the end seem about three feet above the track. I swallowed hard and closed my eyes.

By dusk that evening Colin, Harry Pearce and Peter had arrived in the transporter. Their "uneventful" trip included hitting a "level" crossing at fair speed and bouncing both Coopers nearly out of their runners. Mine was on top and had belted against the framework, creasing the tail. Fortunately the high-mounted fuel pump was unharmed.

Naturally they were keen to see the circuit, so we all piled into the Anglia with me at the wheel. The 'Ring was pretty, late in the evening—the long black ribbon of road winding haphazardly through the trees, up hill and down dale, between rustic wooden fences. The long rays of the setting sun shone down through the valleys and glinted on the bonnets of the Ferraris and Porsches, as drivers familiarized themselves with the tricks of the 14-mile circuit. A blue Alfa Romeo whistled by —Behra; then a Porsche Carrera screeched past on the limit, into the Wipperman—Bonnier. I had covered the circuit eight times before going back to Adenau for dinner and lay awake a long time just thinking about it.

On Thursday morning, after a cup of coffee at the Sport Hotel opposite the pits, we found Graham Hill and Cliff Allison getting set for a lap in the former's Austin A35. A race was soon arranged, Ian and I being allowed a minute start as the Anglia was stock-standard.

We pounded the Anglia along for a mile or so, then ducked up a side road to watch the A35 howl by in vain pursuit. Graham was not to be caught out, however, and keeping an eye open saw the Anglia and gave a derisive wave as he passed. We gave chase, but skimming down into the "Foxhole" the over-worked little Ford gave a death rattle with all its bearings gone. We coasted down into Adenau to leave the car at a garage, but now it was imperative that we should find some sort of car with which to learn the circuit. The 'Ring is one of two circuits left where this is necessary, the other being the Targa Florio, which is 45 miles to the lap.

Roy Salvadori offered us the use of the Volkswagen he had rented with John Cooper and took us all for a few laps. As we circulated, Roy described in great detail every accident that had occurred there. Each hole in the hedge seemed to mark the exit of a distinguished pilot and every set of black tyre marks spiralling into the woods indicated the prelude to someone's mammoth shunt. Roy described this butcher's tour tonelessly as he held big oversteering slides, while John, Ian and I clung to the seats and privately hoped he would stop next time round.

Later in the day Ian and I did another three laps in the VW. I'd now done 16 practice laps and, although I couldn't say I knew the circuit, was beginning to think the task of learning it wasn't quite as impossible as it had seemed.

Roy had discussed the 'Ring at some length with us, but we learned in practice that sections Roy had described as "flat out" were ten-tenths effort for Fangio or Moss. Ian took Roy at his word in a couple of places on his first lap and almost disappeared into the timber.

In learning the circuit I found it essential to start memorizing from the start–finish line, breaking it up into sections separated by top-gear straights. Whenever we joined the circuit half-way round at the Adenau Bridge, I made a point of closing my eyes until we reached the start line, so that I wouldn't confuse myself.

I was a passenger on most of our unofficial practice laps and am convinced this is the best way to get an idea of the circuit. If you are driving a fast sports car, you can get some idea of how a formula car would behave on various fast pieces, an effect not possible in a saloon, as the track looks altogether different when you are travelling 70 mph faster. Straight stretches suddenly become fast corners and a racing car often becomes airborne over rises where a saloon has to change down a gear. As a passenger I find one can keep looking to the side and backwards and get a better picture of the true shape of the corner than from the driving seat.

Friday was the first official practice and after three laps warming up in the Cooper, I started to have a go, flashing past the pits, through the long South Curve, back behind the pits, swinging left into the two sets of "esses" down through the woods. Through the flat-out right-hander, up the steep hill, pull well to the left, brake and steer right, off the ground over the rise, right, left, and swoop down to the sharp right-hander before the Foxhole.

I was really getting with it at this point, but suddenly had a funny feeling something was wrong. As I swung right the feeling strengthened. There was a sudden shriek of tyres and puffs of rubber smoke and I jerked round to see a Vanwall front wheel almost in my cockpit. My biggest worry was that the wheel was still connected to the Vanwall and connected to the steering wheel of the Vanwall by one hand was an irate Stirling Moss. His other hand, in use as a fist, was being waved violently in my direction and continued to be, all the way down through the Foxhole until I lost sight of the Vanwall tail.

At this stage of my career I regarded Stirling as the head prefect. I knew him and he knew me vaguely, but that didn't stop me getting bawled out for mistakes. I stopped at the pits hoping that my little mistake would for ever be a secret between Stirling and myself, but Harry Pearce, looking upset, said, "Moss is looking for you." Stirling didn't find me that day, as I made myself scarce.

My best lap had been an unsensational $10\frac{1}{2}$ minutes and I wasn't cheered to hear bearded journalist Denis Jenkinson discussing practice times with John Cooper at the frankfurter stand. "You can wipe that lot for a start," said Jenks, indicating the group towards the bottom of the list. That made my day and I slunk quietly away.

The next day things were a little better. My standing lap was 10 min 7 sec, and the first flying one 10 min dead. Later in the morning I got down to 9 min 56 sec and Ian managed 9 min 55.3 sec so we were both fairly happy. Back in the paddock Colin and I soon had the car prepared and everything was fine, except for a sort-out over one of my front tyres, which resulted in a tyre I was sure would have lasted the race being replaced with a new unscrubbed one. We locked the box door, but I was a little dubious, as we appeared to be the only ones who had finished with their charges. Everywhere else mechanics were crawling over, under and around racing cars. "Perhaps we'd better find some more work to do," I suggested guiltily. Colin didn't agree, and told me so.

Jack Brabham was in high spirits, as he had set fastest F2 lap at 9 min 44 sec, but Coopers had misread the regulations, which stipulated that each driver had to complete six practice laps. Jack had done only five and was relegated to the back of the grid.

Race day looked as though it could rain if it tried hard. I was on the fourth row of the grid, behind Jean Behra and Harry Schell in their 2½-litre BRMs, and John Cooper had advised me to ignore the starter's flag and watch Schell's rear wheels. When I saw the BRM wheels start spinning I dropped the clutch and followed Harry. I was fifth into the South Curve, with only four F1 cars ahead of me.

Half-way round the South Curve Salvadori chopped past in his Cooper. I had to apply plenty of right-hand lock to cope with the understeer from the new front tyre. Up the straight behind the pits the F1s started to stream by. Down through the "esses" I found myself on the tail of Trintignant's blue F1 Cooper. For half a lap I hung on to Trint's tail as though my life depended on it. I had one or two dicey understeers, but by the time we hit the straight the tyre had been well and truly scrubbed.

Stretching away into the distance I could see the race forming. There was a lone green car (Moss in the Vanwall), two or three red Ferraris and Maseratis, a gaggle of green cars (Vanwalls, a BRM and a Cooper) and a BRM was pulling past me. I didn't know who it was, but it was a faster car to follow. Into the pit area we burst, through the South Curve, and behind the pits a confusion of signal boards were hanging over the high fence. Mine said I was in second F2 place, but clinging to the tail of the BRM down through the "esses" didn't give me any time to think about race positions. I was concentrating on driving as smoothly and quickly as I could and the car was running beautifully.

On the third lap, Colin hung out a full board for me to mentally digest. I was second in the F2 section, nine seconds behind Phil Hill's Ferrari and 18 sec ahead of Barth in the Porsche. Now I had the picture and had seen Bueb, Burgess and Marsh in a bunch behind Barth going down the pit straight as I was coming out of the South Curve. I knew Jack must be out and learned later that he had tangled with Bonnier's Maserati.

For five laps the picture remained the same and the F1 battle raged on. I knew Moss was out, as I'd nearly collided with his Vanwall just before the second Karussel, and Brooks, Hawthorn and Collins were hard at it. Then Colin's pit signals began to show I was catching Hill's Ferrari, with the warning that Barth was closing the gap behind me. I was soon on Phil's tail, but although the Ferrari brakes were fading badly, he wasn't giving in without a struggle. He was slamming the car round the circuit, bouncing off the earth verges, but I felt I could pass him and the stones that shot back only added to my determination. Next corner I ducked through on the inside of the Ferrari and, with one eye on the mirrors, pressed on to widen the gap slightly. Behind the pits the signal board told me I was in the lead, two seconds ahead of Phil, but how close was Barth? Before swinging into the Karussel on that lap I glanced back to see the Porsche starting up the hill barely a hundred yards away. It seemed like inches.

I put my foot hard down trying to forget about the Porsche and think only about the car in front. I was relieved when the signal board showed a five-second lead on the Porsche, next lap I had drawn out nine seconds and then—phew!—I took the chequer. I slumped in the cockpit and took a few big gulps of air, slipped into neutral and coasted through the bottom curve and back to the pits. When I stopped I tried to uncoil my left hand from the wheel and found I couldn't. It was stiff with cramp from not being shifted during the race.

Feeling very proud of myself I was led to the victory dais and stood beside Tony Brooks, while God Save the Queen was played twice. Brooks won in the Vanwall followed by Salvadori (Cooper), Trintignant (Cooper), Von Trips (Ferrari), myself fifth and first F2 car, Barth (Porsche F2), Burgess (Cooper F2),

Marsh (Cooper F2) and Phil Hill (Ferrari F2). I had also managed fastest F2 lap at 9 min 37 sec.

Colin placed the laurel wreath on the nose of our Cooper and we grinned at each other as we pushed it towards the paddock. Not in our wildest dreams had we ever imagined anything like this. Jack Brabham thought it was a huge joke. "I don't know," he said, "a couple of Arabs come over with three spanners and a spare wheel just to fill up the entry list and then they win the bloody race!"

Later I heard about the first of John Cooper's famous victory somersaults. When Roy took the flag for second place it was the best placing the works had gained in a Grand Epreuve and, unable to contain himself, John turned a somersault. Huschke von Hanstein, the Porsche racing manager, walked up with a large cine-camera under his arm and asked John to perform again. "I'll do another somersault when the F2 Cooper comes round in front of your Porsche," laughed John. And he did.

But the day was not without its tragedy. Peter Collins had gone off the road in his Ferrari and died later in hospital. I'd met Peter only once and taken an immediate liking to him. Mike Hawthorn was terribly upset and it was a shock to many people. There had been a growing feeling that the top rank F1 boys were invulnerable and only "new boys" got hurt.

One race was over for the day, but another was just beginning. We had to catch the midnight boat from Ostend to get back for the F2 race at Brands Hatch the next day. The Anglia had been repaired, so Ian and I bundled in and set off for Belgium, while Harry, Peter, and Colin were going to load up and leave as soon as they could, to join us on the midnight ferry.

With about 20 miles behind us the motor developed a light tap; after 60 miles the tap was heavier; by the time we had reached Liège it was a loud knock. We stopped and took the spark lead off to lighten the load on the delinquent bearing. This quietened the noise considerably, but it returned again in full force as we reached the Jabbeke Highway and eventually we came to a grinding halt. It was eleven o'clock on the night of the race and pitch dark and we spent three-quarters of an hour trying to pick up the headlights of the Atkins transporter. Having flagged Harry down and tied the Anglia on behind the transporter with an alarmingly short piece of rope, we bounced into Ostend at 60 mph, just in time to see the ferry sailing.

The Anglia was bequeathed to the RAC man at Ostend and, after bundling our bags into the transporter, we crammed the five of us into the cab and set off for Dunkirk with Harry hunched over the wheel. It was like a Hollywood version of motor racing, with the laurels in the cab, the two cars bobbing in the back and Harry thrashing the lorry along with great gusto. We reached Dunkirk just in time to catch the 1 am ferry and try to sleep, but it was hard to unwind after such a day of excitement.

We reached Brands Hatch at about 8 am and it was easy to spot the people who had been to the 'Ring. They were sleeping on blankets, under transporters, or curled in the back seats of parked cars. I was really exhausted and made a vow that I would fly back from the 'Ring in future. I finished third in the race.

There was another meeting at Brands on August 30th and I managed second fastest time, no mean feat with Moss and Brabham included in the field. Although I could turn in fast individual laps, I knew I couldn't mix it with Brabham, Moss, Lewis Evans and Harry Schell, as I lacked the competition experience. I could do fast laps by myself with no one to distract me, but the others pressed on regardless of the company.

That day also happened to be my 21st birthday and commentator John Bolster led the crowd singing "Happy Birthday" as we made the parade lap. Birthday wishes did not help me in the race, however, and I was placed fifth.

Our sights were now set on the big F2 race at Avus in Germany. So far I'd done 11 races and finished in every one.

Colin and I always tried to be first to scrutineering, first to practice and always to have the car looking as immaculate as possible. I still maintain these three things are important and go a long way towards winning races.

Before leaving for Germany, however, Syd Jensen and I were booked to drive John Coombs's front-engined 2-litre Lotus sports car in the Tourist Trophy. It was the first time I had driven a Lotus. Apart from being front-engined, it felt vastly different to the Cooper. I didn't like the smallish steering wheel and the car felt a bit flexible. The gearshift was terrible—a quadrant-type change, the idea being to push forward for the lower gears and back for high. There was always a moment of apprehension as you let out the clutch, wondering which gear you had selected. It was generally the wrong one, so for the race a sliding bolt, such as you might find on a garden gate, was mounted on the transmission tunnel. Once into top gear you pushed the bolt across the quadrant, so that you could push the lever against the bolt for fourth and back to fifth. You couldn't go wrong—theoretically. Our lap times were not improved by having to chug out of the chicane in fourth and the box eventually broke while I was leading our class and lying fourth. Poor Syd never got a chance to drive.

In the early part of the TT I had a big dice with my old New Zealand mate, Ross Jensen, driving a works Lister-Jaguar. Ross had placed second to Ivor Bueb's Lister-Jag at a Brands meeting a few weeks earlier.

To my mind, it was ridiculous to have a race on the Avus circuit. It proved nothing and was dangerous, consisting of two $2\frac{1}{2}$-mile straights connected at one end by a hairpin and at the other by a very steeply banked corner—and I mean steeply banked. It was around 40 degrees.

This banking was made up of bricks in rough, bumpy pavé fashion. The straights were two sides of an autobahn, but if a car had crossed sides out of control into oncoming traffic, there would have been a most fearful shunt.

The race itself was like a group of schoolboys in dodgem cars with wheels touching, noses and tails bumping, jostling for the lead—but we were doing 150 mph! Slipstreaming was the order of the day on the long fast straights and seven cars battled in a bunch for the first hairpin, with Burgess leading in his Cooper and Masten Gregory trying to carve his way through in a Porsche. Everyone managed to scrape round the hairpin and, accelerating along the back straight, the Porsche began to draw away.

Then it happened. The pushing and shoving reached a limit, at 150 mph just before the banking and Burgess' Cooper bounced sideways, slid wildly across in front of the pack, spun again and hurtled into a ditch beside the track, then leapt thirty feet in the air, throwing out Ian. Miraculously we all missed the spinning car and were gone before car or driver hit the ground. There were now six cars in the lead pack, but the stunning pace hadn't slowed at all. We were flat out, nose to tail, side by side, squashed into our seats by the tremendous centrifugal force on the near-vertical banking at 120 mph.

On down the narrow autobahn, chopping and changing lanes to keep the tow, or lose a would-be towee, and Gregory's Porsche still held the lead. Another mad scramble for the hairpin, going round it three deep. It couldn't go on.

The Porsche pulled further away, leaving five cars in the fray and Allison in the Lotus was towing us all along. Two more frightening laps and, as we were braking on the limit for the hairpin, two more cars collided and went flying into the air. Allison and Wicken. The red Cooper went up over the haybales on the inside, while the Lotus landed backwards up the bank on the outside. Then there were three.

Brabham, Russell and myself, all in Coopers, with the Russell car about five miles an hour faster than Jack or myself—not that this helped him when he was towing us. We settled down to serious slipstreaming, each one hatching his own plan for crossing the line first. First Russell would lead, then Brabham, then myself, or we would be running abreast at full chat about a foot apart. Jack and I were trying to organize the finish between us, but our sign language was spotted by Jim. "I didn't know what I was doing, mixing it with those 'down unders'," he said later. "They were talking to each other as they went by."

After another ten laps, my race finished in a clatter as a rod went through the side on the back straight. Russell had been nibbling my exhaust and almost ran over me when the metal started flying. Then there were two. It was obvious that whoever led away from the last hairpin would tow the other car just short of the line, so that he could break out of the slipstream and win. It was a case of both Brabham and Russell trying to be last through the hairpin. They almost stopped there on the last lap before Jack leapt away trying to snatch a surprise lead. But he was not quick enough and Jim passed him to cross the line only inches ahead. Gregory won the race comfortably and the slipstreaming had carried Jack and Jim well clear of the rest of the field.

Pit signals during the race told me Ian had survived his shunt and I later visited him in a Berlin hospital, where he had been taken with a broken leg, gashed head and four broken vertebrae. Wicken and Allison were unhurt. I stayed in Berlin for the rest of the week to make sure that Ian and Solvei were organized, then drove Ian's Anglia back to England.

My engine was in a fine old state. A big end bolt had broken and caused the rod to leave via the side of the block and the engine position for Casablanca looked grim, until Tommy Atkins again came to my rescue and loaned me the engine out of Burgess' Avus wreck. Colin had already flown back to New Zealand and plans were well under way to get a 2-litre Climax to take out in my Cooper. I was also doing very well in the F2 Championship and it looked as though I might win it in the Morocco GP at Casablanca, which was a combined F1 and F2 race as the German GP had been.

Jack Brabham proved the fly in the ointment. I had assumed Jack would drive a 2½-litre Cooper at Casablanca, as Coopers had two F1 entries and two F2 entries and I understood Jack Fairman and I were to be the F2 works entries. I soon learned things had changed and Brabham was to drive a F2 car. This meant if he won the race, the F2 championship would be his. Jack told me he would *much* rather have driven a 2½-litre car in the GP, but John wanted to make sure that the works won the championship and two chances were better than one.

John told me that he would have preferred Jack to have driven the F1 car, but the fuel company had insisted that he drive the F2 car because *they* wanted to win the championship. Reg Tanner, the competition manager for Esso, with whom I had been under contract since the Crystal Palace race, passed the ball back by saying that Jack wanted to win it this year, "You can win it next year."

It was one of my first brushes with a complicated situation, but after the help Coopers, Jack and Esso had given me, I didn't really mind. The position became involved in New Zealand, however. When the Casablanca results were cabled out the championship points were added up incorrectly and New Zealand read at breakfast the next morning that I had won the F2 championship. In fact Jack had just pipped me.

Nearly everyone connected with motor racing was on the charter plane to Casablanca on the Thursday, the five-hour flight passing quickly during a champagne dinner. John Cooper was waiting for us when the plane landed and the local Esso representative whistled us through customs formalities. That evening we went to the sumptuous home of the President of the Automobile Club and were entertained by his head wife. The other wives watched proceedings through windows in alcoves, but were smartly withdrawn when Salvadori began paying attention.

On the Friday morning the African sun was beating down and Jack Brabham, John Cooper and I wanted a swim. Roy wanted to go shopping in the town, but someone had to attend the Royal reception, so we ganged up on Jack Fairman, who was driving a F1 Cooper, and appointed him Cooper delegate for the reception. Practice was at 3.30 in the afternoon when the fierce heat had died a little and I lost no time sorting out the course, so that I would not baulk the F1 boys when they started later in the session. Jack hooked a tow from Roy's F1 car and dropped his lap time by three seconds. He was using a special 3·85 : 1 ratio and, as I had more revs than I needed on the straight, I fitted a 4·1 : 1 ratio for the next day. Roy had just started towing me when someone dropped a sumpful of oil on the circuit, making further attempts useless, but Jack and I were comfortably fastest of the F2 entry. That night we were guests of Lord Tregard on his yacht, *The Henry Morgan*.

Race day was hot and with F1 times so close it looked as though the race would be, too. The circuit was very fast and F1 and F2 times did not overlap, so the grid was virtually in two sections.

Ten laps after the start the race had settled down, with Moss (Vanwall) and Phil Hill (Ferrari) struggling for the lead. First one then the other broke the lap record, until Stirling turned a really fast one and left Phil sailing down the escape road. Moss was then a lonely first, going like a rocket. On this race hung the best chance Stirling ever had for winning the world championship, but to clinch it he had to win and make fastest lap, with Mike Hawthorn finishing lower than fourth.

Mike was lying third in his works Ferrari, just behind Tony Brooks in the Vanwall. Behind them were a group of Maseratis and BRMs, further back to Brabham, the lone Maserati or Gerini, Picard in the Rob Walker Cooper, and myself.

Ten laps later the picture was similar, but the drama was starting. I had managed to sneak past Gerini and Picard, but a slipping clutch slowed me and Picard passed, only to disappear through the straw bales a few laps later. The clutch became steadily worse and I made a quick pit stop. Nothing could be done and I went on my way with instructions to nurse it. By this time debris was starting to collect, there were several ominous holes in the straw bales and the straw and drifting dust made vision difficult in the blinding sun. Bridger (BRP Cooper) and Gendebien (Ferrari) had shunted, the Cooper rolling a couple of times.

I was pounding down the back straight when Lewis Evans' Vanwall passed. He had just pulled by me when there was a huge puff of smoke from the exhaust, the rear wheels locked and the car slewed sideways. I stood the Cooper almost on its nose in an attempt to stop and Stuart tried very hard to hold the Vanwall, but it spun into the sand and overturned in a clump of trees. A thick pall of smoke hung across the road on the next lap. Stuart died later of burns received in the crash.

The engine broke on Brooks' Vanwall soon after, ending his dice with Mike's Ferrari. Phil Hill, having his first F1 ride with Ferrari, was then reputed to have slowed with engine trouble, but the Italian team manager's signals to the American driver looked suspiciously like "slow down" ones to me and Mike finished second to win the 1958 world championship.

Jack won the F2 section and took fastest lap and I finished second in both departments to my team mate.

That night we mistook the time of the presentation and arrived two hours late, but as Stirling and Katy were with us, we were excused. Stirling had won the race easily, but only mechanical failure by Mike could have given him the championship. The championship couldn't have gone to a more popular driver that year and we were all stunned to hear in New Zealand the following January that Mike had been killed when his 3·4 Jaguar hit a tree on the Guildford Bypass. Mike made himself a legendary figure of the sport while still very much a part of it and the circumstances of his death were tragic.

We all invaded a night club after the presentation and John Cooper and Graham Hill soon joined the Mexican band and were wearing sombreros and waving tambourines and maracas. The band loved it as the boys put on a floor show, finishing the evening with a bull-fight, backed by spirited Spanish-style music.

The charter return flight arrived in England six hours late, touching down at 2 am, having been delayed in Paris with a mechanical fault. Tension tightened and tempers frayed as the delay dragged on, but Masten Gregory and Cliff Allison were oblivious to it all, engrossed in a marathon chess game.

Puncturing my engine at Avus had revised modification plans for my New Zealand car. I had put in a fair amount of work on the head before I went to Casablanca. I smoothed out the ports, narrowed the valve seats, polished the inside of the SU carburettors and streamlined the butterflies with solder. Climax had built up a new block, four new pistons and rods (a rod couldn't be found to match the out-of-date broken one, so a full set was fitted) and new oil pumps. A larger crankshaft was also fitted, increasing the capacity to 1960 cc to take advantage of Formula Libre racing in New Zealand. When it was all screwed together, the motor was giving 178 bhp on Climax's brake and they were most impressed. So was I.

The gearbox had to be rebuilt after Casablanca, as I found a tooth off the crown-wheel, a tooth off second gear and half the dogs off top gear. I fitted a ZF crown-wheel and pinion in place of the ordinary Citroen one, as it was stronger and designed for the 2-litre engine. I accidentally stumbled on the fact that the factory Coopers had been using wider, stronger gears all season and was lucky enough to snaffle a set for New Zealand, so I had virtually a new car. To top it all, I fitted a new screen and painted it British racing green with a silver stripe round the nose. Jack was taking out the Cooper that Fairman drove at Casablanca, but had fitted it with a 2·2 engine.

Towards the end of the season I was approached by several people with offers of lucrative drives for the following season. Two different fuel companies were after my signature, but at that stage I didn't know for whom I would be driving. I didn't even know whether I would be back.

I had run away from school, as it were, when I left my engineering studies to take the NZIGP trip to Europe and that was on condition that I returned to race at Ardmore the following January. When I accepted the trip, I never gave much thought to the fact that I might not go back to college, neither had Pop. At least he didn't say anything. After the first few offers of drives for the next season, I approached John Cooper on the subject of a team drive with Coopers. "Don't worry, we'll look after you, boy," John kept saying, but I was anxious to have it down on paper.

Breaking the news to Pop that I wanted to race again in Europe in 1959 was a more subtle operation. My letters home in the latter part of the year usually had some such reference as "I've had a long chat to so-and-so about a drive next year, but haven't said anything yet." This left things conveniently in the air, to be broached at an opportune moment back in Auckland.

SEVEN

Water, Water Everywhere

COLIN AND I were in Auckland to collect the Cooper when it arrived. Pop was naturally very interested in the car and the changes made from the previous year's 1750 cc model and he soon began itemizing parts we would have to alter! We diplomatically suggested that a season's racing with only one retirement meant that it really wasn't too bad as it stood.

The field for the 1959 New Zealand Grand Prix was probably the most colourful and comprehensive ever seen at Ardmore, mainly due to the efforts of Buzz Perkins, who spent much of the European season following the circus and signing top-line drivers. Stirling was driving a 2-litre Rob Walker Cooper; Ron Flockhart a front-engined $2\frac{1}{2}$-litre BRM; Harry Schell and Carroll Shelby modified 250F Maseratis, owned by American millionaire Temple Buell, and Jo Bonnier a private 250F. Ross Jensen had a specially hashed-up Maserati from the works, that was supposed to be a light-weight Piccolo. In fact, I believe it embodied the chassis of the 250F Bira drove to win the New Zealand GP in 1955, with a smart new body.

Rain stopped the usual parade of GP cars through Auckland's main street and the drivers were taken to the New Zealand première of *Checkpoint*, backed by a few other motor-racing feature films. People packed six deep outside to try and get a glimpse of our group as we walked into the theatre. It was more like a London première.

We were taken on stage singly and introduced to the crowd by one of Auckland's well-known woman radio announcers. I was first up and shook hands; Ross Jensen followed me, shook hands, and pecked her cheek; Brabham shook hands and pecked both cheeks; Bonnier shook hands, pecked both cheeks, and enveloped her in a bear-like embrace; Harry Schell came up the steps and embarked on a real necking session, to the delight of the crowd. This was one day when even Stirling couldn't out-do Harry's efforts.

The race was preceded by two heats, with times deciding the GP grid positions. Brabham won our heat in the 2·2 Cooper, I was second, with Bonnier and Schell behind. Stirling had a cosy lead in the second heat until a half-shaft broke and he had to push the Cooper 400 yards to the line, leaving the heat to Flockhart (BRM), Shelby (Maserati), Jensen (Maserati) and Syd Jensen (Cooper 1500).

The Rob Walker spares kit didn't run to half-shafts, but Jack had a complete Cooper sitting at the back of the pits which he was unlikely to use, so he lent Stirling one. This was a sporting effort, as Jack virtually forfeited the race by putting Stirling back in the running.

Flockhart held pole position, but stalled and the field surged round him. Stirling, starting from the back of the grid, turned on a display of carving that would have honoured a Sunday roast and led the field on the first lap.

He set off to build another of his fantastic leads, while Jack and I battled with Schell, Bonnier and Shelby. I tried a bit too hard on one corner and spun, which let Flockhart, who had made up his lost ground, into fourth place. As I spun the knob on the gear-lever came unstuck and rolled out of reach. This did not worry me at first, but each gear-change on the bare threads was wearing at my glove, eventually tearing it and scraping my palm.

Flockhart's BRM dropped out of third place with a broken oil breather, and my dice with Ross and Shelby for the vacant position gave me little time to worry about my bleeding hand. Jensen's Maserati slowed with an ailing clutch, but the Buell car still sounded healthy and the tall, drawling American was pedalling it fast enough to keep ahead of my Cooper.

I was pleasantly surprised when he took to the pit road on the 41st lap, to retire with cramp in one leg. His seat was quickly taken by Harry Schell, who had retired his car earlier with engine failure, and he forced the 250F back into fourth place behind me, finishing with no brake linings at all. My Cooper was going off song towards the end of the race and I was lapped by both Stirling and Jack.

We found afterwards that the header tank had split and assumed this was the reason for loss of power, though Pop maintained the trouble stemmed from the steel head gasket we were using.

The following Saturday I won a couple of short races at Levin, then we headed off to Wigram. My main opposition was from Jack and Ron and I soon found in practice that they were quite a bit faster.

Race day was terrifically hot and the track was slippery with oil and rubber from earlier races. Jack and Ron shuttled the lead between Cooper and BRM throughout the race and my Wigram luck struck once more, when the temperature needle climbed off the dial and I realized the gasket had gone again. I was able to cut back the revs and still finish third, but we had a major overhaul on hand to cure the overheating problem.

The next race was around the streets of Waimate, a little country town just south of Timaru, about 130 miles from Christchurch. Colin and I pulled the engine apart in a Timaru garage and checked everything before putting it together again with a new gasket. Waimate is a sleepy place and it seemed strange to stage a motor race there, but the townspeople were enthusiastic. The straight ran through the main street, then darted off into the residential area past churches and neat homes, with spectators leaning over their garden gates.

The Cooper handled well on the tight 1·3-mile track and I managed fastest time in practice ahead of Merv Neil and Syd Jensen in their 1500 Coopers and the bigger brigade of Ross Jensen (250F Maserati), Tom Clarke (Super Squalo Ferrari) and Johnny Mansel (250F Maserati).

The cars lined up on the grid in sunshine and I was looking forward to the race. Then a clap of thunder must have scared the starter into dropping the flag and before we reached the first corner it was pelting with rain. The spray danced high in the air, reducing visibility to almost nil. I was leading on the opening lap, but the Cooper took over on a puddle on the back straight and the car swopped ends, with the field barrelling at me in a cloud of spray.

Tom Clarke, who was leading the pack in his big Ferrari, said later he didn't know exactly what I was going to do, but intended to try and stop everyone else hitting me. Somehow he managed it and I sorted myself out and carried on surfing in the middle of the mob.

Johnny Mansel had seized his chance in the mêlée and was flailing along in Stirling's old 250F Maserati, with Jensen catching his spray behind in his bright blue Maserati. The bigger cars were enjoying their advantage over the "mechanical mice" as the Coopers were called, and when the rain at last started to ease they were almost a lap ahead. I have never seen so much water on a circuit. On one back section I began to think we had been detoured into a river bed, with the water more than a foot deep in places and the cars looking more like speedboats as they carved a wave through the miniature lakes. Officials round the track rapidly lost interest in cars they could barely see and were sheltering under trees and verandas. I could see no point in bending the car with another spin in the wet, so settled down to wait for a flag saying the race was to be stopped or for the rain to abate.

A hailstorm didn't improve matters, but it drew the teeth of the thunderstorm, the rain stopped as suddenly as it had started and the sun was shining again. A new hazard came with the sun, as we found ourselves groping through clouds of steam from the rapidly-drying road. Bedraggled pit signals appeared for the first time and showed the bigger cars were rapidly losing their advantage as the track dried.

I was closing the gap to Jensen in the leading Maserati at five seconds a lap and really enjoying the controllability of the leaf-spring Cooper. Ross had his work cut out holding the big Maserati on the road as the gap decreased and a few laps from the end I arrived at a right-angle right-hander to find the blue Maserati parked backwards on the pavement, with Ross trying frantically to get it back on the street, as I carried on to win.

The papers were featuring the rivalry between Ross and myself for the New Zealand championship and I believe Ross thought he might turn the tables on me on the slippery surface at Teretonga, just outside Invercargill. Remembering the dicey do the year before on the pebbles-in-tar surface, I had a sneaking suspicion he could be right.

To sort out the question of tyres, we sneaked out to the track for an unofficial work-out. We took a set of Michelin Xs to fit at the rear, to cure the oversteer we were worried about, but the car performed so weirdly that I could hardly drive for laughing. There was no grip at all at the rear and I seemed to be advancing in a series of spins. Putting the R5s back at the rear made it a different car and I started knocking five seconds off the lap record straight away. We were in high spirits as we loaded the car back on the trailer and crept back to the garage unobserved—as we thought. But Tom Clarke and Ross were waiting in the garage when we got back. "Sneaked out for a few quiet laps, eh?" said Ross with a knowing wink to Tom and they both laughed.

Practice showed that Jack in the 2·2 Cooper, Ron in the BRM, and Ross' Maserati would be my main opponents. The

Teretonga track starts with a straight stretch, disappearing into a long loop which brings it back behind the pits. Jack and I both made good starts and were side by side, fractionally ahead of the BRM as we went into the loop. We obviously couldn't motor through the loop two abreast and although Jack was a nose ahead, I was on the inside. For the first and only time in his career he nodded me through. I hopped into a grateful lead and set off determined not to return the favour.

My Cooper was the single-wishbone model and, although only a 1960 cc car, was handling better than Jack's double-wishbone car on this circuit and I found that I was pulling away from both him and Ron. Jack spun later in the race and Ron finished a popular second in the BRM. Jack was strangely quiet that night and has never waved me past since when we have been in equal cars, but it was the first time I had beaten him fair and square and I was pleased with myself.

Ron was a great favourite with the very pro-Scottish Invercargill crowd and at the prize-giving he started his speech, "Sassenachs, Clan McLaren, ladies, gentlemen and others . . ." He drew further laughs when he said he didn't really mind being beaten by a Maori if he had a Scottish name.

Teretonga was the last event on the international calendar, but I took the Cooper to a race on the airfield circuit at Ohakea near Palmerston North in the North Island. The Cooper was the fastest car there, but it was running rough at low revs, so we set about tweaking the SUs and altering the float levels. We eventually got it running clean low down, though it sounded a bit fluffy higher up. We overcame the trouble by fitting special needles for the 2-litre engine.

I won fairly comfortably, but the colour in the race was provided by Tom Clarke, who headed the 250Fs home to place second in his Ferrari. Tom is a big, bluff and hearty character who started racing with a Mark 7 Jaguar. His description of the first drive in an 8CM Maserati, on a loose metal hill—what better place to tame a wild Maserati?—is colourful!

"Jeez boy—I squirted it once and I was at the first corner. The second squirt and I was half-way up the hill. If I was still on the road, I squirted it again and I was across the line!"

Tom's first races with the Mark 7 were in 1954 and his main rival was Ross Jensen in a Ford V8. In 1956 he tried his hand with a troublesome blown HWM, then dropped it to buy Peter Whitehead's Super Squalo Ferrari for the 1957 season.

He hired Hec Greene, a brilliant Christchurch engineer, to look after the Ferrari. Hec was quite a personality himself, having designed and raced a rear-engined RA Vanguard special. This car embodied several suspension features that appeared later as startlingly new ideas on English F1 cars. His latest creation, a neat little RA Special, features interesting suspension detail and an engine he built around a TR crankshaft.

There is traditional rivalry between Australia and New Zealand and late in 1957 Tom took his Ferrari over to "clean up the Aussies". Unfortunately, he looped the Ferrari on the tricky Bathurst circuit and was on the "dangerously ill" list for several months with serious internal injuries. He pulled through and watched the 1958 New Zealand GP from a swinging couch outside the timekeeper's box. Doctors told him never to race again, but with typical tenacity he had the Ferrari rebuilt and took it out for one last season, climaxing with a second place at Ohakea before he retired. Tom has been one of the big names in the NZIGP Association for several years and his brusque good humour makes him the Duncan Hamilton of New Zealand motor racing.

An interested spectator at Ohakea was Denis Hulme, a young driver from Te Puke, who had cut his competition teeth on an MGA in minor events. He had his eye on Merv Neil's Cooper, which was bored out to 2 litres by that time and after the race he bought it.

When final negotiations indicated I would be going back to England to race for Coopers, my car was sold to George

Lawton from Whangarei, who like myself had started racing in an Austin Healey. George and Denis Hulme became sparring partners over the next season in their 2-litre Coopers and were picked as the NZIGP drivers to Europe in 1960.

I had finally pestered John Cooper into giving me a contract to drive works F2 Coopers in 1959 and had also signed with Esso, who agreed to support me if and when I returned to Europe. With a reasonably solid racing future ahead if I returned to England, it gradually became a question of the family asking me *when* I was going back, not *if*.

Before leaving New Zealand I had suggested Phil Kerr might be able to help Jack with the garage and car sales business he was considering starting. Jack offered Phil a job on the spot, so one of my first chores on returning to England was to find a flat for the pair of us. My rounds of the estate agents and visits to rooms large and small, flats tiny and tremendous, grubby and grand, ended with the choice of a neat little Surbiton apartment in Lovelace Gardens. Phil arrived about a month later and we set up house in the experimental manner that must be followed in bachelor flats everywhere.

I joined the ranks of the domestic motorists in a modest manner soon after arriving, when I bought Betty Brabham's little two-door Morris Minor 1000.

On my first visit to the Cooper factory in March I was surprised to find that there were three cars nearly ready to run. There was a $2\frac{1}{2}$-litre car for Jack and a pair of 2·2 cars for Masten Gregory and myself. John told me things had changed slightly and I would now be driving a works F1 entry instead of F2. "Will that be all right, boy?" asked John. My answer was a definite affirmative.

I took an immediate liking to the dry, drawling, bespectacled Masten, who was to be No. 2 driver. At Goodwood testing early that season Jack was giving the $2\frac{1}{2}$-litre car a work-out and Roy Salvadori was trying the Tommy Atkins Cooper-Maserati. Their times were not brilliant and Roy debited the lost seconds to the wind, saying that it was a slow day. Masten mulled this over behind his ever-present pipe, then shot Roy down in flames by saying, "It's a slow day all right, 'cause Moss and Brooks ain't here." I've never been tempted to blame sub-standard practice times on a "slow day" since then.

Masten's mechanic was to be "Noddy" Grohman, a first-class craftsman, though with a rather difficult temperament. Bill James, a pleasant bald-headed mechanic who had been with Aston Martins, was to look after Jack's Cooper, while I did my own preparation early in the season, until Mike Barney was taken from the production shop to work on my car.

Mike has been with me ever since and I have never had a complaint over preparation. To avoid summoning two mechanics by asking for "Mike", Mike Grohman was ever after called "Noddy" and, by virtue of his size, Mike Barney was "Big Mike".

The works cars for 1959 all had double wishbones with a single-leaf spring at the rear. The nose had been lengthened and, with the tail fin, our Coopers looked attractive. They retained the four-speed Citroen/Cooper gearbox, with the heavy but dead-reliable D-type three-plate Borg and Beck clutch. The new car was wonderful to drive. I had a feeling of complete security, as the cars had been put together by mechanics who really cared about the job and took great pains to make sure everything was just right.

Before the works season officially opened I was tinkering about with my car when Ken Tyrrell wandered into the factory and asked what I was driving at the forthcoming Goodwood meeting. "Nothing," I replied. He asked me if I was driving F2 and, when I told him I wasn't committed for F2 drives, offered me the F2 Cooper he was running in partnership with Alan Brown.

I rate Ken one of the best team managers in the business. He has the ability to size up a situation, technical or psychological, with remarkable common sense. If I were looking for a manager, I would certainly go to Ken.

The new cars were good, but untried, and a testing session was necessary to sort out a few small bugs before the first race at Goodwood.

Some drivers look on test days as boring affairs, but I always enjoy them. Coopers usually hire Goodwood or Silverstone. I like these as testing circuits and lap times set the previous season are good yardsticks to calculate improvements on the new cars. You can remember how last year's car performed on certain parts of the course, compared with the new model. Other teams' test times also make interesting comparisons. Stirling's times a week before, or BRM's best a fortnight ago can usually be gathered at the Steering Wheel bar. If we beat these times, then they were obviously gained from a reliable source, but if our times are slower the rumoured records are regarded as highly suspect and "another of Stirling's yarns".

Testing a new car generally involves doing about 20 laps to run the car in and discover its general steering and handling characteristics. Then suggested modifications begin. Roll bars are changed, roll-centre heights adjusted by shifting the inboard mounting of the wishbones, and tyre pressures altered. The driver must be self-critical and analytical, not making comments or suggestions just for the sake of sounding important. I find it is best to confess if I don't know the correct answers. It is easy to get used to a bad fault, such as automatically correcting oversteer, but if the car was brought in and the back end break-away cured, times would improve immediately.

No matter how well a car handles, it is never perfect, bearing in mind that the following year's models will be even faster. So it is best to try changes, then set out to test their worth.

Improvements must always be judged by the stopwatch. Sometimes a car appears to handle better than ever before, yet records slower times. Jack and I had a test system whereby we staged a mock "dice" and motored consistently at nine and nine-tenths, to set steady, fast lap times for comparison with previous efforts. At the end of the day, when we were right on form, we usually put in a few circuits at ten-and-a-half tenths, really hanging it out to gauge the ultimate lap times of the car in its present form.

There is nothing more appetising than a good session testing on a crisp winter's day—most English days before the start of the season seem to be crisp and cold (or just plain cold)—and I find that when I climb out of the car I can always polish off a big lunch.

From a design view point these test days are very instructive. More can be achieved in an hour of carefully planned testing, than in a week poring over a drawing board.

Our testing was aimed at the first Goodwood meeting. The grid was drenched with rain and we scuttled off into the spray, motoring gingerly with lowered tyre pressures to cope with the slippery surface. Jack was up among the "big boys" with the 2½-litre car, but I sat on Masten's tail throughout the race and we finished fourth and fifth, having had a lot of fun despite the rain.

It was late when we left Goodwood, so we decided to stop at a pub on the way home. We were not the only ones with this idea, as John Cooper discovered when he tried to park his Zephyr and trailer with Jack's car on the back. Visions of the other boys already at the bar prompted John to park on the foot-path, with no tail light and no trailer registration. A report filtered through to the bar that a constable was studying the trailer. John peeped out and returned saying, "He'll soon go away." An hour later he was still hovering round John's car. Apart from coshing the policeman and racing off into the night, we could think of no way out, until I had a brainstorm.

The Brabham Morris was immobilised by removing the coil lead and, while the locals packed all available window space, John hid behind the front door and Jack wandered out for a fruitless attempt at starting his car. Illumination was required to trace the trouble, so Jack politely approached the constable. "Good evening officer, I wonder if you could possibly . . ." Clump, clump, clump, went the official feet while "twinkletoes" Cooper went streaking for his car. The constable was very helpful, even tracing the trouble with Jack's car. Unfortunately we couldn't wait to see the official features when he discovered his bird had flown!

The Cooper factory buzzed with activity as Jack's $2\frac{1}{2}$-litre car was prepared for Aintree. All attention centred on this car to make it the fastest and best-ever Cooper. It had big front tyres, bigger carburettors, special brakes, the suspension was specially tweaked and if it wasn't the quickest car on the course, John Cooper would need a very good reason why. Masten was being promoted to a $2\frac{1}{2}$-litre car for Aintree, but his machine was very much a secondary effort, being almost a mobile junk pile, of all the bits taken off Jack's car.

Masten might well have preferred to drive the 2·2 Cooper, but didn't complain as his car was loaded with narrow F2 front tyres, old-type brake pads and small carbs that were strangling the bigger engine. In practice Jack was turning in respectable lap times and everyone felt proud of the effort that had gone into the car. Masten had been warned not to do too many laps in case something fell off before the race. Imagine the consternation in the Cooper pit when the timekeeper announced that Masten had just broken the circuit record with a lap substantially faster than anyone else—including Jack's car with all the "goodies".

Masten was hastily flagged in. "If that car's bad—leave it bad!" he drawled as he slid out of the seat. Clutch-slip claimed Masten in the race, but my 2·2 went like a bomb and I finished third behind a couple of Ferraris.

Masten made a name for himself at the next Silverstone race by baling out of his Lister-Jaguar at high speed.

Finding himself in trouble approaching Becketts at speed and realizing he wasn't going to make the corner, he decided to go straight ahead. There was one obstacle to this move—a hefty wall. Nothing daunted, Masten decided to part company with the Lister as soon as possible, climbed on the tail and launched himself a second before it wrote itself off against the wall. Masten's flight was short, his landing heavy and somewhere in transit he gashed his thigh, but he was soon limping round the pits and his vivid description of the crash kept us amused at dinner that night.

My efforts in the Tyrrell F2 Cooper made dull conversation compared with Masten's epic; a tooth chipped off the crown-wheel, the exhaust pipe fell off, but although I drifted back to the tail of the field, I managed to finish.

EIGHT

Learning Behind Brabham

THE FIRST championship race for 1959 was at the Mediterranean sunshine capital of Monaco and Phil rashly joined me for a trek in my faithful Minor 1000. I could have sworn there was a respectable amount of tread on the tyres when we drove away from Surbiton, but some off-course dicing with the Citroens on the French cobbles must have done nasty things to the rubber. This was forcibly brought to my notice when it started to rain on a hilly section and it took me nearly quarter of a mile wrestling the wheel to get the Minor pointing in the right direction. I was rather proud of this effort—after all, we *were* still on the road, and it *was* a long way to the bottom of the valley—but Phil only forced a grey smile and took a firmer grip on the underside of the seat. Some people have no confidence.

Our hurricane progress through a French village roused official wrath and a frantic whistle gave rise to speculation that it could have been a gendarme. We decided it would not be diplomatic to see whether the officer had been whistling at us, so continued with the Minor's speedometer needle bouncing off the ignition light. Suspicion that the speck magnifying itself in the mirror was a gendarme straddling a large BMW motorcycle was confirmed as he hove alongside and flagged us to the curb. We put on our best "Who, us officer?" expressions in

French, though neither of us knew a word of the language—none that would have been useful in this situation, anyway.

Quickly becoming exasperated with his foreign "catch", the gendarme began writing a traffic fine of astronomical proportions. Howling tyres heralded the approach of another speedster and an A35 went hurtling past—Graham Hill in a hurry. We managed to convince the gendarme that our meagre francs would not cover his fine, so he reconsidered our offence in the light of Graham's performance and decided we had only broken a fiver's worth of French law. We paid up smartly and hurried after the A35.

The arrangement of works cars for Monaco was baffling. I had been given a 2½-litre car for the race and prepared it myself. It was fitted with Webers and I was looking forward to a good race. When I arrived, however, I found Jack's special seat in my car, which was polished up and ready to go, while my seat was in another car. The first practice session was also my first run in a 2½-litre car and the improvement in performance over the smaller 2·2 Climax was startling. I found myself getting wheelspin all the way up the hill to the Casino. Jack stopped practising with overheating bothers and the next day I practised in my own car, fitted with a 2·2 engine for the session.

In the third session Jack's engine was still overheating and his brakes were giving trouble. Masten's 2½ engine was running well, but the American felt Jack would fare better with the good engine and insisted on a swap. This was done and Jack also borrowed my brakes, going to the Monaco line with the best bits of team cars.

This shuffle of parts caused official ructions. In those days the components of each car were sealed at scrutineering, with a number corresponding to the driver, to stop a major swapping session such as we had done. It often took longer to change seals than to change engines.

Jack had a car in A1 condition, Masten had one with a duff engine, while mine had a good 2·2 engine fitted with SU carbs.

After a good start I was keeping the leaders comfortably in sight in the opening laps, sandwiched between the BRMs of Bonnier and Schell, with the bearded Swede leading. Sweeping on to the seafront before the tunnel my car was suddenly jarred sideways and I found myself on the footpath pointing in the wrong direction. Harry Schell had lost his patience and nudged me. Everything happened quickly and I could hear the tail-enders barrelling out of the Station Hairpin. Startled TV cameramen jumped for safety as I drove behind them to regain the circuit. The car was handling a bit oddly, understeering on left-handers and developing alarming oversteer on right-handers. The rear wheel had been knocked out of line on contact with the sea wall and I made a quick pit stop to check the rest of the suspension.

Finding nothing broken, John suggested that I carry on. It was fortunate I did, as a rash of retirements reduced the field to five, Jack's Cooper in front, mine bringing up the rear. This was Jack's first championship win and he sat proudly at the official table during a swank dinner at the Hotel de Paris, which went with a swing and ended in a battle, with strawberries flying round the dining-room.

I was sore at being pushed off the track and John suggested we should sort out Harry. I was flabbergasted when he swung round and began berating *me* for pushing *him*. A couple of hours after the race Harry came over and apologized.

The F2 race at Pau was next on our list. I was driving Ken Tyrrell's green Cooper. Phil and I drove over in the Minor and stayed at the Citadel Hotel in Carcassonne, a wonderful fortress-style town, high on a cliff. The battlements were floodlit at night and it looked like something from a fairytale. Pau is a street circuit even tougher than Monaco. The race had drawn a fair entry, including Brabham in a Cooper and Jean Behra in his specially-built F2 Porsche.

During the first session we all stayed together and when the official times came out naturally thought one of us would have been fastest. But no, Jack Lewis' Cooper was fastest. Who was Jack Lewis? We checked the times and they were correct. In the next session we all kept a respectful eye on this young Welshman, who drove his Cooper with a smoothly polished style not unlike Stirling. Behra eventually set fastest time, with Jack second, myself third, then evergreen Maurice Trintignant in a Cooper.

I was away to a good start in the race, but Masten had made a jet from the second row in his Cooper and led into the first corner. Trint wasn't to be pushed around on his home circuit however, and when Masten overdid things I lay second to the Frenchman.

Heavy rain started to fall and I was closing two seconds a lap on Trintignant until I came unstuck on a pool of water lying across a 100 mph corner leading into the main straight. The Cooper and I revolved through 360 degrees so quickly that I was off after Trint before the incident registered. On the next lap I saw Barclay's Cooper involved in a terrific shunt, not far from where I had spun. This curbed my enthusiasm abruptly and Trint maintained his lead easily for the rest of the race.

Ken gave me a rocket afterwards. What revs had I been using off the line? I hung my head and admitted it had been quite a lot. "Five thousand," I said. "Five thousand?" spluttered Ken. "That's a lot? You should have screwed it up to seven!" He was right of course. The 1500 cc F2 engine revved safely around 7000, but the $2\frac{1}{2}$-litre was fussier and had to be treated more gently.

Ken took Phil and me over to Zandvoort for the Dutch GP. I was still a new boy on the GP scene and my entry hadn't been accepted, so we joined the spectators. We found Jack and John Cooper staying at the Meijershof Hotel and managed to get a room there. It was a cosy little hotel with excellent food. We stood on top of the transporter and watched Bonnier win the race in the BRM. I enjoyed the race, but I'm sure it couldn't have been as frightening to the drivers as it looked to us.

Jim Russell had asked if I would co-drive his 2-litre Cooper-Monaco with him at Le Mans and having read of the epic race but never been offered a drive, I gladly accepted. My first Le Mans drive may have biased me against the round-the-clock endurance race, but like a lot of other drivers I now think twice before competing there. The Monaco was in trouble from the start of practice with gearbox problems. Soon after the start second gear failed and when I handed over to Jim at 9.30 on Saturday night it was jumping out of top. I was all for nursing the car in an attempt to finish, but Jim had spent a lot of money and time on the Cooper and was reluctant to give up so early.

He started turning in fast times, considering he was not using second gear and having to drive with one hand holding the gear-lever in top on the straights. But oil had been dropped at the fast, tricky Whitehouse Corner and Jim crashed. The Cooper caught fire, he was badly burned and rushed to a French hospital. I was worried about his condition, although he was chirpy enough and it was through Jim's accident that I met Dr Frank Falkner. He has since become a firm friend and has often been of great assistance to me with business matters in the US. He advised us that Jim should be flown back to England as soon as possible.

I hurried back to England after Le Mans to prepare my car for the French GP at Rheims and arrange accommodation for my parents, who were coming over for a holiday. They arrived three days before we were due to leave for France. They both loved England. Mother was thrilled with the shops and restaurants, which always strike the visitor as gayer and more modern than their New Zealand counterparts. Pop, like me, was amazed at the number, variety and quality of cars. A Jaguar carried a high-class stamp at home, but the high cost of running such a car in Britain drops the price.

We decided to motor to Rheims in the Minor. I was driving in the F1 race with a works 2½ and Ken had entered me in the F2 race with his Cooper, so I was in for a full day's work.

Race morning showed promise of a sunny day and we had breakfast in high spirits. By noon the sun was beating down with such intensity that a spanner lying on the ground for ten minutes was almost too hot to handle. All the cars were covered and drivers were dousing themselves with buckets of water. As we climbed into the cars for the warm-up lap, John suggested we should take it easy and keep out of the slipstreams to avoid overheating. Braking into the Thillois hairpin sent stones from the melting road surface flying everywhere as a gentle hint of conditions ahead.

The first few laps were murder. It was impossible to keep clear of the battering hail of pebbles from the lead cars if I was to stay anywhere in the hunt. Tony Brooks took an early lead in the works Ferrari that he was to hold to the finish. I was eighth, Jack was disputing second place with Trintignant, and Masten was lying about fourth, when a large stone hit him and he came into the pits half-dazed to retire. John Cooper retrieved the stone from the cockpit and claimed he could have chocked the car with it.

Half-way through the race I tucked in behind Gendebien's Ferrari in ninth place. The heat was almost unbearable. My knuckles were being burnt by the hot blast of air coming over the screen. I tried licking them, but it didn't help. It was getting past the hot stage and I began to feel strangely cold. Going through the long fast curve after the pits behind the Ferrari was like walking into a furnace. The heat of the vicious Ferrari exhausts added to my discomfort. I could hardly breathe and was desperately trying to scoop air into the cockpit going down the straight. Jack had punched out his screen in an effort to increase ventilation and Phil Hill was almost standing up in the Ferrari seat on the straight.

I had to stay on Gendebien's tail to hold my position, but was taking a fearful battering from flying stones. The mixture of sweat and blood in my goggles was like pink champagne. I raised them and the mess sluiced down over my face.

After that I couldn't see much through my goggles, which I found later had almost been completely shattered by 35 direct hits from flying stones. The lenses were splintered, but still intact. The chequered flag was never more gratefully received and exhausted drivers were lifted out of their cars to collapse on the pit counters, or be brought round with buckets of water. I climbed out, took off my helmet and started to cry my eyes out. I don't know to this day why, but I wept uncontrollably for several minutes. I must have gone queer in the heat.

This was the first motor race Mum and Pop had seen abroad and they were staggered to see it develop into a bloodbath. I felt in no condition for more racing when I climbed out of the F1 car, but there was a half-hour break before the F2 race and I had recovered sufficiently—so I thought. Ken told me to stop if I started to tire, but I felt on top of the world as we formed up on the grid. I realize now how dangerous this was and in the opening laps I did things I wouldn't have entertained under normal conditions. I was hanging the tail out through the fast bends, almost as though I had been drunk and unaware of the consequences. Jack had already stopped. After a few more laps I decided I would be a lot safer sitting on the pit counter, so pulled in to join him.

Stirling won the race and passed out at the back of the pits after the presentation. I signed a mental pledge that afternoon never to drive in two full-length races on the same day.

I had a Tyrrell entry in the F2 race at Rouen the following weekend. With Nora and Ken Tyrrell and my folks, I motored to Paris for a couple of days en route. Huge blisters had formed on my fingers, where they had been burned during the race, so I called at the big American hospital in Paris and came out bundled up with tape and thick bandages, which I had to endure for a couple of days. My hands were still fairly painful and I kept the bandages on for the first practice session, which made things a bit awkward, but on the second session drove with only the tape on my knuckles and for the race itself removed the tape as well, to drive with tender fingers.

While in Paris we did the usual shopping tour and at night took in the Lido and a couple of other shows. If Mum and Pop enjoyed Paris, they thought Rouen was wonderful. The track itself, just outside the village of Les Essarts, winds up and down through a forest—like a miniature Nürburgring—and the city is quaintly old and entertaining. Practice usually finished about five o'clock in the afternoon, leaving plenty of time to clean up and select a restaurant for those enjoyable dinners that extend themselves into a mild party.

Mum particularly liked the Jeanne d'Arc, a timbered building reputed to be the oldest restaurant in France. It overlooks a market square, with a concrete plaque in one corner to mark the spot where Joan of Arc was burnt at the stake. According to the fourteenth-century date of construction, diners in the top floor of the restaurant must have had a balcony seat for the ceremony.

Ken entertained us with stories of life in England and we replied with some New Zealand tales. A display of folk dancing in the square prompted Ken to ask if we could oblige with a Maori war dance! We visited a shooting gallery where Ken and I eventually retired with a bottle of wine as a prize. I asked Jabby Crombac, a French racing personality, if the wine was all right. "So long as you don't want to drink it," he said in his clipped French accent. "It would be fine for washing in, I suppose."

Results were not impressive at Rouen. The right rear tyre started going down soon after the start, but I kept going to finish third.

When we got back to England, Coopers were in turmoil preparing for the British GP at Aintree. In my absence Mike Barney had been delegated as my full-time mechanic and we got along famously. Practice at Aintree was damp and fastest time was set by Jack in the Cooper. This was surprisingly equalled by Roy Salvadori in the works GP Aston Martin. But it was the brief moment of glory for the marque in GP racing and after a few more ventures with little success (the days of big front-engined cars were numbered in 1959) they returned to retirement. Both cars are now raced "down under" with 3-litre sports car engines installed. I was on the third row, with Stirling in the light-green British Racing Partnership front-engined BRM and Carroll Shelby in the other works Aston Martin.

In the opening laps I followed Trintignant's Cooper and had a valuable free driving lesson. In Trint's wheel-tracks I found my lap times were improving, though I was motoring more gently through some corners than previously.

Up front it was Jack's race. Stirling was trying hard in the BRM, but a stop for new rear tyres spoiled his progress. I had passed Trint and found myself third, though still some distance behind the Moss BRM. I was turning laps around 1 min 59 sec and maintaining my position comfortably, but when I caught a glimpse of the pastel BRM accelerating away from the pits as I went by, I realized that Stirling had stopped again and that I was in second place behind Jack.

Coopers first and second. John would be enjoying this, I thought, and set off on the irreverent task of keeping Moss "The Master" behind me. The Cooper was all over the place. I was really caning it and using most of the track with spinning wheels and a sliding tail.

After a few laps I began to think I might be making a clown of myself in front of Stirling. I saw the BRM nose come alongside the cockpit going into the fast wiggle at Melling, but left my braking a little later than usual and stayed in front. I could see people in the pits getting excited watching our dice. Stirling was braver than I through the flat-out right-hand sweep at Waterways and I tailed him into Anchor Crossing. I got back alongside when he missed a gear going through the tight Cottage loop and, wondering if Stirling was getting annoyed, glanced across.

To my surprise, Stirling was thoroughly enjoying himself

Right, McLaren leads Dan Gurney into a bend at Avus, Germany. Below, ploughing to victory at Waimate in conditions more suitable for speedboat racing

Left, McLaren walks back to the pits at Spa, Belgium, in 1962 after a broken bearing ended his interest in the race. With him is Cooper mechanic Mike Barney. Below, with wife Patricia at the same meeting

and gave me an encouraging thumbs-up sign. He was driving neatly as always and I tucked in to follow. Our pace hadn't slowed and I made several attempts at passing. Jack was cruising round well in the lead, but Stirling and I had captured the crowd with our dice, which was lowering the circuit record on nearly every lap. It was finally credited to us both at 1 min 57 sec (93·31 mph).

Coming out of Tatts, the tricky right-hander before the start-finish line, I pulled up beside the BRM, but Stirling had my measure and took second place, with the Cooper nose abreast of his cockpit as we crossed the line.

The following week-end, Masten and I were in France again driving the Tyrrell-Brown F2 Coopers at Clermont-Ferrand. This five-mile circuit in the Auvergnes is one of the best. It is really beautiful, climbing and twisting with hardly a straight section and, unlike many road circuits, has a billiard-table surface. Henry Taylor and I had a great dice, spending most of the race side by side or nose to tail. He beat me into second place with Masten a little behind us, fourth.

Chris Bristow, a young rising star with a pleasant personality and Cockney accent, put up a good showing at Clermont in his Cooper-Borgward, gaining a front-row grid position and leading for the first five laps before retiring with a blown gasket and handing the race to Stirling.

Ivor Bueb crashed his Cooper-Borgward in this race and died later from his injuries. He had been a sparring partner of mine the year before in F2 racing and was always a great sport.

August 7th found us back at Avus—not by choice—for the German GP. Jack, Masten and I all had 2½-litre Coopers, Jack managing fourth fastest in practice to scrape on the front row with Tony Brooks (Ferrari), Moss (Cooper) and Dan Gurney (Ferrari). The Ferraris were in their element on this flat-out circuit. Brooks' eventual winning average was 143·6 mph and his record lap 149·14 mph.

In practice it rained. I was scared stiff, scorching down the straights at 180 mph on the slippery surface—and I wasn't the only one. We all got together and protested to the organizers, who later barred passing on the banking in the event of rain and no one was allowed above a line painted around the "wall of death". This would have been both dangerous and difficult. In the sports car race the day before the GP it was raining steadily and the brick-faced north banking was like glass. Behra lost control of his Porsche, which spun to the top of the banking, struck a concrete flagpole base and the little French driver was flung against the flagpole and killed.

We were all glad to see sunshine on race day. At the start, Masten tucked in behind Brooks' Ferrari to be towed to the head of the leading bunch.

He played a diminutive cat among the red pigeons, ducking out of the slipstream at 170 mph to snatch brief leads over Brooks. I was sandwiched between the BRMs of Schell and Bonnier in the second group (Jack and Stirling had dropped out with transmission bothers) and as the Ferrari came up to lap us just before the end of the first heat, there was a big out-fumbling session to snatch a ride in a Ferrari slipstream. I was the lucky one and was drawn into fourth place. Masten harrassed Brooks and Gurney for 120 miles, before a big-end bolt broke and almost sliced the engine in half.

Brooks was motoring carefully out in front, looking after his lead with an eye to his prominent championship standing and at the hairpin slowed and looked carefully on both sides to make sure no tail-ender was likely to shunt him.

I was on the front row for the second heat and climbed aboard Gurney's slipstream. The drag behind the Ferrari was terrific. Moving sharply across behind the faster car you could actually feel the Cooper being jerked forward.

Stripped drop gears finished my race and Jack retired again with a broken spiggot shaft. Both our transmission troubles were caused by the bleed-screws on the clutch-slave cylinders of our cars being mysteriously missing and we had been driving without clutches for much of the second heat. Sabotage is an unmentionable word in racing, but it struck us as strange that *both* bleeder screws should be missing.

German driver Hans Herrman gained himself world-wide publicity at this race when he looped the BRP BRM. The car leapt high in the air and Herrman was tossed out to escape with bruising. Photos showed the BRM, with various pieces falling off, poised above a flag-marshal post. All the marshals were in flight except one, who was carefully studying his programme, unaware a shunt was in progress until the BRM descended in front of him.

Bristow put on another meteoric exhibition in the F2 Bank Holiday race at Brands Hatch. The race was in two heats with aggregate times deciding the winner. In the first heat, Bristow cleared away from Brabham and Salvadori, while I couldn't get above fourth. Jack took over the second heat with Salvo second, but Bristow hung on in third postion with a safe win on aggregate.

We were using double wishbones on the rear and the car was not so controllable as previously. With the single wishbone set-up we had more oversteer, but it could be controlled and it was safe to hang out the tail. With double wishbones the car would hang on longer in a corner, then let go with a bang and it was hard to drive quickly and neatly.

The Kentish "100" for F2 cars was at Brands the week-end after the Portuguese GP and, having learned our lesson, we had our Coopers changed back to single wishbones. Stirling hadn't been there for the first race and was the only one to turn up at the second meeting with double wishbones.

With the Portuguese and Italian GPs scheduled close together at the same end of Europe, the Cooper transporter took off loaded to cover the two. I flew out to Lisbon with my parents. The race was to be run on the Monsanto circuit, just outside the Portuguese capital, with cobblestones to contend with in places.

I was lying fourth behind Stirling, Jack and Masten as we began to lap the tail-enders, but Cabral, a local driver in a Cooper-Maserati pulled across in front of Jack, forcing him off the road at about 120 mph on a fast curve. The Cooper mounted the footpath, jumped hay bales and smashed down an electricity pole, throwing a tangle of wires across the track. Jack was tossed out of the car and landed almost in front of Masten, who took evasive action, lifted both feet off the pedals and steered over the fallen wires with his fingertips, "to minimize the chances of electrocution if the wires were live," he said.

Arriving on the scene after the shunt, I could only see Jack's bent Cooper against the pole. There was no sign of him and this worried me, so that I was secretly relieved when the drop gears broke again. At the pits I learned he had been taken to hospital for treatment and when we called to see him we found he had escaped with bruises, scratches and strong views about the inclusion of inexperienced drivers in Grandes Epreuves.

He insisted on driving at Brands the following week-end, although he was still stiff and sore and turned on a staggering display, driving everyone else into the ground. Bristow led initially, but spun in front of the pack at Kidney filling the outfield with spinning cars and flying turf. After that no one got near enough to challenge Jack. I placed fourth. In the second heat Stirling stayed with Brabham at first, but was soon back with the "boys" as Jack drew rapidly away.

The Press gave banner headlines to the "Moss Jinx" and implied that Brabham had won only on the strength of Stirling's bad luck. This "jinx" talk was annoying a lot of people, especially where Stirling had been beaten fairly and squarely and I think he himself was getting embarrassed by the inference that others were winning only when he was hampered.

This viewpoint accentuated the pointed lack of acceptance of Brabham's ability and the idolizing of Stirling during the season before Jack's two-year championship reign.

For some reason my luck leaves me—not that I was having

much at this period anyway—when I step from a Formula car into a sports car or saloon. The 1958 TT in the 2-litre Lotus had been appalling; Le Mans hadn't been much better with the Russell Monaco, and for the 1959 TT Jack and I were lined up for a Cooper-Monaco entered by John Coombs. It was a dead loss. Jack drove for a few laps, until a bolt securing the right front steering arm sheared and the car was retired. I sat on the pit counter and watched Stirling win in an Aston Martin, after he had transferred to the second team car when the one he was sharing with Roy Salvadori caught fire in the pits.

In practice for the TT, Huschke von Hanstein, the Porsche team manager, produced a prototype of a F2 Porsche and asked Moss to take it for a few laps. Stirling was busy with other things and I was offered the drive. Keen to balance Cooper performance against the new German F2 contender, I jumped at the chance and was starting to get warmed up when Stirling decided that he mightn't be wasting his time with the Porsche —he was to race one for Rob Walker the following season— and I was unceremoniously hauled out.

Masten had another more serious attempt at self-propelled flight when a brake pipe broke on the Tojeiro he was driving with Jimmy Clark and he went straight ahead at Woodcote. He climbed out of the seat and was hurled over the bank, as the Tojeiro smashed into it.

The Italian GP at Monza was now out of the question for Gregory, who was lying in hospital with a broken leg and shoulder, so the spare works Cooper was to be driven by local boy Giorgio Scarlatti. John Cooper had set off for Monza just before the TT, to get the hastily-assembled spare Cooper race-worthy to make up team numbers after Jack's shunt in Portugal.

This meant I had two cars to sort out in practice. I never fancy this situation, as inevitably one feels car "A" would surely be better with "B's" gearbox, or that "B's" chassis with the engine, gearbox and brakes from "A" might be a race-winner.

As it turned out, Scarlatti was in the pits on the first lap of the race and lost a further two laps before his broken gear linkage was repaired.

Tony Brooks in the works Ferrari was Jack's main worry in the championship and Brabham must have felt better when he saw the Brooks' Ferrari trundling to a halt with a broken clutch on the opening lap. Stirling took the leaders away with his Rob Walker Cooper, fitted with wire wheels at the rear in case a tyre change was necessary. Jack was happy to sit in fifth place and I stayed in his slipstream, having bother with second gear on the slower sections.

We were bombing down into the South Curve and I was easing my foot off the throttle when a rod went through the side of the engine with a colossal bang. With no braking from the defunct engine I went into the corner too fast and, with no sane hope of making it, braked hard and skidded nose-first into a bank.

After my dust-up with Stirling's BRM in the British GP I began to realize I could put up a fair show against the "big boys" if I was on the spot at the right time. My motto had always been to drive neatly and carefully and finish races, but after Aintree I thought perhaps a little more was expected of me and, instead of pussy-footing, I had better have a go. This was also the start of a too-lengthy list of retirements.

In all my races I had reckoned on finishing, but I had a spell of gearbox bothers and a few stops that could have been put down to bad luck—or the more popular "jinx"—but in fact this was when I started to drive as fast as possible, rather than neatly and smoothly.

On an average circuit I can be half a second or more a lap quicker by changing gear on the limit and not letting the revs drop too much in the process, letting the clutch take the brunt of the gear-changes, and pounding the brakes. But all this is hard on chassis, suspension and brakes, to say nothing of the engine, gearbox and clutch. Leaving braking really late also improves lap times, providing it doesn't spoil the particular line on the corner.

This was the way I was driving for a while, but the cars kept breaking and I resolved to pay more attention to my role of reliable support as No. 3 driver in the team. It was to pay off immediately with almost staggering results.

NINE

My First Grand Prix Win

I CAME CLOSE to missing a drive in the US GP at Sebring. Coopers had entered two cars—one for Jack and one for Masten, but Masten's broken arm made it doubtful whether he would be able to drive. As I was on my way back to New Zealand anyway, John decided I should go, just in case.

Sebring was the decider for the 1959 championship; it lay between Brabham, Moss and Brooks. Jack was in strongest position with 31 points, ahead of Moss ($25\frac{1}{2}$) and Brooks (23), but the complicated permutations showed that if Jack failed to win and Stirling did, with fastest lap, the title went to Stirling. Poor Brooks was a little further from the title, as he had to win and take fastest lap, with neither Brabham nor Moss in the first three places.

So the title virtually hinged on who took fastest lap. We considered running one of the cars with light tanks, so that Masten or I could go out to do just that. But at that stage I didn't consider myself capable of it—not against Moss, at any rate. As Masten wasn't fit enough for the task, the idea was forgotten.

At Sebring there is always a meticulous medical check and this gave me the drive in place of Masten, who failed to get by the doctors.

It was the first time F1 cars had been seen in the US and speculation was rife among American fans about the margin by which Rodger Ward's "Leader Card" midget would beat us! Rodger is a quiet, likeable character and I think he knew he wouldn't be able to compete against the cream of the current F1 machinery, but his crew had other ideas and John found himself with 20 dollars staked that Rodger's midget wouldn't get within 20 sec of the best F1 time.

"Maybe you'll go by on the straights with your $2\frac{1}{2}$ litres," said the condescending Americans, "but Rodger will slide right round the outside of you when you come to the corners."

John got into an argument on how fast the F1 cars would lap. He maintained the best lap would be around three minutes for the $5 \cdot 2$-mile airfield circuit. This was greeted by guffaws. The sports cars were doing only 3 min 25 sec, so how did we think the smaller F1 cars would manage to get round quicker?

On the first day of practice most of the quicker boys were around 3 min 10 sec and Moss had clocked 3 min 5 sec. In the final session Stirling got down to 3 min dead, with Jack just 0·03 sec slower, but many of us were in mechanical trouble. Jack had ploughed through the tyres and hay bales in the middle of the "esses", putting a fair-sized dent in the side of the car and we were worried that the chassis might have been damaged.

My car had stripped its drop gears yet again and was over-heating, which in those days meant only one thing—cylinder head sealing rings. It looked as though the Cooper team was in for a night of hard work. Tim Wall, Jack's personal mechanic, was also on his way "down under" and, to save an air fare, helped look after the works cars. As he was a good engine man, he had the job of taking the cylinder head off my car and renewing the seals.

When I stripped the gearbox I found some of the teeth off the broken drop gears had mangled through it. This meant a major operation.

We were garaged in a hangar beside the Webster straight. It was rented by Briggs Cunningham, who had laid it on exclusively for Coopers. The BBC TV men were well aware of the championship drama, and tried to capture the atmosphere in the garage as Tim and I worked on my car and Jack, John and Noddy toiled away on the No. 1 car under floodlights, with the mechanics cursing as they tripped over cables and dodged round cameras and lights. Briggs, seemingly oblivious of all the excitement, was sweeping the floor to give us the cleanest possible working conditions and keeping us supplied with hot coffee and chicken soup. His hospitality was almost unbelievable. This was our first real contact with Briggs and no one could have made a better impression.

Dr Frank Falkner was helping manage the team and he bundled Jack and me off to bed just before midnight.

Next morning I was at the garage early to run the car round some of the service roads, to bed in tyres and brakes which I had been unable to do after the gearbox broke, and to make sure the cylinder-head bothers were cured. This turned out to be a pleasant warm-up for the rest of the day.

It was a lesson to see how spick and span the car looked. Tim had worked all night and was sitting back waiting for me with everything ready to roll.

The weather was good. The mayor made a speech. The high school band struck up and the drum majorettes flaunted about. We were on the grid. Then the pantomime started.

Harry Schell had a Cooper with only a 2-litre motor, yet had been credited with a time of a little over three minutes. We all knew this was probably ten seconds out and that he should have been well back in the grid. Officials placed him on the third row, but Harry argued vehemently that his time had been published as just over three minutes and he should be on the front row. He eventually talked his way there, but this put Brooks back to the second row and Tavoni, Ferrari's team manager, almost cried. Brooks had to be up front with Moss and Brab-

ham to have that equal chance. But Harry was firmly en-
trenched in the front row and there he stayed.

Rodger Ward was on the back of the grid after numerous
bothers in practice and had been 43·8 sec slower than Stirling's
best lap, leaving John looking smug with 20 dollars in his
pocket.

When the flag fell I made my best ever start. The car left the
fourth row like a rocket and at the first corner, if memory serves
me right, I went in side by side with Moss. Discretion being the
better part of valour, I let Stirling through and followed him
closely, with Jack snapping at my exhaust. Going into the next
hairpin I moved across to let Jack through on to Stirling's tail.
I didn't know then, but in that first lap behind me, von Trips
had shunted Brooks up the escape road at Websters, bending
Tony's Ferrari and dropping him well back after a pit stop.

Off we went, Moss, Brabham and myself. Behind me I could
see Allison and one of the other Ferraris, and Trint in the other
Rob Walker car. That was the way we settled down. Stirling
had opened a gap on Jack, who had drawn away from me.
Then Stirling was standing at the side of the track, looking dis-
consolately at the broken gearbox in his Cooper. Another
world championship had eluded him.

So Jack's championship was now in the bag and, with the
pair of us out in the lead, Jack gave me a thumbs-up wave and
we settled down to some careful but quick motoring. This was
one of the first of a series of occasions when I was to follow
Jack. With a few laps to go we were making a comfortable pace,
when John started to point anxiously at the signal board giving
the time gap to Trint, who was only about 12 sec behind. With
each lap the gap dropped by about a second and I was making
signals at Jack. I couldn't have gone much faster, but if Jack
had slightly increased his speed, he could have towed me along.
I was getting worried. If we continued at our present comfortable pace we would finish about five seconds ahead of Trint,
but this seemed cutting things too fine. Jack knew what he was

about, however. Here was the championship in his grasp and another GP win coming up, so he wasn't keen on speeding up.

With about two laps to go and the gap to Trint down to about six seconds, Jack slowed and pulled to one side, waving me by. I was staggered and looked across at him in utter dismay. I'd slowed right down myself, so picked second gear thinking that as Trint wasn't too far away I'd better get on with it. I think I only had a lap to go.

And suddenly there was the chequered flag and I'd won a GP. It was staggering. I couldn't believe it. I was amazed, excited and the victory lap after taking the flag must have been the most pleasant I have ever done. I stopped at the pits and was mobbed by Pressmen and photographers, while Jack slowly pushed his car across the line to a heroic finish, nearly collapsing in the heat. He had won the world championship, Coopers had won the manufacturers' championship, and I had won my first GP. It was a very happy occasion. John was beside himself, so were we.

It transpired that Jack, often a last-minute change man, had gone slightly smaller on choke-tube size, which made the engine run a little bit richer and the fact that he had been towing me in his slipstream helped save my fuel—and exhaust his. Moss had gone down two millimetres on choke tubes in practice and had found a considerable improvement. Jack had spotted this by looking at Moss' carbs and changed his accordingly. Probably Moss would have run out of fuel as well had he lasted the distance, as the tanks on both Coopers were presumably the same size.

But Jack and I were pleased with ourselves and with Coopers. It was a smooth-running team and a nice set-up. We didn't reckon we could find a better one. On the flight to New Zealand I had time to think back on the race and it was a pleasant feeling. I was to recount that story of my first GP win scores of times to my NZ friends.

The brief visit to New Zealand for the season in 1960 now

seems an almost forgotten interlude between two exciting and important motor races.

It wasn't a bright year in New Zealand from an international point of view. Brabham and Moss were the big names, with David Piper (front-engined 2·5 Lotus) and Ian Burgess (Cooper) making up the ranks of visitors. I had the second works Cooper and in the opening laps of the NZ GP Stirling, Jack and I had a battle. After 10 laps Stirling was out with clutch trouble, leaving Jack and me sparring in front. During the closing laps we really got down to business. It was the nearest I had been to winning the race, but Jack had the better of me and finished two seconds ahead.

Luck deserted me at Wigram. In practice a piston collapsed in my 2·5-litre engine and the connecting rod twirled round, virtually cutting the engine in half. This calamity came on the Friday afternoon and with the race on the following day the organizers and the oil company sponsoring the works Coopers were anxious for me to get the car mobile again. I convinced them of the difficulties involved in patching such a blow-up overnight, 14,000 miles from the factory, and it looked as though I was to be a spectator.

But a sporting offer by a friend, Malcolm Gill, found me on the grid the next day in his impressive-looking Lycoming Special. This car, built by Ralph Watson a few years earlier in Auckland, featured a flat-four Lycoming aero engine turned upside down, converted to dry-sump and fitted with a fuel-injection system of his own design. At the front end Austin A40 suspension and brakes had been used and at the rear a De Dion axle, with rearward-facing radius arms, was fitted in a similar fashion to the Spanish Pegaso.

It says a lot for this special that Brabham, Burgess and Piper were gaining only slightly on each lap. To be sitting bolt upright near the back wheels with the engine in the front was a novel change from the Coopers and an interesting experience. It was necessary to change gear only a couple of times on each lap.

The immense torque of the flat-four engine from 1000 to just under 3000 rpm had to be sampled to be believed and there weren't many cars to match me in acceleration.

Shortly after this race I was globe-trotting again, to Argentina, for the first round of the 1960 world championship, but feeling more confident and experienced than two years previously.

Well-wishers at the airport told me to start the season with a repeat of Sebring form, but I warned them I couldn't be that lucky again.

The cars Jack and I were to use in Argentina in February were the ones we had driven at Sebring the previous December, but delays in getting the cars back to England meant the mechanics had only three days to prepare them before they were shipped again. That was nothing to the problems we met in Argentina.

Having flown for nearly two days on a Super Constellation, I arrived in New York to find my Comet flight south with an Argentinian airline had been cancelled and I had just missed a Pan-American Boeing. It took me nearly half a day to persuade the airline to hand over my ticket, which they were holding for me, and I finished up pounding down to Buenos Aires in a DC3, another vintage piston-engined aircraft. This took a further 36 hours and I arrived in the Argentinian capital two days late and a physical wreck.

From the airport I was whisked to an hotel in the heart of the city, where a long sleep in a comfortable bed was priority. When I woke after twenty hours and tried to find the Cooper team, I had my first experience of the infuriatingly casual "maybe tomorrow, señor" flavour of South American service.

The general reply to a long series of phone calls round the city was, "The Cooper team is somewhere in Buenos Aires, we don't know where . . . perhaps we shall find them tomorrow . . . perhaps the next day!" Finally I located John and found the boat carrying our cars was not expected for another two days, as a piston had collapsed and it had broken down. That meant the cars should arrive on Friday, two days before the race. There wasn't much we could do, but wander round in the sun at the autodrome watching the BRM's, Ferraris, Lotuses and Cooper-Maseratis practising.

BRMs had two of the previous year's cars and three drivers, so Dan Gurney and Graham Hill flipped a coin with Graham winning. Jo Bonnier was the No. 1 driver then. The BRMs were motoring well, the Cooper-Maseratis seemed to have found a little more power and the Ferraris looked bigger and better than ever. Large bulges accommodated the side-mounted fuel tanks and the engine was mounted a little further back, but their lap times hadn't shown much improvement. Froilan Gonzalez, the "Pampas Bull", was driving one of the works cars, but in a fairly smooth manner. This was certainly not the fiery Gonzalez I had read about.

The new rear-engined Team Lotus cars shook us. If anyone had been beaten to the punch, we had. These new Lotuses were very similar to what we had on the drawing boards back in Surbiton.

They were rear-engined, small and light and obviously a lot of thought had gone into the independent suspension on all four wheels. It looked ridiculously light to us, but was lapping very quickly and we realized the new Chapman car would be a real threat.

By Friday night the boat still wasn't in port. It hadn't arrived on Saturday morning; by midday there was still no sign of it, not by two o'clock or even three. John and the mechanics were out at the mouth of the River Plate peering at the horizon and waiting for the boat to appear.

It eventually did and they kept pace with it along the river road to the docks, watching the ship's cranes lifting the crated cars from the holds. While the ship was still berthing the wharf cranes were swinging over to drop the crates on waiting trucks. This surprising excess of enthusiasm and efficiency was certainly untypical, so I guess the sheaves of telegrams from Coopers must have had some effect on the authorities.

The ship nosed alongside the wharf at quarter past five, and by seven the still-crated cars were being unloaded at the circuit 20 miles away. There was frantic activity as they were rolled out, numbers went on, petrol in, water, the brake discs cleaned of grease and, with only a few minutes of light left, Jack and I set off on a dozen laps to find which way the circuit went. On race morning there was a little more practice, but it was just before the race, so we could only scrub tyres, bed brakes and hope. . . .

Most important modification that morning was to fit thermos flasks in the cockpits to carry ice-cold orange juice. All week it had been getting hotter and shortly before the race it was up to a sizzling 110 degrees in the shade.

Suddenly, with mechanics fleeing from the grid, the flag was up and down and we were on our way. Surprisingly, no one was run over. Even more disconcerting were the hordes of photographers lining the circuit on that first lap, making passes with their cameras like matadors with a bull and side-stepping the cars at the last minute. On the corners they formed an unnerving human corridor through which we drove.

The BRMs, Lotuses and Stirling's Cooper were soon out in front and there didn't seem much we could do about it. They had opened a gap down to Jack and I was further back in the field trying hard to settle down on the strange circuit.

Carlos Menditeguy, the Argentinian all-round sportsman, expert polo player and tennis man, was just ahead of me in a Cooper-Maserati and I could not catch him.

So far the only good thing about the race had been the cold orange juice. The luxury of that cold drink in the heat was beyond words. It was agony when it ran out later. But the race was taking a sudden turn and the cars ahead of me were dropping out like flies. Some were stopping for water, to revive both engine and driver. Both BRMs had dropped valves and Jack's gearbox had broken.

Dicing on the go-kart track . . . Brabham takes the lead as McLaren's "kart" corners on two wheels

Jaguars at Brands Hatch . . . McLaren spins off after a "tap" from number 134, Mike Parkes, who takes the lead closely followed by Roy Salvadori

A line-up of motor racing's ace drivers: from the left, front row, Jack Brabham, Stirling Moss, Graham Hill, Jo Bonnier, John Surtees, Bruce McLaren and Dan Gurney

McLaren motors past the wrecks of Ginther's BRM and Trintignant's Lotus on his way to victory in the 1962 Monaco Grand Prix

Stirling had been battling hard with Bonnier's BRM and was bouncing the Cooper over kerbs in his pursuit, until a suspension arm snapped. He then took over the other Walker car from Trintignant, who was suffering from the heat.

So I was fifth . . . then fourth . . . third . . . second . . . and suddenly I saw FIRST on the signal board. I didn't need any more orange juice!

A Ferrari only eight seconds behind me seemed too close for comfort and, with something to drive for, I opened a 20 sec lead before the chequered flag came out. Lucky, lucky me!

As I rolled the car into the pits I thought I had found a riot. There were spectators fighting, police struggling with them, officials pushing, cameras shoved in my face, people screaming. I was dragged into the grandstand. I tried to walk but my feet weren't touching the ground—I was being propelled by three burly, sweating Argentinian policemen on each arm. Down in South America they don't just show enthusiasm—they go mad!

Soon it was all over bar the shouting and even that was dying away. We had been lucky and knew it, but had learnt two things: no matter how impossible things seem to be, keep trying, and that we had to get quickly down to work with our new Coopers. The BRMs had out-cornered us, Lotus had the edge on acceleration and Ferraris were not too far behind, but we had a championship start on them and were going to try and use it to our advantage.

We had contracted to do two races in Buenos Aires—or so we thought—for we were under the impression that the race the following week-end was on a different circuit in the city. News soon filtered through that it was at Cordoba.

"Cordoba? . . . Ah, Señor, just a short distance . . . just down the road," they said. We looked at a map and found it was about 500 miles. Unquestionably we should go back to England. Jack's gearbox was broken and there was plenty of development to be done with the new cars.

I had blisters all over my hands from the vibration coming

9

through the steering due to the rough surface in the braking areas. Several of us had blistered feet from the heat and all in all we weren't very happy.

When we suggested we might not be able to prepare our cars in time for the next race, officials gently hinted that our air tickets might not be ready ... or perhaps there might be a hitch with our passports ... and of course they could not be held responsible for the actions of the rather excitable public, if it was learnt we did not intend to fulfil our obligations and go to Cordoba.

We didn't mind too much as we had discovered a delightful night club that was open during the day. It had a swimming pool where we spent most of the day in an effort to get fit. Besides it was so hot and trying to get anything done was impossible. We had to get the cars from the autodrome to Cordoba and the club had assured us they would handle this. They told us the trucks would be ready to take the cars inland on Tuesday morning, so they were frantically prepared on the Monday. We were down at the autodrome bright and early on the Tuesday morning to help them load up ... but there were no trucks.

After struggling with a phone for a couple of hours we contacted the club and the gentleman there seemed perturbed. Of course the trucks would be there. When? In just a few moments. So we waited until six that evening and still the trucks did not arrive. We had been phoning the club every two hours and eventually it was admitted that perhaps the trucks would be coming the next morning. Once again we were out at the track early, once again the morning dragged on with no sign of the transporters. By now we were getting worried as the cars were not quite ready to race and we were wasting valuable time.

At four that afternoon, when the Cooper tempers were nearing a dangerous edge, a couple of huge transporters arrived. To our horror we realized they intended pushing the cars inside, shutting the doors and letting them rattle round inside for the 500-mile trip!

John was livid and to make matters worse could find no one at the club who spoke English this time. It was too much. John walked out of the booth leaving one unit of the Argentinian Telephone Company's intricate communication system lying scattered on the floor. We scrounged around for six hours collecting rope and chocks to secure the cars and eventually stood back to watch the big wagons rumbling off to Cordoba.

Everyone was charming on our flight down, but only because Fangio was acting as our courier. That evening we were taken out to a villa in the country to a barbecue with delicious kid as the main dish.

For some reason we weren't allowed to drive on the roads in Cordoba, so we were given a chauffeur—an elderly gentleman who drove everywhere at 15 mph. The first thing we wanted to see was the circuit, so we set off at our sedate pace along a bumpy, winding road. It soon became apparent that motor-cyclists were a wild breed in Cordoba, as they flashed past at great pace, using all the road. Then we spotted flag marshals and realized we were on the circuit with a motor-cycle race in full swing! We hastily impressed on our driver that he must get us off the circuit.

The track was a cross between Monaco and one of our rustic New Zealand road circuits. John was horrified, "That's it. Three laps practice and three laps in the race and we're off home!" We thoroughly agreed.

Fangio tried his hand in a F2 Porsche for a few laps, then hopped into a 250F Maserati. This must have been his last drive in a single-seater and it was sad that it should have ended in a spin which bent all the wheels. Fangio was lucky to escape injury and had our sympathy.

Race day was a scorcher—even hotter than Buenos Aires. We had learnt our lesson there, but our feet were still getting burnt, despite tubes carrying air into the cockpits and large nose scoops. The start of the race was chaotic. Regulation timing boards from "THREE MIN" down to "30 SEC" were flashed to us, but it took less than 60 sec from the first board to the flag. After Buenos Aires I was well aware that anything could happen and made a good start, braking into the first corner level with Jack.

The pair of us had such a lead on the opening lap that John thought the rest of the field had stopped. He had told us before the race started that if we took it easy we'd walk away to win, but I foolishly started dicing with Jack and, trying too hard, hit a hay bale, jolting the nose just hard enough to crack open the oil radiator. With the engine starting to overheat I stopped at the pits and Jack soon joined me with a vapour lock in the fuel lines. The BRM challenge died when Bonnier stopped with cooked brakes and the gear-lever on Gurney's car broke off. Menditeguy's transmission failed and, after a rock-steady race under the blazing sun, Trintignant came in an easy winner. Just as John had prophesied.

Despite our miserable result we felt it had been good practice for Monaco and, as I had collected fastest lap, we knew the cars weren't as slow as we had feared.

TEN

The Lowline Cooper Arrives

JOHN COOPER, Jack Brabham, Mike Grohman, Mike Barney and I arrived back in Surbiton on March 17th and before the May Silverstone meeting the 1960 lowline Cooper was built and developed. Records show this was one of the most successful Grand Prix cars ever built. Later that year Jack was to win five consecutive Grands Prix and we finished first and second in the drivers' championship.

No doubt the new Cooper's progress was speeded by the unveiling of the first rear-engined Lotus in the Argentine, but even before that the general outline had been decided.

Owen Maddox, chief Cooper designer, had spent five months designing a completely new five-speed gearbox and the patterns had just been completed, so castings could be made. Materials had been bought for gears, selectors and other internals, to be produced by Jack Knight at Battersea. Owen was then on his own in the drawing office and, using my little technical experience at college and university, I started to help by drawing wishbone assemblies, suspension units and components so that manufacture could start as soon as possible. Gallons of midnight oil were burnt at Coopers during those two months.

Jack would spend a few hours each day perusing the new

drawings and putting forward ideas, while John, his pockets full of scraps of paper with figures and sketches heavily under-lined, was phoning or calling on all the engineering and com-ponent manufacturers who were supplying and helping us.

Charles Cooper threw a spanner in the works by insisting the car must be designed so that the old Cooper leaf spring could be put on the back, if these "new-fangled" coil springs did not do the job for which they were designed.

We quickly assured him that this had been kept in mind all along! Soon we started constructing the first chassis. The pace had been so hectic that John needed a few days' rest and Charles, always a very sound but necessarily cautious man, insisted that only one chassis be finished—and therefore only one car built—until it had been tested and proved.

This didn't fit our plans, as we knew the first car could not possibly be finished until just before Silverstone. We couldn't leave it that late to start a second car, so I found time, while he wasn't looking, secretly to build a second chassis. In fact we managed a third, in case of accident.

We all had great faith in this new car. In design it followed a process of evolution, but every single part of the high old leaf-spring car had been re-examined. The same principles were used, but the theme was simplification, lightness, strength and efficiency. The first day's testing was at Silverstone a week before the race. Jack turned in a lap at 1 min 34·5 sec—a clear *six* seconds inside the previous lap record.

The grin on John's face was only excelled by that of Charles, who promptly claimed the coil-spring rear suspension as his own idea! This was an advance in racing car design surpassed only when Colin Chapman produced the monocoque Lotus 25 in 1962.

The rear-engined Lotus and BRM had, of course, been designed late in 1959, but lacked the vast amount of rear-engined experience the Cooper Car Company had gained since the days of the 500s.

The Cooper could be likened in a sense to the Type 35 Bugatti, which on its first outing looked right, was a clean and simple design and very quickly became a race-winner.

In racing car design some basic essentials must be borne in mind. These are rudimentary, but also the most important.

If one has an engine with a given amount of power, the lighter the car, the better its acceleration. The smaller the overall dimensions, particularly the frontal area or cross-section area at the largest point, the faster it will go down the straight. The lower the whole car is built, the faster it will go round corners. The more balanced the arrangement of weight distribution (i.e. about 50 per cent of the weight on the front and rear wheels, perhaps with a bias towards a little more on the back) the more stable the car will be under cornering. And the lighter the wheels, shock absorbers and axles (the unsprung weight), the more the tyres will keep contact with the road and again the faster the car will negotiate corners.

These are the basic requirements and any designer with a car embodying them all is certainly starting off on the right foot.

From there one goes on to what I regard as secondary technical points, such as the actual suspension layout (geometry), which governs the angles which the wheels take up and the movement of the chassis relative to the road.

There is still a primary object—to keep the wheels as near perpendicular to the road surface as possible. These are the basic things which have always been right about Cooper racing cars since the days of the 500, Cooper Bristol, the rear-engined sports cars and rear-engined F1 cars, all of which set a standard practical form which has proved successful.

The secondary considerations that help make a good car even better are such things as roll-centre height, roll stiffness, chassis torsional strength, spring rates, shock-absorber rates, bump and rebound travel and pitch centre, etc.

Since early 1960 there has been a strong resemblance between F1 racing cars. They now all have rear engines and independent suspension all round by, in effect, double wishbones. In some cases this is achieved by using radius rods and links, but the resultant geometry is basically double-wishbone. The cars have similar weights, disc brakes made by proprietary companies and almost equal power outputs, so performances are very similar.

This has led to increased importance of chassis. Just as the major criterion was once to have the engine tuned to its utmost, now it is also necessary to have the chassis properly tuned.

The May Silverstone was a week before Monaco, so we were going to do both a trial run and run-in period for the cars, as well as gain some estimate of our chances for the rest of the year.

Coopers had been thought lucky to win the 1959 championship. Probably they were. Ours was the only rear-engined car running in GPs and one of the few which then handled well enough for the driver to "throw it about". After our day's testing we were confident another good year lay ahead.

Team enthusiasm was tremendous and Brabham was on top of his form. My driving was slowly improving and we were ready to enter the fray with banners waving. On the first practice day Jack and John went to Silverstone, but it rained continuously. The rest of us stayed at Surbiton to try and finish my car.

This was the memorable day when Stirling Moss had an accident accelerating away from the pits. The new Aston Martin had just been unveiled to the public for the first time and Silverstone was to be its first race. The car was standing in front of the pits waiting for a driver, when Stirling "the rain master", shot on to the wet track in the Rob Walker Cooper. He lost control in front of the pits with everyone watching and spun backwards into the new Aston Martin. The Cooper took the crash fairly well, but the new Aston was damaged beyond repair, certainly for that week-end.

I went to Silverstone on the Friday morning. The boys had

worked all night to get my car ready for the final practice. It was still teeming with rain and the track was almost under water.

My 1959 car was there and I was set for a splash around, but John was terribly agitated and didn't want either Jack or me to go out at all. It was Friday the 13th and I didn't have the heart to tell him I'd left at Surbiton the little *tiki*, a Maori native charm which I normally have in my pocket. I did about five laps just to get on the grid, then stopped at the pits and John told us to put both cars away.

Ireland, Surtees and Stacey had already had minor accidents, then in the last ten minutes of practice the rain eased and the track started to dry. Much against his better judgement, John let us go out again. We all wanted to go just that little bit faster. Moss had put up a very fast time and we wanted to get down to something reasonably near it.

Then it happened. Harry Schell spun his car on the fastest corner of the circuit, smashed sideways into a brick wall on the inside of the corner and died almost instantly from his injuries. Late practice was cancelled as a mark of respect to a charming character, who had been in racing a long time and there were many moist eyes in the pits that afternoon.

We waited until the second new Cooper arrived at 8 pm, just in time for me to try the gearbox by running it round the paddock area before dark. The parade lap next day, the quiet one we use to warm up the cars before the race, was also useful to get some idea of how it was going to feel.

I was well back on the grid, but made a good start. It was the first time we had used the five-speed box and it seemed very fast off the line. I even had to back off a couple of times to avoid running into slower cars.

Jack botched his start, going straight from low gear to fourth —a theoretical impossibility, as we had an interlock device which let one go only to second gear! With a four-speed gear-box, low and second are on one side, third and top across to the other, but with a five- or six-speed box, low and second are to the left, third and fourth in the middle, and fifth and sixth to the right—one could change from second straight to fifth if one weren't careful. This wouldn't do a racing engine much good, so some sort of interlock device is usually fitted to help sort out the gears in their correct order.

I was settling down after 12 trouble-free laps when I started having trouble entering corners. I found I was having to brake earlier and gear-changing was getting difficult. Finally on a corner I realized something was really amiss. It felt as though the throttle was stuck about a quarter open and rather than risk crashing I switched off, rolled to the side of the track and opened the bonnet. Not finding anything obviously wrong, I drove to the pits by putting it in top gear and keeping the brakes on.

The mechanics soon found the locknut on the throttle return stop bolt had not been tightened and had wound right out, holding the throttle open.

Better for it to happen at Silverstone with its open corners than at Monaco. As it had cost me three laps, I just cruised on to finish. The car felt fine and for a brand-new machine it was a good first outing. I couldn't get below 1 min 37 sec, but wasn't sure whether that was me or the car—probably me at that stage. Stirling was doing 1 min 36 sec in the old leaf-spring car and driving fabulously until it broke. And Innes upset us all by doing 1 min 34·2 sec in the Lotus. Jack had lapped at around only 1 min 35 sec, but still managed to win by about two seconds. We were a bit tongue-in-cheek as we hadn't expected the Lotus to be faster than our new car. But we didn't have time to worry, with the Monaco GP the following week-end. Jack and John took one of the new cars to Brands Hatch to make sure they could get around the tight corners and also started setting up the carburation.

We felt ground clearance at the front was about an inch too high, as the springs were designed for 35 gallons of fuel. The car was also rolling a bit much, with the roll centre five-sixteenths of an inch under the ground at the back, rather low.

Practice for the Monaco GP is always frustrating and tiring. It is one of few races where drivers are forced to qualify. It is a short circuit and only 16 cars are allowed to start, so the 16 fastest are taken. More than 20 cars were trying to get in and we were out to practice bright and early on the Thursday afternoon. The idea was to take it easy at first and get familiar with the shape of the stone walls and kerbs. The carburation on my car turned out to be hopeless. It wouldn't run at all at low speed and this is a major problem at Monaco. Failure to accelerate cleanly out of the corners in low gear spoils one's lap times there.

We tried to improve the car during practice, but were unsuccessful and that evening I resolved to have a big session with the carburettors. I restricted the accelerator pump travel, changed the needles and seats, lowered the float levels, went leaner on idle jets, and leaned the pump jets a little—and thank heavens it worked on Friday morning.

The carburation was so good that on my second lap I shot out of the Gasworks hairpin with wheels spinning and slid the tail into the kerb! Ten minutes later the broken wheel was changed and I went out to practice again with a caution from the irate John.

John never pushed a driver over the limit. If the driver said he was going as fast as he could and that wasn't fast enough, then it was just too bad. He would never ask anyone, particularly on a circuit such as Monaco, to drive beyond his capabilities.

After a few laps I managed to get down to 1 min 38·6 sec. This was apparently satisfactory and out went a "Come In" signal—a large arrow on the board pointing to the pits. My time was sixth fastest, with Moss, Brabham, Bristow and Bonnier ahead of me and we were sure that the picture wouldn't change much. But the unpredictable Monaco timekeepers credited me with only 1 min 39·2 sec and as half-a-dozen cars were in that half-second down to 1 min 38·6 sec, Saturday evening practice was to be all-important.

We had fitted new front springs and brake pads for the race and after a couple of steady laps to check the handling and bed in the brakes, I was due to start motoring. Then I upset things. The gearbox bung dropped out of my car and put a sudden stop to practice. It's surprising what a gallon of castor oil will do at Monaco.

Not only did we stop practice—but French television as well! The cameras were trained on activities in our pit and a tele-photo lens zoomed in, bringing viewers face to face with John, who was red in the face, and telling the mechanic in words loud and clear what a quaint thing it was not to wire the gearbox plug and what an unusual sort of chappy he found the mechanic. Only he didn't say "quaint" and he didn't say "unusual", and he didn't say "chappy". French viewers had their English vocabularies enlarged by three words that afternoon!

Then started perhaps the most dramatic practice session we have ever seen. Before I'd dropped my oil, a couple of BRMs had got just under 1 min 39 sec, making a total of 19 cars under the 1 min 40 sec mark. Trintignant, Gregory, Halford, Surtees, Ireland and Stacey hadn't then managed to qualify. Moss was out shepherding Ireland and Stacey round, while the others strove for elusive fractions that would put them in the race.

Suddenly I was among the ones that might miss out. It was incredible that on an oily circuit everyone should be three seconds under the old lap record. I went out again, as it was imperative to improve on that official figure of 1 min 39·2 sec. I again did 1 min 38·6 sec and was signalled in. We sat back to relax, but now Trintignant was nearly out of control trying to qualify and Ireland was trying like mad. This was crazy! Then the loudspeakers announced that I was sixteenth fastest qualifier—still with 1 min 39·2 sec!

Trintignant had just done 1 min 39·1 sec and Lotuses had

notched up 1 min 38·8 sec, so now it was in the lap of the gods. They had missed my time again. We had just filled the tanks to try handling when fuelled for the race and only three minutes of practice was left.

With full tanks this was impossible. I managed 1 min 39 sec before the chequered flag went out and practice was over. Apparently I had just made it—last qualifier. Halford had missed out with 1 min 39·6 sec—a very quick time two days previously. Between 1 min 38 sec and 1 min 39 sec were 12 cars.

The American Scarabs had unfortunately failed to qualify. Built by likeable, wealthy young Lance Reventlow, they were to have competed in their first European race. They were sharing a garage not far from us and we spent a lot of time with the crew helping as best we could to improve the handling of their cars, but at that stage they were far too slow.

Came Sunday morning and the first good news was that my times had been registered at 1 min 38·6 sec after all, which shifted me to eighth on the grid. But our problems weren't yet over.

The heat on the previous day had apparently upset the rubber seals in the brake calipers, or maybe the master cylinders, anyway the brakes were sticking on, so we changed calipers, then bled the braking system.

We had just ten minutes before the start, when we found that the rear master cylinder wouldn't return—it was stuck down. And in the meantime a newly-designed plunger in the gearbox had jammed open. By now we had the car on the grid, but the nose was off, the tail was off, the gearbox was in pieces and the brakes were stuck on. John and Charles were demoralized. I didn't mind too much, as a last-minute panic is sometimes a good thing. I knew our boys would get it sorted out and it was just the frame of mind in which to start a motor race.

The flag fell and I made a fine start, at least until Graham Hill almost stalled in front of me. This caught me unawares and I dropped back to the tail of the bunch.

But the Cooper was going like a rocket and I was able to work up through the field until suddenly I found no one in front of me—just a long gap. Rain started spattering down a few laps later and as I came over the brow of the hill at the Casino, I saw to my amazement a line of cars in front of me— Bonnier, Brooks, Brabham, Hill, Moss; they were all there just a few yards ahead and in a lap I was with them. What a race!

The previous year I'd bounced off kerbs occasionally, but now that was tame. Phil Hill and I were dicing wheel to wheel, even bouncing off the walls beyond the kerbs at times. The inside of our tyres were ringed with white paint from the kerbs. Thank heavens those tyres were strong.

Then I had my first incident. Accelerating around St Devote, just before the uphill run to the Casino, I spun completely, ending up facing backwards on the footpath. Jack had done the same thing a few laps earlier in the rain and was still there surveying his bent car. Mine felt all right, so while Jack signalled that the road was clear, I blipped the engine, slipped into low gear, dropped the car back on the road, spun round to the right direction and rejoined the race.

By then it was really slippery. Twice I came to a stop on the hairpins, completely sideways with full opposite lock on to try and stop the car spinning. I once scared Phil Hill by blasting out of the tunnel at 110 mph on the footpath! Come to think of it, I don't suppose Phil was the only one frightened. I seem to remember three marshals leaping the sea wall to dodge the Cooper. One magazine report said I left the tunnel backwards, but this wasn't quite true—it was only sideways!

I was having trouble with my goggles and could see only with my right eye, as the other lens was completely steamed up. At Monaco there is little time to take a hand off the wheel and sort out such situations.

I've never been quite so glad to see the finishing flag. This was certainly my best drive so far, even in second place. I was thrilled with the car, but we were going to have to watch the

BRMs and Ferraris. Moss, of course, was fast in anything and he romped home to yet another victory at Monaco in his new Lotus.

With one first placing and a second in championship events, I had a fair stack of points and the title table read: McLaren first, Moss second, Allison third. Allison had been unfortunate enough to shunt the Ferrari in practice at the chicane and was to suffer as a result of the accident for more than a year.

Jack's Cooper had to be whisked back to Surbiton to be straightened. This meant day-and-night work for the already-tired mechanics, with the next Grand Prix only a week away at Zandvoort in Holland. They left early the next morning with the car in the back of the transporter and detailed arrangements were made for the Cooper to be flown across the channel, collected by trailer and taken to the works.

I drove quietly to Zandvoort for my first race on the circuit. The previous year my entry had not been accepted because I was an unknown, but this time I was going there as leader in the world championship. But when some of the other drivers asked, "How is the world champion today?" I was embarrassed, because I knew I was leading more by luck than skill. I prefer a result to be obtained the hard way, as I don't think easy success is ever appreciated.

It was also getting awkward with Jack, the No. 1 team driver not having scored a point, but it was typical of Brabham's character that this made him more determined than ever and round the sand dunes at Zandvoort he proved he was made of stern stuff.

I'd done many practice laps to learn the circuit well and was about half-way up the grid. Moss was fastest, closely followed by Brabham. Innes Ireland was third fastest, motoring very fast at this stage, but reliability wasn't the Lotus team's strong point.

The race became a terrific dice between Brabham and Moss, until Jack clipped the inside of a corner and lifted a brick which Moss struck with a front wheel. This broke the rim and let the tyre go flat, forcing a pit stop and wheel change for Stirling and handing the race to Jack on a platter—his first win of the season.

I'd gone only about 10 laps and was moving into third place when a universal cross joint failed and I was suddenly left with no drive to the rear wheels. I coasted to the grass at the end of the straight and leapt from the cockpit to find what had gone wrong. I soon discovered the trouble and trudged back to the pits.

As I arrived something made me glance up and at the same instant spectators in the grandstand came to their feet and screamed as Dan Gurney's BRM ploughed off the end of the straight at unslackened speed. It hurtled high in the air over the sand dunes, then across a gangway between spectator areas. Dan escaped with a severe shaking, but the BRM in its crazy flight had struck an eighteen-year-old youth who died later from his injuries. Again the rear disc brake of the BRM had failed.

Jack was back in the championship placings with 8 points, Moss had 11 and I had 14.

The next round was Spa in Belgium—a race most of us wish we had missed. Spa must be one of the hardest tests of driver-car combination in the world. The average speed is up around 130 mph, with sweeping corners on a perfectly surfaced, but not wide road between pine trees and brick buildings.

This was to be our first one-two race result in Europe, with Jack first and myself second, but it was a race of tragedy and a result on which we never look back as worthwhile or memorable.

The first accident happened during practice. Moss had been recording very fast times and when I saw him leaving the pits as I swooped down from La Source hairpin, I jumped at the opportunity to follow him and learn more about the circuit. I sat in behind as he accelerated up the hill, up through the woods to the long left-hander before the plunge down to Burneville corner. He left me going down the hill and opened a gap of a hundred yards or so.

We swung into the long right-hand curve made blind by farm houses immediately beside the road. I had a strange feeling something was wrong and backed off a fraction.

But I was shattered to see Moss' Lotus spinning wildly on the road in front of me. It hit the left side of the road, rocketed across to the right and bounced wildly in the air. There was so much dust that I lost sight of the car. I had the brakes on hard and slid to a stop as the Lotus came to rest.

At first I thought Stirling was still in the cockpit and, well aware of the ghastly risk of fire, raced back to the wrecked car. To my amazement it was empty! Stirling was lying in a patch of soft bracken where the car hit the left-hand side of the road. He was having trouble getting his breath, so I loosened his helmet and overalls.

Stirling was asking for artificial respiration, but with the thought of possible internal injuries, I persuaded him to lie still and keep his mouth open until his breath came back. I felt sure he was only winded. The only thing I had forgotten was that he had false teeth and might have swallowed them. Fortunately he didn't.

Within a couple of minutes we had virtually the entire field of 15 cars lined up on the side of the road, each driver having recognized the broken blue Lotus. We were worried at first as we had no idea how bad Stirling was, but we found blankets and pillows and were able to make him comfortable and warm. He was conscious and talking, concerned about what he might have broken.

We assured him his arms and legs were all there and he looked just fine. But why wasn't there an ambulance? We had been waiting 10 minutes and it was a further 10 before the ambulances finally arrived. We were all incensed about this delay, but there had been another accident at almost the same moment as Stirling's.

Further around the circuit the steering had collapsed on Mike Taylor's Lotus, which had plunged off into the pine trees and Mike was also badly injured. This had been a bad day, but worse was to come.

On race day we were paraded round the circuit in open sports cars. Alan Stacey was in the car behind me and as we entered the pits again at the end of the lap, I noticed that he looked nervous. I tried to offer him a couple of cheery words, but he barely appeared to hear.

Early in the race Bristow's Cooper went out of control at around 140 mph on the corner where Moss had had his accident the previous day. As I flashed past I knew it was a Yeoman Credit car, which meant either Brooks or Bristow and I knew it was bad; in fact I knew it was as bad as it could be, for as I went past an ambulance man pulled a blanket over the driver.

Within a quarter of an hour there were two huge black lines 200 yards further down the track leading off into a bushy area on the right.

On the next lap the whole area was a bonfire. This accident looked even worse than the one at Burneville, but the race was still on and I was dicing with Graham Hill and Gendebien. A piece of rubber matting glued to the undertray of the car worked its way in among the pedals. I slowed down to retrieve this and threw it out of the cockpit, but this cost me just enough time to let Hill and Gendebien open a gap. Within a couple of laps Gendebien was out with a broken gearbox and a piston had collapsed in Graham's car.

Jack and I, the worried victors, stopped at the pits. All we wanted was to be told who had crashed. This was perhaps one of the worst things about Alan Stacey's accident. We had no idea who it was. For all I knew, it might have been Jack, and vice versa.

I haven't heard an account of Bristow's accident and I haven't asked very much. Chris and I were good friends and it's easier to try and forget as soon as possible. To think at all is bad. It may sound callous and hard to accept accidents, but if you're going to keep on racing, you must do so.

Alan Stacey was one of the most likeable people in motor racing—a quiet, modest young man and a natural driver.

A priest who was first on the scene said he found the remains of a bird splattered over Alan's goggles. Something like this is easier to reconcile, on the basis Battle of Britain flying aces adopted. If your number was up, that was it and there was little you could do about it.

An accident of this kind could have happened at any time in any one of Alan's cars and because of this we can excuse ourselves for motor racing and perhaps excuse the accident as not being directly attributable to it.

Unquestionably we still feel it is one of the finest sports in the world, it's just a pity the penalty for a misjudgment or mistake on the part of any member of the team—whether a designer who draws a faulty part, a mechanic who assembles it poorly, or a driver who overdoes it or drops concentration—can be so final.

This risk and drastic penalty for a mistake does not add to the excitement. I am sure every Grand Prix driver who sees an accident in a racing car immediately loses the keen sense of enjoyment and competitiveness of this demanding sport.

After the disastrous week-end at Spa, our next race was Rheims, where Phil Hill and the Ferrari team were to be our main opposition. We knew they would be well up on top speed, so were anxious to get there and find how the Coopers would compare. There were 100 bottles of champagne for fastest lap on first practice day; another 100 on the second, providing the fastest lap bettered the previous day's best, and the same applied on the third and final day. Played carefully, there was obviously the chance to gain a store of champagne, if nothing else.

Wednesday was first practice day and Jack soon turned in some excellent lap times, substantially under the old lap record and doing 180 mph on the straight, which earned him fastest lap and the champagne. The next day competition was a little harder as Ferraris had arrived, but driving with quite a bit in hand Jack still gained fastest time with 2 min 16·8 sec and another vanload of champagne. Phil Hill was getting close (2 min 18·2 sec) with the Ferrari as we expected and I wasn't far behind with 2 min 19 sec. Jack's engine was really singing. We felt we just had to win—the car was immaculately prepared, team spirit was high, and there was a tremendous air of confidence.

At the Friday session it would have been possible to go a little faster again and win another 100 bottles of champagne, but John decided we had quite enough and there was no point in extending the machinery more than necessary. The race, after all, was on Sunday. And that day Jack and Phil had a duel that will long be remembered.

Phil was really the man to charge the big Ferraris round and Jack thoroughly enjoyed the dice. Phil is a really safe driver in a GP car. At Monaco I had diced with him side by side for lap after lap and he had twice let me through when he felt he was baulking me. To drive on a circuit like Rheims in close company with another car at 160 mph, you need confidence in the other man.

Phil and the red cars were to carry all before them the following year, but right now they were taking a beating. The Ferrari V6 engine produced more power than the Coventry-Climax four-cylinder, but contrary to our expectations they were no faster than the Coopers on the straight, this was purely a question of the relative size of the cars.

The Ferrari was still a racing car in the old tradition, front-engined and much bigger than the Coopers. It was also much heavier. This superiority of Coopers during 1960 was eventually to result in a lean year for the British cars in 1961. It was felt in many circles, particularly and logically, I suppose, by Coventry-Climax, that because we were able to beat the Ferraris we must have more power. Or, if not actually more power, a greater amount of area under our power curve in the rev range that we used. This, of course, wasn't the case at all.

Even in 1960, when we had only 240 bhp, Ferraris probably had 265 bhp or more from their V6, so that in 1961 when Ferrari took the British form—small and rear-engined, with independent suspension all round—we had lost our advantage.

For the second race in succession I had a long, hard dice with Gendebien, but this time it was my car that was in trouble. A piece of the ducting inside the nose had loosened itself and folded back across the radiator, sending the water temperature rocketing up. It says a lot for the engine that during the latter part of the race, when the temperature gauge was reading 115 degrees Centigrade, it continued to run satisfactorily. The oil pressure fell right off and the oil temperature went up to about 140 degrees Centigrade.

Although I finished only third behind Gendebien, it was a happy day for Coopers. They finished first, second, third, and Henry Taylor in another Yeoman Credit Cooper similar to Gendebien's (a 1959 car) was fourth. Now Jack and I, both with 24 points, were joint leaders of the championship.

The new Vanwall had made an appearance in practice, but did not perform particularly well. Tony Brooks, who had won three times previously at Rheims, was having a very difficult drive and was in the pits after a couple of laps.

There had been quite a mix-up on the starting grid. Halford's Lotus, Trintignant's Cooper-Maserati, Bianchi's Cooper, Brooks' Vanwall and Graham Hill's BRM were all involved in a mighty shunt, which nearly knocked the whole rear end of Graham's BRM and severely damaged Bianchi's Cooper. Poor Graham was having a rough season in GP cars.

At this time the Cooper flag was flying high. It seemed as though there wasn't another car to compete with them. By driving my car steadily I could guarantee to finish in the first three and Jack, driving hard, could lead the race from start to finish. It seemed to be getting a piece of cake and the British GP was needed to shake us out of our complacency. This race at Silverstone cast many shadows of forthcoming events. Any prophet could surely have taken down the facts and predicted the Grand Prix picture in two years' time.

Graham was left badly at the start with a stalled engine and lost 35 sec, but during the race not only made up that 35 sec, but came right through the field to catch and pass Brabham! That drive will go down in history. Graham had still to win a major race, but he was the fastest driver on the track that day. His time was clearly to come.

Battling for third place were two new names—John Surtees and Jimmy Clark. Clark retired with mechanical trouble and the Press made a big thing of Surtees' performance. I had been able to race alongside both of them that day (I finished fourth) and it was the Scotsman Clark who impressed me. They were both fast, but Clark was the smoother of the two, driving in an extremely relaxed fashion.

I had led the race for the first two laps, then let Jack through to win like a good team driver should, but I was disappointed with my fourth placing. This was further down than I'd finished for some time and Jack was well aware that he had been lucky Graham didn't finish. But as Fangio has said, "To win a race, you have to finish." Jack had no reason to feel too bad, as it was a driver error, not a mechanical breakdown that cost Graham the race.

ELEVEN

Racing Sports Cars in the US

THERE WAS A rash of smaller meetings after Silverstone and before the Portuguese Grand Prix at Oporto. These did not count towards the world championship, but were international races with the first one for F2 cars at Solitude—one of the best road circuits in the world—just outside Stuttgart and won by von Trips in a Ferrari, a rear-engined prototype of what was to be the 1961 F1 car. The only man able to stay near it was Jim Clark in the Lotus and in fact he was gradually drawing away from the Ferrari until retiring at the pits with mechanical failure.

A week later there was another F2 race on the south circuit of the Nürburgring. Denis Hulme and George Lawton, the two NZ GP "Drivers to Europe", were racing as a team under the management of Feo Stanton and had loaned me their 1958 F2 Cooper, as Denis was racing in Italy with his Formula Junior car.

There wasn't much chance of competing on level terms with the new Porsches, but at least Coopers were represented. Jack had an interim-type F2 Cooper, which he was running privately. It was a lightened version of the factory car and a fairly reasonable performer, but we couldn't hold the might of Porsche and the German cars finished first, second, fourth, fifth and sixth, with Jack squeezing into the vacant third place. I was ninth and Dan Gurney tenth, but Dan and I felt we'd come first and second in our particular race. The first eight cars had been supplied with special Dunlop SP rain tyres and as there were only eight sets available, the rest of us were running on the older normal tyres. Race day was atrocious and we couldn't keep pace with the lucky ones who used their new SPs to advantage. Towards the end of the race, fog drifted across the circuit and in places it was possible to pick out the edges of the track only by spotting the tops of trees as the mist thinned. Not ideal racing conditions!

The following day we were back at Brands Hatch in the F1 cars for the GP-style race on the enlarged circuit. The popular kidney-shaped mile circuit had been extended to nearly three miles.

Most of the British F1 teams were there and it was a good race, with Jim Clark again showing signs of things to come. Brabham and Clark duelled furiously in the opening laps, until mechanical trouble once again claimed the Lotus. Graham Hill then took over second place, while I followed him home in the other works Cooper. Innes Ireland tried the SP tyres he had brought back from the German race, but it wasn't raining at Brands Hatch and he soon found that, although they were fine in wet conditions, on a dry road his Lotus was uncontrollable. Poor Innes had the crowd on its toes as he spun regularly, until convincing himself that discretion was the better part of valour and retiring. Had it rained, he might well have won. So far as we were concerned this was just a fill-in period while waiting for the Portuguese GP.

Portugal always puts on a motor race bursting with colourful Continental personality—thousands of sun-browned, excitable spectators in a blaze of garish colour, amiable policemen and officials and glorious sunshine from dawn to dusk.

Oporto is a road circuit in the true sense of the word, with everything from tramlines to cobblestones, to tax driver and car. Practice was hectic, with Henry Taylor and Jim Clark having a big accident right in front of the pits. Jimmy's Lotus tried to climb a pole, but he escaped unharmed. Henry lost a bit of skin.

Dan Gurney had struck form again and was turning in fast lap times in the BRM. He had been a man to watch in the Ferrari at Lisbon a year earlier and once more Dan'l was proving Portugal to be the Gurney stamping ground. Surtees also lapped fast and Moss was back in the Walker-Lotus for the first time since his Spa accident.

Stirling had been circulating for a few laps when Jack made his opening tour warming up the Cooper. As Moss flashed past Brabham, one or two journalists became ecstatic in praise of their hero. Here, they said excitedly, was Moss passing Brabham as soon as he got back in a racing car! The story grew out of all proportion before the day was over.

In the race Surtees went into the lead, only to get in difficulties when braking for a sharp left-hander at the end of the main straight and thump the straw bales. Jack had a narrow escape when he tried to out-brake one of the BRMs while straddling the tramlines. When he wanted to turn left he found he was stuck in the rails and was forced down the escape road, fearing he would ride the rails down to the depot!

Mechanical casualties were high. I drove steadily and by the end of the race was a comfortable second behind Jack, who took the chequered flag to notch five wins in a row and confirm that he was to be 1960 world champion. The Cooper Car Company were also established in an unassailable lead for the manufacturers' championship.

The next round was at Monza, where the organizers had decided to combine the road circuit with the banking. This steeply-banked oval circuit, used mainly for record-breaking attempts, had become bumpy and was dangerous not only if a driver lost control over the bumps, but also because banking of this nature imposes a far greater load on the suspension. All sorts of mechanical components could either give trouble or fail completely.

The road racing circuit, set in the grounds of the autodrome, is perfectly satisfactory, but the organizers wanted to combine the two. British constructors felt this to be dangerous and, in hopes that the banking might not be used, met and decided they would not appear at the Italian GP. Things became a bit political, with considerable lack of understanding or co-operation between organizers and constructors. So far as Coopers were concerned, the race was immaterial—the championship was in the bag and there was little point in racing on what we felt was a dangerous track. Eventually none of the British teams went to Monza and the race was won by Phil Hill's Ferrari.

The Gold Cup meeting at Oulton Park in Cheshire rounded off the European season. A Moss-Brabham clash had been advertised, but in the opening laps Ireland and Clark in the Lotuses set the pace. Clark dropped out after getting involved with a slower car and climbing a bank, leaving Innes to demonstrate an ability that is often overlooked, as he began to pull away from Moss and Brabham. But his moment of glory was short-lived and he was soon in the pits. Then it was Moss against Brabham with a vengeance.

I was the meat in a BRM sandwich not far behind them, with Jo Bonnier just ahead and Graham Hill behind me. I was trying to pass Jo and Graham was trying to get past me—a feat he accomplished with Jo's help in one of motor racing's neatest tricks.

At the end of the straight and just before Knickerbrook curve, I tried to pass Bonnier on the right. He moved over in front of me, so I pulled left. He also pulled to the left and slowed, so that I had to do likewise, This let Graham get alongside me on my right. I then had Jo in front, the grass on my left and Graham on my right as we braked for the corner. Jo braked hard, slowing more than necessary and waved Graham through. I couldn't do a thing, as I was hemmed in, while Graham was able to ease off his brakes, nip past Jo and leave me stuck behind the pair of them!

Jo was soon out, however, and I resumed my dice with Graham, tailing him home behind Moss and Brabham. The crowd were delighted.

After this I accidentally moved into a new and strange phase in my career—sports car racing in the US. Brabham had placed tenth in a sports car "Grand Prix" at Riverside, driving a prototype of the E-type Jaguar owned by Briggs Cunningham. On the following week-end he was signed to drive the Ecurie Écosse Cooper-Monaco at Laguna Seca, so Phil Kerr, now installed as Jack's manager, phoned to say he could fix me the drive with Briggs. Soon I was on a plane heading for California. This was the first time I was to drive for Briggs and ever since I have had a high regard for him and the way he goes racing.

I hadn't much idea where Monterey was, or whom I should contact when I arrived, but as we had cabled the race organizers with my flight details I fondly imagined I would be met at the airport. I arrived in the early hours of the morning to find barely a soul around, apart from a couple of sleepy porters and a bus driver, whom I persuaded to take me to the nearest hotel.

I had brought a crown-wheel and pinion for the Ecurie Écosse Monaco, and thought finding them would be no problem in the morning. If there was a motor race on, everybody would know about it. I woke bright and early and asked at the desk for the race office. Motor race? The girl knew nothing about it. She had seen some stock cars in town on Saturday night—perhaps the race was over? I assured her these were not the sort of cars I was talking about! I phoned the Chamber of Commerce . . . they knew of the race, but had no idea who was running it or where the office might be.

There was nothing in the telephone book to help me, so I wandered out into the sunshine, wondering what the next move was, when I heard a reassuring noise—a raucous bellow of an open exhaust from a garage across the road, where one of the Reventlow Scarabs was being prepared for the race. I had no idea to whom the car belonged, nor who the characters were with it, but assumed they would soon be setting off for practice and asked to hitch a lift with them. I explained I was driving the Jaguar for Briggs Cunningham and they were singularly unimpressed, but volunteered to give me a ride to the circuit.

Out there I found a few more familar faces and asked for the Cunningham équipe. I was told to look for the biggest transporter and semi-trailer in the paddock. Sure enough, there was a huge mobile workshop and, parked alongside it, a car transporter with a couple of Maseratis, a gaggle of Formula Junior cars and a big white Jaguar.

I introduced myself to the crew and took an immediate liking to the group of enthusiastic mechanics from the Momo Corporation, headed by seventy-year-old Alfred Momo. Much-loved Alfred, whose Italian accent was so thick I had great difficulty at first in understanding him. Fifteen years in New York had done little to Americanize his particular brand of English. There can be few more popular men in racing than Alfred, who treats drivers, team managers, mechanics and almost Briggs F. Cunningham himself as though he was their father. Mary Momo looks after "her boys" in a similarly generous fashion. A wonderful couple. Andy, Pete, Jo, Victor and Marcel make up an efficient team. These long-experienced, soft-spoken, friendly Italians soon had me sitting in the Jaguar to make sure I could reach the wheel and pedals comfortably. The car had a solid feel about it.

I started the engine, blipping it a few times, and the whole car resounded and rang with the drum of the exhaust as though it were all one solid, bell-like unit. It felt good.

Walt Hansgen, long-time No. 1 driver for the Cunningham team and one of the best and most experienced in the States, gave me a run-down on the circuit. I was keen to get on the track as soon as practice started, but the idea shocked Walt.

"Wait for at least four laps," he counselled, "just take it easy and let them sort themselves out." I soon saw what he meant! I've never seen so many cars go off a track in such a short space of time. After the first four or five laps things started to settle down, the cars that had immobilized themselves were pulled off the track, those that hadn't were being driven with a little more caution and the straw bales and corner-markers were gathered up and replaced, while the more experienced drivers got down to some serious practice.

The E-type was fun to drive on this tight little circuit. You could spin the wheels nearly everywhere and controllability proved to be one of the car's better points. It was the sort of car you could get very sideways on, and still have it in control. My main problem, however, was getting into the race. It wasn't just a question of arriving, tooling around and turning in some sort of lap time as in Europe. Only 22 were allowed to start and, as there were some 40 sports cars and specials of all shapes and sizes, this meant 22 fairly fast cars. Someone hinted it would be harder than Monaco and I took their point.

There were several 2- and 3-litre front-engined Maserati birdcage sports cars; Moss and Gurney had a couple of still-very-new Lotus 19s, and Jack had the Cooper-Monaco. Lance Reventlow's F1 efforts had not been so successful, but his Scarab sports cars were earning well-deserved reputations as fast, well-built, race-winning cars. Augie Pabst, a young American with a lot of ability, drove one of them and was quite a sight to watch out of the slow corners. His Scarab was the one I'd seen earlier that morning and "Red", the chief mechanic, was one of the best-known in America, noted for his dry humour. I had asked that morning as they were warming-up the Scarab amid fantastic noise, how the car performed.

"Well," he drawled, "even if it doesn't go fast, it sure scares hell out of the natives!" I agreed—the garage walls were reverberating with the blast of the exhausts.

Besides the Scarabs there were several other Chevvieengined specials; "Old Yaller" was a Buick-engined machine with a colourful history and there was the usual collection of Ferraris of different shapes and sizes.

Qualifying was nerve-straining and exciting. It was arranged for one car at a time to go out and do three laps—one warm-up, one flier, and one slowing-down for the return to the pits. Everything depended on the flying lap. I drew a position near the end of the qualifying line, which gave me the doubtful advantage of knowing roughly how fast I had to motor to get in the race. It also meant I had to sit there for about two hours just waiting.

Phil Hill went out in an old V12 Ferrari just ahead of me and even though he threw the car around, it looked as though he wouldn't be quick enough to qualify. To make the grade with the Jaguar, I knew I had to clip at least three seconds off my previous best time and that was quite a problem.

I left the line like a scalded cat. There were two fast left-handers on an uphill part of the circuit and on the flying lap I had both inside wheels well off the track on the inside.

The revs shot up as the rear wheel spun on the loose surface, but I didn't dare lift my foot for fear of losing time and blazed all the way up with the hitherto unseen reading on the rev counter. I just made it, qualifying about nineteenth fastest, which pleased the Cunningham crew, who hadn't expected the E-type to get in the race.

The race was run in two heats the next day. Cars blew up and spun off all round the circuit and somehow I managed to collect fifth-place prize money. I'm sure this couldn't have been right, but I didn't waste time arguing.

I talked to an American of about my own age at the airport on the way back to England the following day. He had been driving a Porsche and seemed to have fared reasonably well. We became firm friends on the flight to New York and agreed to get together next time we were both at the same motor race. His name was Roger Penske.

Back in Surbiton, the F1 cars were being prepared for the American GP at Riverside. The first US GP in November 1959 had been poorly supported by the public, largely because F1 racing there was and still is virtually unknown. It was a pity, therefore, that the second US GP was not better handled.

It was organized by the people who run the Sebring 12-hour sports car race in Florida, a task they perform reasonably well, but it wasn't very diplomatic for anyone from California's rival sunshine state to promote a race on the West Coaster's door-step. Partly as a result of this, I think, little publicity was given to the race in the big newspapers of either Los Angeles or San Francisco.

A public relations firm handling advertising for the meeting were proud of the one or two small Press notices they had been able to obtain, but we explained to them that this was nothing like the coverage given a corresponding championship race in other countries. Apparently only football or baseball interested the newspapers and as championship events—from boxing to billiards, chow-making to chess—were being held with monotonous regularity in California, a motor racing champion-ship didn't mean very much. I expected far more interest.

We kept meeting people who wanted to know what all the "limeys" were doing in Riverside. On telling them we were there for the motor race, a blank stare greeted us. So we went on to explain it was a world championship F1 race at Riverside and that we were driving European cars.

"European cars? Oh, you mean Jaguars and Porsches!" We politely described our single-seater racing cars and this brought a drawl of information about speedway cars. These conversa-tions usually died uneasily, as we tried to explain the difference between our cars and Indianapolis machinery.

The race itself paled in significance compared with Lance Reventlow's party, highlight of the week. A couple of buses collected us from our hotels and delivered us to his sumptuous Beverley Hills home. Lance's wife, Jill St John, was the perfect hostess and for about half-an-hour the British GP contingent and a few dozen American journalists stood chatting formally about the weather and motor racing and taking care not to drop cigar ash on the rugs. But only for 30 minutes.

Malayan boys were handing round apparently innocuous rum-based drinks with large lumps of pineapple on a stick. These went down particularly well and all seemed to take effect at once.

Just then dozens of Jill's starlet friends made an entrance and the party woke up. Before you could say "Stirling Moss", Innes Ireland was down to his underpants, splashing into the indoor swimming pool, while Jill handed around towels for those who cared to join him. We all thoroughly enjoyed ourselves and many of the Britishers were found to be not so stuffy after all.

New Zealand seemed quiet in comparison with all the American hilarity, but the line-up for the 1961 Grand Prix at Ardmore was the biggest and most impressive ever. Graham Hill, Dan Gurney, Jim Clark, John Surtees, Ron Flockhart and inevitably the old sparring pair, Moss and Brabham, had all been signed up. Most of them were flying direct to Warwick Farm, Sydney, for the Australian GP a couple of weeks later

Socially the season was a great success. Activities started on the right foot with a quiet dinner for drivers and members of the Grand Prix Association, so that everyone could get acquainted. Social jaunts were organized, as well as a deep-sea fishing expedition and a 150-mile run to Rotorua and the Lake district. Highlight was the trip on Ross Jensen's launch after practice, on the day before the race. Suitable company, food and weather had been laid on, setting the stage for a session of sky-larking and water ski-ing in Auckland harbour.

Australian driver Arnold Glass was the acknowledged expert and embarked on the unenviable task of tutoring the GP aces. Graham Hill must have established a new under-water ski-ing record! Graham reasoned that if he hung on to the ski rope long enough, he would eventually ski on the surface. We had told him to stay in the ski-ing position and hold on. He followed instructions to the letter, the only trouble being that the skis were on top of the water and G. Hill underneath!

Dan Gurney was star of the day, managing to stand straight up on the skis at his first attempt. There were too many counter-attractions for Innes to spend much time on skis. The combination of strenuous exercise, salt water and brilliant sunshine resulted in several sunburnt and sore drivers on the grid the next day, and it was darkly hinted that the whole thing had been a McLaren plot!

John Cooper was running the Cooper team and must have been tired of people asking whether the cars would be running to team orders. I'm afraid most New Zealanders believed I had to finish second and was not allowed to beat Brabham. My argument that I couldn't head Jack anyway, was always greeted with a sympathetic smile and a wise nod. John silenced the queries by telling a reporter I was free to beat Jack if I wanted. This was splashed across the front pages to everyone's delight. Except mine, as Jack was now more determined than ever to win.

In practice we found a problem that was to recur with the F1 1·5-litre four-cylinder Climax at Zandvoort and Spa later in the year. In an effort to improve carburation through the very slow hairpin at Ardmore, where the engine was coming down low in the rev range, we were running the fuel pressure and float levels relatively low. Both engines were on a methanol blend of fuel and, when driving the car really hard with the throttle nearly wide open from half-way round the hairpin, they would start to die just before reaching the end of the straight. We discovered later that it was caused by fuel being used out of the float bowls faster than it was going in. This was partly due to the low fuel pressure and partly because, with the needle valve floats set in a lower position, the needle valve governing fuel entry into the float bowl was not being fully opened before the floats reached the end of their travel. The engine coughed in this manner two or three times in the last few laps of the race while I was chasing Jack for the lead. But it was one thing catching Jack and another getting past. We crossed the line nose to tail.

The memorable race of this series was the Lady Wigram Trophy at Christchurch, where—unusually—it rained solidly for two days during practice and the race. The Friday practice session was postponed to Saturday morning, when it was hoped the sun would be shining. It wasn't—practice started in a torrential downpour. Ten minutes later there were three cars in a deep ditch on the outside of the first fast corner.

Johnnie Mansel, one of the most colourful New Zealand drivers of recent years, who was to lose his life when his Cooper-Maserati crashed in the rain two years later on the Dunedin street circuit, was first in the ditch. He was driving a single-seater, hopefully christened Tec-Mec. It was a 250F Maserati chassis fitted with a Corvette V8 engine and, due to shipping delays, had only just arrived in the country. This was Johnnie's first lap with the car and he skated straight off the road after hitting a puddle. He was trapped under the Tec-Mec, but having a physique like a weight-lifter, shouldered off the car. He was scrambling up the bank when he saw a flash of red and something struck him on the back.

In the spray and confusion he was dragged up the bank to find two other cars were also in the ditch. A 4CLT Maserati had arrived soon after the Tec-Mec and a Super-Squalo Ferrari had followed Mansel's wheel-tracks. The rear wheel of the Ferrari hit Mansel before the car bounced on the upturned Tec-Mec and slithered down the ditch. Mansel nursed a Dunlop R5-patterned bruise on his shoulder for several days.

When the race was due to start it was still teeming, with treacherously large pools of water forming across the track. The organizers called a drivers' meeting to ask our views on shortening the race. Jimmy Clark's suggestion of 10 miles shook them, as they apparently expected us to be delighted at the prospect of a race in the rain and thought we would be upset at the idea of shortening it. The distance was dropped from 150 miles to 100 and when the soggy flag dropped we ploughed into slashing rain. I made a poor start, getting boxed at the first corner. Brabham, Moss and Bonnier were away fairly well, but Stirling tangled with a slower car and bent the steering on his Lotus.

Bonnier had a monstrous spin and ended among some parked cars with the Yeoman Credit Cooper, leaving Jack, Jimmy and myself to battle for the lead. I was hard on Jimmy's tail as we entered the fast left-hander at the start of the straight, where the cars had gone off that morning. Suddenly Jimmy was sliding wildly sideways in front of me, throwing up columns of spray. I was completely blinded, couldn't do much about avoiding and spun, too. Jimmy roared away before me, but in a few laps I managed to get past him and was soon back with Jack. We had a hectic sorting-out session almost rubbing wheels into the corner past the pits and shot on to the straight, to find Denny Hulme right in our path with the 2-litre Cooper. Jack went one side of him and I the other. I remember catching a glimpse of startled Denny's face as I went by—*backwards!*

Getting started again in the mud and slush I lost about a lap and a half. Jack was out in front battling through the murk. Jimmy finally abandoned the Lotus bogged down in the infield!

Frank Shuter, a local driver with a 3-litre front-engined Ferrari, also lost control on the swimming straight and almost cut his car in half colliding with a timing car foolishly placed near the track side. He was uninjured. Angus Hyslop did well to hold down second place with his old 2-litre Cooper ahead of Stirling's Cooper for much of the race. Stirling passed him in the closing laps and the final order was Brabham, Moss, Hyslop and a very damp and muddy McLaren.

Hyslop's steady drive in the appalling conditions marked him as next "Driver to Europe".

Wigram was my last race in New Zealand that year and I headed back to Sebring for the 12-hour race, to drive one of the new Type 63 Birdcage-Maseratis for Briggs Cunningham.

The term "birdcage" derived from the frame of the car, consisting of hundreds of pieces of small-diameter tube ($\frac{1}{2}$ in and $\frac{3}{8}$ in) forming a sort of trellis-work chassis. It was certainly a unique form of construction and the story went that, when it was first built, a canary was released in the centre of the frame and anywhere it could escape another tube was welded in!

The Type 63 birdcage was a rear-engined car with an immense and ferocious-looking V12 engine. It looked and sounded fantastic. You couldn't call it attractive—forceful, perhaps—and we soon discovered it went around corners like its appearance—somewhat unusual.

One seemed to have a very fine line in a corner on which to have the car balanced, almost like a ballet dancer standing on the tip of one toe. A little push on the steering wheel and over one went, but it was very fast and there was a chance we could win.

Briggs had quite a group of drivers. I was to share with Walt Hansgen, the others being John Fitch and Dick Thompson in a front-engined birdcage, with Briggs himself and Bill Kimberley driving a 2-litre front-engined birdcage.

Being in a relatively large team like this was new to me and I learned a lot. One of the best things about the team was the way Briggs acted, not only as team manager but a sort of uncle. We ate together, a large table being kept for the team each evening, at Harder Hall hotel, normally a golfing resort. We all tried not to be late and waited until Briggs joined us before eating. Over dinner we were able to discuss team tactics and any questions we had to raise.

Another feature was our private briefing meetings. Team manager Alfred Momo would often arrange a briefing meeting of all drivers and a couple of Italian Maserati engineers, with himself and Briggs presiding, for a quick run-down on the day's instructions. There was no excuse for anyone not knowing what was going on and what he should be doing.

Briggs once got warmed up on the subject of not over-revving the engine, saving the brakes, treating the gearbox gently and not abusing the clutch, saying, "Remember now, there's no point in haring off, we've got to finish." I was tempted to tell him I'd been driving Grand Prix cars for several years, that it was my job and that I knew all about this. But the big thing in long-distance sports car racing is to finish. The percentage of mechanical failures is very high, particularly on a gruelling circuit like Sebring. Before the 12-hour race there was another smaller endurance race with a 1000 cc limit for small GT cars. Austin Healey Sprites and Abarths were the main contenders. It was to be a four-hour endurance run and Frank Falkner had arranged for me to drive one of the BMC works Sprites.

In practice I found the Sprite terrific fun. I had one with a soft top, as did Moss. Walt had a special stream-lined hard top on his, but it didn't seem to make much difference. It was a Le Mans start; in other words from the other side of the road, run across, open the door, leap in, ignition on, starter-button pushed, engine running, clutch in at the same time and out (it has been left in gear) wheels spinning and you're gone.

I was fifth in line but first away and entered the corner alongside Pat Moss, Stirling's sister, who had been No. 2 in the line-up. Stirling headed the queue. Being a gentleman I let Pat lead me through this first corner, then as we approached the hairpin she ran a little wide and I ducked inside and set off after Stirling, a few yards ahead. But it wasn't Stirling I had to worry about on that first lap, as the Fiat Abarths closed on us with Gurney and a couple of other fast Americans aboard. Soon they established a lead we couldn't do much about. Stirling and I were having a tremendous dice, however. We

screamed down the straight side by side, sliding the little
Sprites playfully through the hairpins and tight right-angle
corners on the airfield circuit.

The Sprites, for us, were just one step above a go-kart. Top
speed wasn't high and you could do almost anything with them
on a corner. After the serious business of the powerful rear-
engined Maserati and our 180 mph formula cars, these were
what Americans call "cars for funnin' ". Down the straight
Stirling and I were virtually able to talk to each other. He
would push back his window and mouth, "How many revs
are you getting?" I'd hold up five fingers, then six, to indicate
5600 rpm. He would glance at his rev counter and indicate
five five, or five four. We managed quite a bit of conversation
and after an hour and a half found Walt Hansgen had gradually
crept up on us. Then the three of us started pounding round
together, nose to tail.

Soon two hours were up and we had to stop for fuel. My pit
stop was long and slow as the man filling the tank was too
intent on it being absolutely full and wasted precious seconds
getting in the last gallon or so. I joined the race again hopeful
Stirling and Walt would be held up as long as I had been, but
they were both 30 sec quicker and I had to work hard for the
next two hours to make up the half-minute.

In the closing laps I caught Stirling, but we couldn't quite
overhaul Walt, who somehow managed to beat one of the Fiat
Abarths by a second. A terrific drive on Walt's part. It had been
fun and the three of us have often laughed about it.

The 12-hour race did not go so well for the Cunningham
team, although our Maserati was the only one to give the
Ferrari sports cars driven by people like Phil Hill and Gendebien, the Rodriguez brothers, Richie Ginther and von Trips,
and Baghetti and Mairesse something to think about, getting
up to third or fourth at times. We were in trouble, however.
The gearbox was making funny noises and the engine had a
bad oil leak. Each time it roared past the pits a cloud of smoke

was pouring from the back. Only the Cunningham/Kimberley 2-litre car finished in our team and even they had trouble with a broken lead on the ignition condenser. Hill and Gendebien won the race.

On the Monday morning I was on my way back to England for a fairly busy season. Jack had been driving my car over the week-end at Snetterton and won the Lombank Trophy. I was hoping Harry Pearce hadn't let him into too many of our secrets. Harry said Jack was delighted with the car and I hoped to maintain his sort of performance.

TWELVE

The 1961 Formula One Season

THE 1961 COOPERS were simply slimmed-down versions of the 1960 cars, fitted with a new six-speed gearbox and the Mark II 1½-litre, four-cylinder Coventry-Climax engine. BRMs had bought Coventry-Climax engines to run in their BRM chassis and Lotus had built a new car (the 21). Yeoman Credit had two 1960-type Coopers similar to the works cars and John Surtees was to drive one of them.

Coopers were building the Indianapolis Cooper for Jack, and as "Indy" and the GPs were the only races the works intended to contest that year, I looked set for a fairly lean season.

Then Tommy Atkins approached me with the proposition that he might run a Cooper sports car if I were to drive it. I suggested that it would be much better to build a Cooper single-seater to run in the 1½-litre F1 races which Coopers didn't attend and also to run as a 2½-litre car in the Inter-continental Formula races at Goodwood and Silverstone. There were also the races in New Zealand and Australia to think about.

I had many ideas I wanted to try on a 2½-litre car. I'd done considerable testing with Ken Tyrrell's Formula Junior cars and found lifting the rear roll centre had a pronounced effect and a particularly good influence on lap times.

Previously Jack had been chief test driver and I didn't always completely agree with the way he liked his car set up, so when the Atkins Cooper was completed we rushed down to Goodwood for some extensive testing.

At the Easter Goodwood meeting I had a great dice with Stirling, actually managing to get past him at Lavant Corner when he slid wide, but I was watching him so closely in my mirrors coming out of the chicane that I put a rear wheel on the grass and had to lift the throttle momentarily to keep the car straight. That gave Stirling the break he needed.

We went into Madgwick side by side, with Stirling on the outside and my Cooper on the inside. He was certainly putting faith in my judgment. As we roared down towards Fordwater he just had his nose in front and he kept that advantage for the last couple of laps to the flag. But we had given him a good run for his money and he came up afterwards, clapped me on the shoulder and said, "Terrific dice, old man—let's face it, we both made a mistake, and I got the better of the last one!" Tommy was pleased and mechanic Harry Pearce overjoyed.

Next on our calendar was the Brussels Grand Prix with the Atkins F2 Cooper. The circuit consisted of part of the autoroute and connecting roads on the outskirts of the city, almost within shouting distance of the famous Atomium. The main opposition were the works Porsches of Gurney and Bonnier, Jack with his F2 Cooper, Moss in a Lotus and Salvadori and Surtees with two new Yeoman Credit Coopers.

Three entirely separate races were run, with a points score over them deciding the winner. Practice was amusing. Jack was fastest of the British contingent and, despite the gear ratio not being quite right on my car, I was only just slower. So I asked if he would show me round the circuit to help me trace the extra second or so. I had in the back of my mind that, if he would tow me round for a couple of laps, I could slipstream him down the straight, pass him before the braking area and pick up quite a lot of time, having by then rectified the gear ratio.

With a few minutes of practice left we set off. On the second lap I passed Jack before the braking area on the very long straight and whipped up to the chequered flag which was out to signal the end of practice. When I pulled back to the pits I found I'd managed a time which put me on the front row between the Porsches and dropped Jack back to the second row. He was naturally a bit upset.

The start of the first heat caused controversy. Jack and I left the grid as the flag was falling to make perfect starts, but the rest waited until it had fallen. The difference was subtle but significant. We were penalized a minute for jumping the start, despite our claim that we didn't have to wait until the flag had fallen, as officials maintained we were on our way before the flag started to drop. Jack and I were third and fourth after our penalty had been taken into account for the first heat. In the second heat Bonnier scorched into the lead and Surtees pulled out all the stops in the Yeoman Credit Cooper in an attempt to catch him. He caught him all right—squarely in the tail at the hairpin, putting both cars out of action and letting Jack and me through to first and second placings.

Stirling, having trouble with his Lotus, did not finish in the earlier heats, so his efforts in the final heat couldn't affect overall results so far as Jack and I were concerned. I was in trouble, anyway, as low gear in the Colotti gearbox was giving trouble, and at Brussels there were three tight 15 mph hairpins that really needed that gear.

Innes Ireland made a tremendous start with his Lotus, but on the second lap spun over a bank, somehow missing telegraph poles, traffic lights and bollards in his path, and trickled back to his pit on the public section of the auto-route, having left the track completely.

I couldn't stay with Jack and Stirling who kept up their tussle for the lead right to the flag, with Brabham holding the advantage just a fraction ahead of the Lotus. On overall points Jack won and I placed second.

Our next race was also a one-two for Coopers, this time with the new six-speed FI cars in the rain at the Aintree "200". The new gearbox was working well and we were doing our best to see from how many people we could keep it secret. It rained, as is common at Aintree, and the Coopers handled particularly well on the wet surface. The new gearbox seemed to help in that, independent of the actual corner, engine revs could be kept fairly constant and the whole car fairly well balanced for sliding about.

After our success with the Atkins Cooper in Intercontinental and F2 events, we were looking forward to the Empire Trophy at Silverstone. Once again we had two days before official practice to adjust the car to the circuit. On the fast corners at Silverstone the Cooper's maximum speed was largely limited by the speed of the steering. A deflection of the wrists was enough to change the direction of the car, but this was too critical, as when the car slid in the middle of a corner, the movement on the rim of the steering wheel to correct it was too fine to have any reasonable accuracy. We discovered a lower steering ratio helped considerably.

The car was well-balanced on all the corners except one—the fast left-hander at Abbey. This could not be taken on full throttle, as the front end of the car sledged out across the road. It was right in the middle of the power range of the Climax engine and as the nose was lifting under full power, the front wheels lost adhesion.

To counteract this we made the right-hand rear wheel point out an extra degree, so the car ran slightly out of line. This meant I could enter the corner under full throttle, locked over and have the car run through smoothly. The only effect on the other right-handers, generally slower anyway, was to make the tail stay in a little more.

On both practice days I had fastest time by a fair margin, and on the Friday in the garage Stirling snatched the chance while Harry was having a meal to run a tape measure over the car, trying to see where we had picked up our improvements.

Our advantage didn't last long. Surtees, Brabham and Moss were all running Coopers and by the second Silverstone meeting, before the British GP, their suspension set-ups and wishbone angles began to look very similar to ours.

Both Silverstone meetings were disappointing for me. It rained hard on both occasions and Moss won easily. At the May meeting Moss, Brabham and myself were closely grouped for the first few laps until I hit a puddle in the middle of the fast, bumpy Woodcote corner. The car spun wildly, going backwards at high speed, then as I braked the front swung round and I was pointing in the right direction. I nearly had it under control, but the tail was just on the grass and this was my undoing. It came round and I was backwards again, still doing about 30 mph, and sailed into the earth bank bending the tail.

Moss was on top form that day. He was rounding most of Woodcote corner with the car power-sliding, as he made infinitely quick small corrections on the steering wheel. No one else was doing anything like it.

Racing hard in wet weather is dicey. If the track is damp, in other words pools haven't formed and the surface is just generally wet, it is not too bad as the behaviour of the car is predictable. If you go into a corner too fast, you'll just slide off. If you brake too hard you'll lock the wheels and not be able to steer. If you apply too much power you'll spin the back wheels and if you're in a corner this means you'll probably spin the car.

You can experiment quickly if the surface is uniformly damp and soon find a reasonable limit to the speed at which you can drive. However, when there are puddles, the light modern racing cars with fairly large tyres will actually hydroplane or ski over the tops of the puddles at speed. This is an uncanny sensation. Hitting one of these pools with a light single-seater makes the steering go completely free, as though the front wheels had been jacked off the ground. If it is just a small puddle in the middle of the corner, the front will skate sideways as it hits it and stop again on dry road. Then the back will slide sideways. It feels as though the car has been given a quick shake, but when you strike a bigger pool of water at higher speed, the process becomes a bit more involved.

Of course if you go slow enough on a wet circuit, this won't matter, but after all a race is a race.

At the July Silverstone meeting, mindful of what had happened in May, when the rain started I took things cautiously and the order was Moss, Surtees, Graham Hill and myself over the finishing line.

Meanwhile the F1 championship races had been running to a sickening pattern—for the English! At Spa Ferraris were first, second, third and fourth, and even on the first lap there wasn't another car anywhere near them.

The Englishman to have a real try on the fast Belgian circuit was Surtees in the Yeoman Credit Cooper. Descriptions of his progress through some of the fast corners were frightening. He had raced on the circuit many times as a motor-cyclist and with four wheels under him, instead of two, he probably felt safer.

Besides the Atkins Cooper and the F1 works cars, I had organized two other drives with Peter Berry Racing Ltd, a newly-formed team running two 3·8 saloon Jaguars and one of the new E-types.

My first encounter with this team had been at the Easter Goodwood meeting. I tried the 3·8 saloon I was to race on a private test day a week beforehand. Saloon car racing was new to me, but I'd always enjoyed watching Salvadori and, earlier, Mike Hawthorn and Tommy Sopwith throwing the Jaguar saloons about and was looking forward to doing the same.

At Goodwood the 3·8 saloon certainly seemed different. Compared with the light single-seaters, where one sits out in the open with the wind buffeting and noise and machinery more or less all round, the comparative quiet and calm of the saloon was a little unreal. One hardly seemed to be racing, particularly when the windows were wound up.

It's strange how important the sense of sound is when driving a racing car. I'd never thought of it before. It felt like watching a silent movie.

But soon came a snag. After a few laps on the Monday I stopped at the pits and said there was a little too much oversteer. The tail of the car was sliding out too far and I thought I could go faster if this were corrected. On suggesting a heavier roll bar on the front I was gaped at incredulously.

"You mean change the suspension?" they asked and I was staggered to find they didn't have a heavier bar.

In formula cars I was accustomed to making an infinite number of suspension changes without a second thought. I suggested they might try to get a roll bar to fit for the Thursday practice session.

To my surprise I learned permission was needed from the Jaguar factory, because they weren't allowed to make basic changes without asking. Next day Peter Berry told me the matter was being discussed at the factory. I could hardly believe it. At the track on Thursday I asked the mechanics if they'd had much trouble fitting the heavier roll bar. There was an awkward silence before someone admitted the bar hadn't been changed. The factory had said the roll bar was designed as a compromise to be best for overall conditions and they weren't allowed to change it.

It wasn't my car and I had only just joined the team, so I left it at that. Race day was wet and I noticed Parkes and Salvadori were fitting RS5 roadspeed tyres, as these were apparently better in the wet than the normal Dunlop racing tyre. Unfortunately we didn't have any. I didn't think it would matter too much, but when the flag fell Parkes leapt into the lead and Roy and I arrived at the first corner side by side behind him. He just managed to lead me into Fordwater and for the rest of that first lap.

Parkes had opened up a slight lead in front of us and I was getting a little excited. I figured Roy was baulking me, so next time around Fordwater and down into St Mary's (a corner I knew I could get through nearly flat) I ran in fast on his tail.

I thought by staying close I would find a spot to get through. Unfortunately Roy braked more than I'd allowed for and I gave him quite a nudge. It didn't affect him much, but as we were both sliding at the time the bump stopped the nose of my car and the tail came whamming round to send me careering into a cabbage field.

I ploughed back to the wet track and set off again in pursuit of the leaders. I thought I was catching on to saloon racing fairly quickly when I gained on the leaders again. I went into tricky Woodcote, braked hard as late as I could, but suddenly the back was swinging out again and before you could gulp "Jaguar" I was on the grass.

The commentator apparently remarked, "McLaren has spun again. He must be enjoying it!"

I found the circuit again and re-joined the race, deciding to take it a little quieter. There was obviously more to saloon racing than met the eye; regularly disappearing backwards off the track in clouds of spray seemed pointless.

After the race, "Lofty" England, now managing director of Jaguars, said "My boy, Jaguar drivers are only allowed two spins a year, and you've had your two." He turned out to be wrong, as I had a couple more before the season finished.

The next one was at Silverstone in a cloudburst. About 15 of the 22 cars in the race crashed or spun off in the atrocious conditions, so at least I had company. It was close company in the immediate vicinity of my spin. As I went into Club Corner I was again just behind Roy, but suddenly, although I was travelling straight ahead, had a side view of his car. Something was wrong. I lifted off abruptly to try and slow but struck the same huge pool of water as Roy and joined him sliding backwards into the earth retaining wall. Looking at the two bent cars, it was obvious Jaguars would have orders for two new body shells.

When we arrived back at the pits, "Lofty" England had a word with us. "What happened?" he asked Roy. Having never quite forgotten the Goodwood incident, Salvadori blandly replied, "McLaren shunted me again, Sir." I denied it emphatically, but it was too late. Roy was in first.

My fourth and final spin was at Brands Hatch in a ding-dong saloon battle. The day before I had raced at the Nürburgring in the German Grand Prix, so the short Brands Hatch circuit seemed small and the Jaguar a piece of cake after the F1 car on the tricky 'Ring. Parkes and Jack Sears in the dark-blue Sopwith Jaguars were out against Salvadori in the Coombs Jaguar and myself in Peter Berry's car.

Sears took the lead, I was second, Parkes third and Roy fourth on the opening laps. I was doing my best to get past Sears and the car felt really good, motoring sideways through the right-angle corners round the back of the circuit. Here was one race in the saloon that I thought might make up for the rest of my misdemeanours.

At Brands Hatch there is a short uphill pull into a tight 180-degree hairpin called Druids. You come charging up to this, brake hard, throw the car into the corner and slide round with the tail hanging out.

I dived in on Sears' tail with the tail out nicely and the power on, when someone rammed me really hard in the boot and my car spun so quickly that I didn't have a hope of catching it. There was so much smoke and dust that I could barely see which way to go when the car lurched to a stop. I got back on the road just as Salvadori went by and followed the three Jaguars sliding and drifting round the circuit. Mine felt a little odd and I thought the back axle might have been shifted in the bump, so settled for fourth.

Strangely enough, there was barely a mark on the car, the only damage being to one lug of the knock-on wheel nut that

Royalty on the racing scene: above, after receiving the Monaco Grand Prix cup from Prince Rainier and Princess Grace, McLaren stands to attention with John Cooper on his right as the National Anthem is played. Below, explaining the workings of the Cooper to Princess Margaret at Silverstone while Lord Snowdon makes a closer inspection

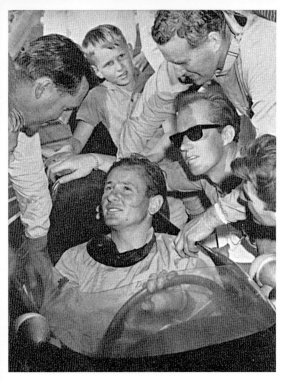

"Well it was like this . . ."
A grimy Bruce McLaren
explains to beaten rivals
Jack Brabham and Bib
Stillwell how he won the
1963 Longford race in
Tasmania. His secretary,
Eoin Young, in sunglasses,
and mechanic Wally Will-
mott listen in

Coaxing the 1963 works
Cooper V8 round the
Station Hairpin at Monaco

had been bent at right-angles, making it touch the spokes.

On the same day I drove the Berry E-type. I had finished second in this car at Silverstone to Stirling in the 250GT Ferrari and tailed him home again at Brands Hatch. At least I was running consistently in the E-type. There was also a race for Intercontinental cars, in which I drove the Atkins Cooper. Never a dull moment!

Brands Hatch hadn't been treating me very well. Earlier at the Silver City Trophy meeting for F1 cars, I damaged one of the works cars in spectacular manner and for a few seconds it looked as though the Atkins car would end in a similar way.

In practice I had made second fastest time to Moss and was ready for a good dice, but when the flag dropped Masten Gregory in the UDT Lotus jumped into the lead, with Moss, Surtees and myself ganging up in line astern. Masten went a little wide on one corner and Moss slipped through, then Surtees dived inside on the next bend. When we reached Druids I was determined to get by, before Moss and Surtees got too far ahead.

I placed my front wheels close to Masten's rears as we went into the corner, hoping to get through on the inside. Then he twitched a little sideways which slowed him and suddenly my front wheels were between his front and rear wheels. In a second his car was broadside on to mine and, as we emerged from the corner, I was pushing him downhill. We both went ploughing off on the grass at the inside of the corner.

As the dust settled I selected low gear and roared back on the track. Out of the corner of my eye I could see Masten crashing round in the small trees with bits of his car's body and nose flying into the air.

I felt sorry for him, as I'd got off fairly lightly, but thought I should call at the pits to make sure that nothing had fallen off my car. I could tell the nose was crumpled. I slid to a stop at the pits, yelling at Harry to look at the front end. He quickly checked the steering, wishbones and brake hoses. These were undamaged, so he grabbed a jack handle and levered the nose opening into some sort of ventilating shape. I was quickly back in the race, but had lost nearly a minute and didn't think there was much chance of making this up on Moss and Surtees. But it was worth a try and I raced after them, setting a lap record in my pursuit. It earned me a trophy for fastest lap at Brands Hatch that year and still stands as the outright record for the circuit.

British teams were taking a hammering from Ferrari in F1 racing and only a couple of wins by Moss with the Rob Walker Lotus at Monaco and the Nürburgring helped to ease national embarrassment at being caught napping with the change of formula.

Cooper hopes were pinned on the development of the new 1500 cc V8 Climax engine. As it neared completion, Coopers used a mock-up V8 (the shape of the engine with the carburettors bolted on, but only a bare casting with no internals) to build a special chassis. Consequently it wasn't long after Climax finished bench testing that Jack, John Cooper, the works mechanics and myself, took the completed car secretly to Silverstone.

Wally Hassan, chief Climax engineer who has been connected with motor racing and engines since the Bentley days, was on hand with chief draughtsman Peter Windsor-Smith and a couple of the engine testers.

We hadn't heard the engine running then and waited eagerly while the Climax men fiddled with the mixture before starting it.

It screamed into life with a piercing howl and sounded wonderful. According to the technicians, however, it wasn't then firing on all eight cylinders, so we switched off and they changed spark plugs. It then fired up with the noise that was to become part of motor racing and put British manufacturers back on the map. Long, gradually outward-tapering exhaust pipes gave the new engine a strange, high-pitched note.

Jack took the car out for a few laps and came back obviously tremendously impressed. I had my overalls on and waited hopefully with crash helmet in one hand and goggles in the other, hoping Jack would soon finish so I could have a try, but it was fairly late in the day before I was allowed a couple of hurried laps.

The new V8 had tremendous and obvious potential. My second lap had been 1 min 38 sec and I felt I could have knocked at least another two seconds off that, which was pretty respectable in those days.

After the four-cylinder engine, the V8 was very smooth. On opening the throttle on the four-cylinder, one felt something of a kick—not so much as on the $2\frac{1}{2}$-litre cars, but a reasonable sort of "kick in the back". This sensation changed with the V8. It became more of a smooth push and there was virtually no vibration.

The Cooper V8's first competition run was in the German Grand Prix on the Nürburgring. It was still very new and on the first practice lap the water temperature went sky high. First we thought this might be just a faulty radiator cap, or a leak in the system, and it was checked carefully before the second session.

Although it wasn't my place to say so, I was convinced the fault had something to do with the cylinder head sealing and that the combustion pressure was leaking out into the water system, causing the overheating. This sort of thing isn't always consistent but one can generally tell by opening the throttle once or twice with the radiator cap off, if there are tiny bubbles in the system, you have got problems.

If out on the circuit and the temperature needle starts to jump about on full throttle down the straight, this is a sure sign that there is hot gas getting into the cooling system.

That evening Wally Hassan took the cylinder heads off the engine, carefully examined the cylinder sealing rings, the heads, and the cylinder blocks for evidence of leaks. There was nothing apparent, so it was debatable whether there was a leak.

With racing engines, if one spots the temperature jump (in other words one picks the leak virtually at the moment it occurs), when the engine is stripped and the joint faces examined, any fault is very hard to detect.

A similar fault on a saloon car is a different thing. If a lady brings her Morris in to a garage, complaining it isn't running right and you discover there has been no water in it for the previous week, if a gasket has blown, this will be obvious when the engine is pulled down as the fault will have been present long enough to leave its mark.

We couldn't tell whether or not the engine was going to overheat in the race, as Jack covered only about one mile!

Half an hour before the start, rain began to spatter lightly and a set of Cooper wheels were sent off to have the D12 rain tyres fitted. I had my own car to worry about, but can remember Jack, Coopers and Dunlops just 10 minutes before the start having an argument among themselves when Jack discovered there were rain tyres only for the front wheels and none for the rears. As it was too late to do anything about it then, Jack had to leave things that way. He found the softer-mix front tyres gave considerably more grip than the rears, which made the car uncontrollable on the first sharp corners down through the woods. Jack disappeared through a hedge, fortunately without much damage to man or machinery. I had a more comfortable and uneventful race to sixth place.

Before the Italian Grand Prix at Monza Coopers had a larger radiator built, in case the Cooper cooling system was at fault. It wasn't. The car retired with overheating, once again it was a cylinder head sealing problem.

In an effort to gain good water circulation round the top of the cylinder liner, there was no location, as such, at this point. There was an abutment well down on the liner, which determined its position, but there appeared to be two problems—one that the top of the liner tended to move about through the mechanical loadings involved; secondly, when the aluminium block expanded at a greater rate than the steel liner, it reduced the loading on the sealing rings between the liner and the cylinder head.

It wasn't until the following year when the design was re-fashioned so the liner was held in an aluminium sleeve and located at its top surface, that the overheating problem was cured.

BRM's had their new V8 at Monza in a car which looked so small that it was almost a plaything. It seems hard to believe that a year or so later the same car, although a world championship winner, was one of the biggest and heaviest in the field.

This was the year of the bad accident at Monza. Besides the normal road lay-out with relatively flat corners and normal road-type conditions, we were also using the banked oval section, mainly used for high-speed record runs. These bankings could be taken at around 140 mph and to ensure that our cars didn't hit the bumpy surface, it was necessary to set the springs up and fit much longer bump-stops. This may have made some of the cars a little unstable.

Soon after the start two cars touched. One of them, the Ferrari of von Trips', climbed a bank and ran along a safety fence knocking down many spectators and throwing out the driver.

I was with a group of four cars a couple of hundred yards behind when it happened. Our first warning was a huge cloud of dust, as one of the cars in the group ahead shot on to the grass at the side of the road. We were too busy trying to slow down and find a clear path through the wreckage to look closely at what had happened. We just hoped everyone was all right and raced on.

I sat close behind Dan Gurney's Porsche until he dropped out with transmission failure and finished third as the first four-cylinder car and first British car across the line.

But it was a sad day. Von Trips had apparently been killed

outright and there were terrible stories about the number of people killed in the crowd. Jimmy Clark had been involved in the accident and was looking badly shaken.

Dinner that evening was very quiet. Someone suggested the best thing to do was have a party in the bar.

"You can't have a party after a day like this," came a shocked reply.

"The last thing Taffy would have wanted was you lot sitting around moping," said one of his friends.

I guess he was right. Most people managed to forget at least some of the events of the day in the hours that followed.

THIRTEEN

Back to the States

BY SEPTEMBER I had bought the Intercontinental Cooper off Tommy Atkins and preparations were in hand for the 1962 season in Australia and New Zealand, but when the Cooper Car Company found they had a cancelled Cooper-Monaco order on their hands I remembered the fantastic prize money and the fun of the race in California the previous year.

I thought if I could set up a Monaco sports car to the specifications of the Intercontinental car and fit the 2·7 Indianapolis engine which Climax had agreed to sell me for the Australasian season, I would have a competitive chance.

There was only one snag. Money. I'd already paid for the Cooper, the 2·7 engine, enough spares for the "down under" season and four round-the-world air tickets at £500 apiece. The total project was going to cost some £10,000, which couldn't be recouped for the best part of six months—the time it took the race organizers to deliver their starting money by bank drafts to England.

I had quite enough on my financial plate. Finding someone else to buy the Monaco and back the sports car project seemed the ideal solution and luckily I was able to sell the idea to Peter Berry.

The prospect became brighter for him when he learnt I

would be able to use the 2·7 Climax engine in the Monaco if he decided to back the venture. Peter immediately obtained a promise of financial help from Castrol and signed a contract with Coopers to buy the chassis and gearbox the next day. Frank Falkner, my American manager, phoned the Riverside and Laguna Seca organizers to arrange starts for the car and I made sure I could ship the 2·7 engine straight from San Francisco to Auckland after Laguna Seca. I was sending the single-seater chassis and gearbox direct from England to Auckland.

Tommy Atkins had agreed to lend me Harry Pearce, to be my mechanic in New Zealand, so I assumed that during the Christmas period we could re-build the engine in Auckland and fit higher compression pistons for the methanol mixture we would be using there.

I started assembling the Monaco chassis right away. Coopers loaned one of their mechanics to give a hand and after three busy weeks we had the car together and running. I spent a couple of days testing at Silverstone to check the handling, then sent it with tyres and spares by air to America.

I had been quite pleased at Silverstone. The car was a second quicker than Stirling had been in the Lotus 19 and I felt reasonably confident our chances would be high. Peter was convinced we should win!

The United States GP that year was at Watkins Glen, a week before our first scheduled race with the Monaco at Riverside. The GP was exciting and I was in the thick of it until all the teeth divorced themselves from fifth gear in my six-speed box. Any other gear wouldn't have made too much difference, but fifth probably failed because it was the hardest-worked cog in the box and I certainly used it a great deal at Watkins Glen. When that went, I had to use either sixth or fourth.

But there were many might-have-beens in that race, with any one of about five people potential winners. Roy Salvadori in the Yeoman Credit Cooper was going great guns late in the race, only to have his engine blow up. Innes Ireland, who had a hectic spin early in the race when he was leading, finally came back through the field to win—something he had deserved for a long time—and score the first-ever GP victory for Team Lotus.

Innes' spin had been spectacular. There is one corner at Watkins Glen where you turn right, go down a dip and up the other side, still turning right. The middle of the dip is completely blind. After the first practice I drove round the circuit with two of the club officials, advising them on flag-marshal positions. I suggested that if a car were dropping oil, it would tend to gather in the middle of this dip. As this spot was completely blind, it would be important to have someone stationed there, within sight of a flag marshal just before the corner, so drivers could be warned of anything untoward, such as oil in the dip or a car spinning.

In the race Innes came haring into this dip holding a tenuous lead over Jack Brabham, Stirling, Jimmy Clark, Surtees, myself and Graham and he spun like a top.

We were all more or less side by side behind him, with me on the inside. It looked for a moment as though he was going to spin to the inside and most of the group dived to the left. I started to use the grass and the bank on the right, when Innes' Lotus spun back towards the outside of the circuit, leaving me with a clear run through. I left the others to sort themselves out and kept on motoring. Jack and Stirling with the two V8s were ahead and I was third with the first four-cylinder.

Early on Monday morning after the Grand Prix, I phoned Glenn Davis of the *Los Angeles Times*, the newspaper promoting the Riverside race for sports cars, told him we would be in town the next day, and asked for the shipping agents handling the Monaco and equipment to ensure everything had been cleared through Customs and taken to the garage at Riverside.

Peter and I had arranged to borrow Mike Barney from the Cooper works team to help look after the car. Mike had been with Coopers since I started doing well with the team and had been responsible for the preparation of my car since the British GP in 1959. Apart from being an excellent mechanic, he is good company and we were looking forward to the fortnight in California, although we knew it would be hard work, particularly during the first few days.

The car had been hurriedly built. Since leaving England I'd thought of one or two things I wanted to modify and there would be only a couple of days free before practice in which to to them. We knew the car would be basically very sound. Bigger brakes were fitted for the first time on a Monaco, with large calipers from the Aston Martin sports cars and slightly thicker discs on the front.

The engine had just been rebuilt and tested by Climax. It was the one Jack had used in the race at Indianapolis and turned out plenty of horsepower. Harry Pearce had tuned the carburettors at Silverstone and I was to do final adjustments to suit the Californian conditions. The whole transmission unit was a new one I had completely checked and set up to run freely, so we didn't expect any trouble in that direction.

One job we had was to fit a new type of drive shaft with which I'd been experimenting. We'd had trouble with the bigger-engined cars when we were using our normal drive shafts, which tended to make the rear suspension very stiff under full power through friction in the splines. Having had my eye on a Citroen DS19 large-diameter sliding spline drive-shaft for some time, I'd procured a couple and modified them to fit the Colotti gearbox on the Atkins Cooper.

I knew the sports car would benefit from these even more than the single-seater. They were certainly having a busy life. I'd used this particular pair on the Cooper works car at Watkins Glen and we had taken them with us to fit on the sports car. This was to be one of our major jobs and I knew we'd have a problem getting the gearchange linkage to clear them.

When we finally arrived in California, I was horrified to learn that although the shipping agents had said everything was under control and the car and equipment were sitting in the garage at Riverside, this was not the case. Before driving the 70 miles out to Riverside, I phoned the garage and found they hadn't seen or heard of the car.

Warren Olsen, then manager for Lance Reventlow and his Scarabs, was looking after us while we were in Los Angeles. He suggested I should call at the airport and check that the car had passed through Customs.

It was good advice. Mike and I arrived at the customs area to find an official sitting on the ground surrounded by hundreds of bits and pieces of specialized racing equipment—bearings, bolts, bushes, pipes, cylinders, pistons—all unwrapped and lying on the ground as though some naughty child had been delving in the spares box.

I felt furious, but this was no time to show it. Being as friendly as I could under the circumstances, I asked the Customs man if he was having trouble.

"Say," he said, looking up. "Do you know anything about all this stuff?"

"Yes," I replied, "I'm going to drive it when you get it all together for me!"

"Say, there's a huge pile of parts here," he drawled, "are they all on this list?"

I assured him they were and he asked, "Well, what'n hell's a slave cylinder?" I picked up a small aluminium casting, showed him and he ticked it off.

"Clutch throw-out bearings?" I picked up another small packet and he ticked it off his list. It was all a bit futile.

"You may as well tick them all off," I suggested desperately. "It's all there—brake pipes, radiator caps, drop gears, differential palls—you don't have to worry."

He was apparently beginning to realize the immensity of the job ahead according to the rule book, so agreed and quickly checked off the whole list. I shudder to think what would have happened if we hadn't gone to the airport. We would probably have still been waiting for the car and spares.

Late that evening we had the car in Riverside and set to work behind locked garage doors. We knew the opposition. Moss and Gurney were there with their Lotus 19s, but we felt these couldn't last. It was a long race and although the Monaco may have been a bit heavier than the Lotus, the extra power from my 2·7 engine would help compensate for it.

Jack was our main rival with a Cooper-Monaco he had borrowed from Texan Hap Sharp. Jack's personal mechanic, Tim Wall, had been in Texas a week or so, getting the car into the sort of trim he knew Jack would want and besides this I knew—although Jack probably thought I didn't—that they had the other 2·7 Climax, the practice engine from Indianapolis. I took a quick look at the number of the engine in the Sharp Monaco when it arrived at Riverside and sure enough it was the other 2·7. So Jack and I were up to the same game.

We soon learned how lightly the organizers were taking the regulations. Our Monaco was fully equipped with a generator, lights that worked, a full-size windscreen and two proper seats.

Jack's Monaco was a lightweight affair with none of these refinements, but we thought it would be better to leave our car somewhere near the regulations, just in case we did win and were protested out of the prize money.

Practice went off as I had expected. On the first day I was a couple of seconds faster than Jack, with Stirling another second slower. Gurney hadn't then arrived. Between us we were comfortably faster than anything else in the field.

Towards the end of the second day Stirling had found his extra second and Jack was only a fraction slower, but I wasn't pressing my car very hard and we decided to pack up and keep it in good trim for the race.

"It's all yours," I told Mike as I helped him load up. "I'm going to take it easy and maybe watch the others."

There was a lot of activity round Jack's car, so I had a quiet look. He was fitting the soft-rubber D12 rain tyres. I asked what he thought he might be doing. "Just giving them a run," he said.

Surely he wasn't going to use them in the race?

But wily Brabham knew something we didn't—that there was 200 dollars for fastest practice lap. Jack, with the rain tyres on, found the extra seconds and won the dollars.

Stirling and I thought it was taking a risk to use rain tyres under these extremely hot conditions on a powerful heavy car like the Monaco, but it was Jack's neck. We didn't think they would last the race, but I had a quiet chat with Peter that night and he agreed to have our rain tyres ready. If there was a cloud in the sky we would fit them, but if it was going to stay hot, it would have been impossible to risk a blow-out. Or so I thought.

When we lined up on the grid the following afternoon, there was Jack with a full set of D12s on the Monaco and temperature scorching at 103 in the shade—if you could find any!

The race settled down as I expected after half an hour. Moss had led in the opening laps until he dropped out with the brakes cooked on his Lotus. I'd been nursing my brakes and didn't expect any trouble. This left Jack and me running nose to tail in front, occasionally swapping the lead. Jim Hall was a comfortable minute behind with his Chaparral, third.

Jack pointed at his signal board as we passed the pits—BRAB—MAC—PLUS 60 HALL. I knew what he meant. There was no point in wearing out our cars, so we both backed off. We would cruise until the last 10 laps, so that one of us would have a better chance of finishing first, rather than try to beat hell out of each other for the full 200 miles.

With a quarter of an hour to go we started to race hard. Both cars were running well and I was leading when we came across a bunch of slower cars to lap. I got by them on the straight and knew Jack would lose time trying to get past through the wriggles. This was my chance to make a break and I pulled out all the stops.

With four laps left I was five seconds ahead, but a lap later the Monaco suddenly broke into a tremendous slide on a tight right-hander on the back of the circuit. I thought I must have been relaxing my attention and on the next corner was more careful, but again it slid viciously. Going down the main straight I noticed the water temperature needle was starting to climb and lifted my foot a little as we shot down into the long loop before the pits. Half-way round came another slide and going by the pits the temperature needle was hard against the stop and the engine started to seize or tighten up.

My choice was to ease up or blow up, so I backed off, Jack went past and in another lap the chequered flag was out. Jack had won the race, 7,000 dollars, and a Pontiac Grand Prix saloon. With the bonuses added, he had probably won around £4,000, but I had some small compensation in collecting lap money for leading on about 75 out of the 200 laps.

After Riverside, Laguna Seca was an anti-climax. Mike and I changed the cylinder head sealing rings, which had caused the water leak at Riverside, sending the temperature up as water gathered in the under tray and sloshed on to the back tyres. We found the cylinder liners had apparently settled in the block about five-thousandths of an inch and we had to make shims to fit under the sealing rings.

Had we fitted them before Riverside, they would probably have been worth £1,000 each!

At Laguna Seca we had a piston failure on the 2·7 engine, a problem which was to recur fairly frequently. One of the piston ring lands generally breaks off after four or five hours' running. The piston manufacturers tried various remedies, one of which was to make a piston with only two rings instead of three and to make the sections between the rings wider and stronger. These pistons generally made the engine use a considerable amount of oil, by letting it pass up into the combustion chamber.

After Laguna Seca, I flew back to New Zealand to get

married. Patty and I, after a two-year engagement, were wed at St Paul's church in Christchurch and flew to Fiji and Tahiti for a two-week honeymoon, with not a motor racing circuit within 3,000 miles.

After a fortnight of sea and sunshine—I had also started to water ski—we were bronzed and fit.

Besides racing in Australasia that season, I was determined to improve my prowess as a water-skier. I had my chance, though not quite as I would have wished, in the first race of the series—the drenched New Zealand GP at Ardmore. There was a cloudburst minutes before the start and in places around the track the water must have been deep enough for ski-ing.

I led the field as we ploughed into the blinding rain towards the first corner and held my position on to the back straight. I was wearing a visor—a curved plastic shield which clips on a helmet protecting your face—which was fine until half-way down the straight on that first lap it started to steam up as hot air and moisture rose through the cockpit. Some anti-mist solution would have prevented this, but in the rush and rain at the start I had forgotten it. I could barely see a thing.

First Moss came by in the Walker-Lotus and I tried to follow him as we splashed our way through the Cloverleaf—two rights and left again—then back into the pit straight where I snatched a moment to wipe my visor. To my horror I realized the light wooden markers at intervals along the grandstand side of the track were on my right, instead of the left. A quick glance showed I was off the track running almost against the fence in front of the main grandstands.

That was enough. A few minutes more of trying to plough along blinded in spray might have been suicidal and the whole project, the car and myself could have been finished. I slowed to a saner pace, leaving Moss and Surtees to it. Stirling kept up a very fast pace, sliding about wildly on the swimming track and lapping the field before the race was cut short and abandoned after 100 of the 150 laps.

Once Moss had an alarming sideways slide on the fast left-hander before the pits and later told me this was one of the few occasions when he had been really scared. He thought his number was up.

All I can say under such conditions is good luck, mate! To win when the track is submerged and you are half-blinded most of the time will send the Press mad with their praise. Banner headlines in the evening papers proclaimed Stirling "Boss Moss" and he had certainly shown his legendary form. As he freely admitted, however, it had been dangerous and had he crashed, the same Pressmen would have condemned him for being foolhardy.

Neither I nor Angus Hyslop with his brand-new $2\frac{1}{2}$-litre Cooper were very popular that night. 'Gus had won a race earlier in the day, but in the sodden opening laps of the Grand Prix slid into marker hay bales crushing in the nose and was content to circulate at a subdued pace to finish. We both wanted to live and race again on a finer day.

We proudly maintain that New Zealand offers sunshine with its motor racing, but 1962 was out to damn all our public relations work. The following week-end at Levin it started to rain just after final practice and on race morning the little town was flooded. So was the racing circuit. But Jack was out to make it a Brabham day despite the water and set off at a great pace with Stirling on his heels, this time using the Walker-Cooper. I spun out of third place after hitting a pool of water sideways and had battled back past Salvadori in the Bowmaker-Cooper when Tony Shelly's 2-litre Cooper hit a huge pool of water at the head of the pit straight and hurtled the length of the straight on the grass, scattering mechanics and officials as it pirouetted between the track and the timing tower.

Seconds after Shelly had set off again, Hyslop spun even further in the same place, throwing up huge columns of mud and spray. This left me in third place with Stirling desperately trying to catch Jack. Suddenly, after only eight laps, the

Above, Bruce McLaren takes his Cooper through a bend during the Nürburgring Grand Prix, unaware that a few laps later his car would be in ruins (below) and he on his way to hospital

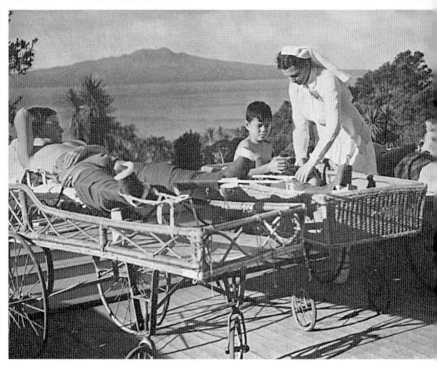

Above, after contracting Perthes Disease Bruce McLaren, left, was laid up in hospital strapped to a Bradshaw frame. Below, a picture that tells the story of how he conquered the disease and went on to achieve international fame

chequered flag was out. Jack said he couldn't quite believe it, so kept on motoring and Stirling, hard on his heels, did likewise, while the rest of the field slowed.

Stirling was livid after the race saying that if the organizers intended stopping the race after only eight laps, they should never have started it. Jack smiling broadly, reminded Stirling that he had not objected to the Ardmore race being curtailed when he was a lap in front.

The Wigram race saved Kiwi faces climatically, but I was still out of luck. We were all using D12s in practice and I managed fastest lap, 0·1 sec faster than Jack. Race day was a scorcher, with sunshades protecting us from roasting as we waited on the grid. Although Stirling had been only third fastest, more than a second behind Jack, he was confidently fitting D12s to the Lotus for the race. In the terrific heat I thought this a little foolhardy—even Jack was running on D9s —but Stirling was backing the lighter weight of the Lotus and it paid off. I made a bad start off pole position and in my efforts to overhaul the leaders, spun and couldn't better fourth place behind Moss, Brabham and Surtees.

Three races for three lowly places were beginning to perturb me, but Teretonga Park revived the McLaren stock.

The Cooper suited the tight little circuit ideally and plenty of water ski-ing beforehand had put me in top physical form.

As the circuit was mostly made up of left-hand corners, and the race only 75 miles, we didn't have to carry very much fuel, so Harry Pearce removed the right-hand fuel tank. This gave us a two-fold advantage—the car was lighter, with the fuel now all on the left-hand side. There were only two right-handers, against half-a-dozen lefts, so I proposed to pick up ground by this move.

There were two race heats before the final and I was paired with Stirling, but our pre-race strategy in removing the tank paid off and I managed to head him home fairly comfortably. In the final I was on pole position, took the lead going into the long loop and I had one of my most pleasing drives, picking up more than a second a lap on Jack and Stirling. On the long, almost 180-degree, left-hand loop at the end of the straight, the car would drift through under full power, sliding out and feeling really stable. With only a couple of laps to go, I saw the tail of Jack's Cooper ahead, but the chequer was out before I could lap him and Stirling was well behind me.

There was another race that day—a free-for-all with a rolling Indianapolis-type start. Stirling made the best of this and led into the loop. I sat tight on his tail for a lap and a half, then nipped by, underbraking at the end of the straight. On the next lap Harry had a grin all over his face and was holding out a PLUS ONE signal, next lap it was PLUS TWO, but on the following lap he was holding out a signal I didn't understand, as it didn't seem to be directed at me.

Afterwards I found he was giving a signal to Stirling. On the board he had chalked what looked like a large "Q"; in short, it meant "pull your finger out!" To the delight of the pits and bewilderment of the crowd Stirling acknowledged with a lofty "Victory V" as he blasted by at over 100 mph.

Before leaving New Zealand for the Australian Grand Prix at Warwick Farm, Ken Tyrrell wrote that he was running another team of Formula Junior Coopers, which were nearly built, and as the Cooper F1 car was well on the way to being finished, John Cooper would like me to come back and test them both.

After the second race in Australia, at Lakeside near Brisbane, there were two free week-ends before my final race in the series at Melbourne's new Sandown Park circuit, so I wrote Ken (sending a copy to John) that I was prepared to fly back and go testing every day for a week. I also suggested that, if by any chance they didn't have either of the cars ready and my trip was wasted, I expected them to pay my return fare from Australia to London.

With only a week between the Teretonga race in New

Zealand and the Warwick Farm meeting at Sydney, the schedule was tight and we had to rush the cars back to Wellington for shipping on the *Johan van Oldenbarnevelt*, which reached Sydney on the morning of the final practice.

The Cooper arrived with hours to spare, but I had already found which way the track went by borrowing Bib Stillwell's Cooper-Monaco. An interesting circuit, snaking about inside a horse-racing track, it was ably managed by Geoff Sykes, who had left an official position with the British Automobile Racing Club to supervise sport at the Farm. Roy Salvadori had a bad crash at the end of the straight, when his Cooper turned sharp left and demolished a marshal's barrier made of railway sleepers. Roy was thrown out and it was feared that he had fractured his skull, but everyone was relieved next morning to learn "Dad" was sitting up and talking, with bad bruises and a very black eye the extent of his injuries.

Moss and Brabham had sent spare cars direct to Sydney before the Teretonga race, so they made good use of the first day of practice to sort out gear ratios and carburation. We had a battle royal in the opening laps until Surtees broke his crown-wheel and pinion on the ninth lap and I spun on the causeway soon after, but I had collected the lap record during the tussle and carried on to finish second. Jack and Stirling had been giving the Aussie crowd a thrilling race as Brabham sat out in front despite all the tricks in the Moss manual, but Jack's gearbox broke after 20 laps and Stirling went on to a comfortable win in the Walker-Cooper, with my Cooper 20 sec behind, second.

If Wigram had been hot, the Lakeside race was unbelievably hotter. The newly-built circuit was largely the work of promotion-minded Sid Saczewski, who runs a contracting firm among other things in Brisbane. A small lake, only a few feet from the circuit, was a godsend and we spent almost as much time in the water as on the blistering track. Sid's son is a water skier of international repute, so I was able to improve my own performance—until a bad tumble burst a small blood vessel behind my eye.

Three tons of ice were carted up to the circuit on race morning and we commandeered a large drum of it to cool the fuel. Drivers were filling their pockets with ice and planting it round their seats in an effort to keep cool as long as possible. Angus Hyslop stopped his Cooper on the warming-up lap and dived into the lake with overalls and boots on!

I had won my heat the previous day, but Brabham and Stillwell were quicker in theirs and beat me away from the grid in the main event. I managed to get by Stillwell, who was driving fast on the tricky up-and-downhill circuit, but almost immediately my gearbox started to make ominous noises and I had lost fourth gear. Colotti gearboxes don't grow on trees, so deeming caution to be the financially better side of careless valour, I retired. All the teeth had disappeared off fourth gear. Jack went on to win from Stillwell, who stayed close behind him throughout the race.

I flew down to Sydney after a rousing party at the Caravilla motel where we were staying. At one stage Angus Hyslop returned to his room to find a stack of D12 tyres being "tested" in his shower, and his bedroom half under water!

A Boeing 707 took me quickly and smoothly to London, where the British Racing and Sports Car Club annual dinner-dance was being held, so within a few hours I had caught up with the latest news. During the evening I was called to the telephone to take a call from America. With an ability that seems to exist only with American telephone operators, they had traced me from Sydney to Surbiton and from Surbiton to the Park Lane Hotel. It was Frank Falkner. He said Briggs Cunningham was flying over to Monza in three days to test the Type-64 Maserati sports car and a Cooper-Monaco, which was being fitted with a 3·8-litre four-cylinder Maserati engine at the factory in Modena. Frank wondered if I would fly down and try the cars, also whether I would be available to drive one of them at Sebring a week after the Sandown Park race at Melbourne. Sydney to London, London to Milan, Milan back to London, London to Melbourne and Melbourne to Sebring—all in a fortnight! I was in for a busy time.

Jack had left Coopers to build his own cars and run his own team. As the new No. 1 with Coopers and with a drive in a very competitive car at Sebring, the future looked promising for me.

The new F1 Coopers were considerably improved structurally from the 1961 cars. The chassis of both had been designed by Owen Maddox, Cooper chief draughtsman that winter, and the cars had a fully ball-jointed suspension.

Before leaving for America and the "down under" season the previous October, I'd spent a few hours with the drawing-office staff. I said the cars were handling quite well, particularly the Atkins-Cooper, and suggested the general suspension geometry, spring rates and roll stiffness shouldn't be altered.

The new cars differed considerably on these two scores, however. The springs had been designed to run in combination with long rubber bump-stops, to give a progressive rate, and the anti-roll bar layout had been changed completely. From a handling point of view we would have to start all over again to get the car balanced perfectly.

Heavy snowfalls made testing impossible, so I flew down to Italy and some sunshine with a clear conscience. Walt Hansgen, Roger Penske and Alfred Momo had come over with Briggs on his shopping spree and we went straight to Monza. The Type-64 Maserati had a 3-litre V12 engine in back, similar to the Type-63 Maserati that Walt and I had driven at Le Mans in 1961—that is, the one I would have driven had Walt not parked it in the sand before I had a chance to try it! Improvements had made this later model a full five seconds a lap quicker round Monza.

I didn't make myself very popular with the Maserati design

staff when I lapped far quicker with the Cooper-Monaco Maserati, knocking two seconds off the lap record.

We also took the cars to Modena, where I had a chance to drive a Formula Junior Stanguellini with Fiat 1100 engine, which Briggs was thinking about buying. I even knocked 1·5 sec off the lap record, much to Signor Stanguellini's delight.

While at Modena I had the pleasure of meeting racing drivers from the days when cars were monsters. Dr Farina and Gigi Villoresi, although getting on in years, were both anxious to try the cars. Villoresi talked his way into the Maserati and set off without goggles, because they would not fit over his spectacles. We had trouble calling him back to the pits.

A typical piece of Americana came from Roger before we had a chance to stop him. As we were introduced to the famous old drivers he drawled, "Who is this guy Villoresi?"

Briggs really had a buying spree. Besides the Type-64 Maserati and the Cooper-Monaco Maserati, he bought a beautiful silver-grey Maserati 5000 coupé. He also took delivery of three 1000 cc GT Abarths for the three-hour race at Sebring and to top up his shopping basket added three special-bodied Fiat 1500s—because he liked the look of them!

Back in England again the snow was still falling, but we did manage a few days' testing before I flew back for the race at Melbourne.

Before leaving England I asked Tommy Atkins if he would like to employ a keen, intelligent young New Zealander as second mechanic to Harry Pearce. This was twenty-one-year-old Wally Willmott, who had gone across to Australia with the motor racing teams for a holiday, became bored with just looking on and at Lakeside asked Harry if he could help on my car. After he had been working only a few hours, Harry said quietly, "This boy's good." The thing that impressed me was that he worked as though he wanted to do a good job.

Melbourne, capital city of Victoria, was very excited about its big motor race. Each day there was publicity over television and radio and in all the newspapers. Nobody in Melbourne can have been unaware of the race.

This was the first one on the new Sandown track, which had been built round the outside of a horse racecourse with a huge, modern grandstand, from which almost the full circuit was visible.

For their inaugural event, the Victorians saw what was probably the best motor race ever held in Australasia. From first light, roads to the circuit were crammed with cars and about ten o'clock we drivers were ceremoniously flown there in helicopters. As we were staying at a motel not far from the gates of the circuit, we had to motor back to the city to meet the helicopter.

The cars and drivers were led in a long line past the grand-stands to the grid. Each car had a marching girl parading in front with a banner proclaiming the driver's name. All very impressive and Americanized, with marching bands adding extra life to an already colourful scene.

That morning John Surtees and I battled wheel to wheel in a race heat, with John taking the decision by a wheel. In the afternoon the main event was just as torrid—and we had Jack to deal with as well. Or should I say Jack was dealing with us, as he won eventually.

In fact the three of us were evenly matched and it was a determined no-quarter-given race from the start. We diced nose to tail for the whole distance and finished only seconds apart. Jack and I had virtually no brakes at the end of the race. We had cooked the pad material to a glass-hard state and Surtees was not much better off, as his different pad material had almost worn completely away.

Our pace had been so torrid that we had lapped Stirling's Lotus, locked in combat with Chuck Daigh's Buick-powered rear-engined Scarab, just after half-distance. This Scarab had been brought out by Lance Reventlow and was his first attempt at a rear-engined car. Chuck was just the man to drive it and the Scarab's blast of acceleration away from corners had to be experienced to be believed. Stirling could vouch for the car's punch . . . although his Lotus could out-manœuvre and out-brake the Scarab, his advantage disappeared under the merciless acceleration. A strong case for the old American adage, "There ain't no substitute for cubic inches!"

FOURTEEN

Moss Crashes at Goodwood

SOON AFTER THE final race of 1962 "down under" series at Sandown Park, Patty and I were on our way to Sebring in southern Florida, with a busy programme, as I was to drive the Cooper-Monaco Maserati with Roger Penske, also one of the 1000 cc GT Abarths in the three-hour endurance race the day before the 12-hour main event.

The Cunningham stable was as fantastic as ever. All the cars were housed in the Cunningham private hangar and these included, apart from the Type-64 Maserati and the Monaco, a much-modified E-type Jaguar, the three Abarths, the prototype Cooper Formula Junior for 1963, which I had tested in England, one of the first new Formula Junior Brabhams, and a 1961 Formula Junior Cooper powered by a Fiat 1100 engine with transistorized ignition.

A stable like this called for race preparation on grandiose lines. Six racing mechanics, two Maserati engineers from Modena, John Cooper, a factory mechanic to look after the E-type and Alfred Momo to keep an eye on his mammoth staff. There was even a man to sweep the workshop floor, look after the spares and keep the freezer stocked with soft drinks.

Prospects for the three-hour race were interesting, if a little frightening. Abarths had a representative at Sebring to look after the Cunningham cars and John Cooper was curious to know how one man could keep a thorough check on all three.

"They don't need looking after," said Briggs with a grin, "just put in oil, water and gas and race them!"

That may well have been the case, but those Abarths would have benefited from some attention to the handling, braking and steering.

I wasn't particularly keen on driving one, as the Cooper-Monaco required attention before the race. We intended fitting larger brakes and quick-change front wheels, which meant a change of hubs, bigger steering arms and so on.

We all went out to practice, but by the end of the session each driver was asking the others incredulously, "Is yours as bad as mine?"

It seemed that at every corner you were in danger of landing on your head! The Abarth was fast, the 1000 cc twin-cam engine having bags of power for its size, but the engine hung way out behind the rear axle and it was a case of the tail wagging the dog.

There were several of them racing and on nearly every corner you would come upon one spinning crazily, either on its wheels or roof.

Briggs said we didn't have to drive them if they really were that bad and I offered mine to any likely takers, but Patty finally talked me into having a go in the race. She and Lissa Penske, Roger's wife, had been standing on the outside of the tricky Websters turn, a sharp right and an equally sharp left only a few yards later, and their accounts of Roger, Walt and I dancing through in the Abarths was hilarious. Roger had spun his once and mine went so far round that it might as well have done the same.

I was slow away in the Le Mans start, as I had no intention of going anywhere in this particular car before strapping myself in securely. Then I stalled when I dropped the clutch and had to start all over again. This meant I had lost many places, but it was raining and Americans are not generally good wet-weather drivers. In England we get plenty of practice at it, so I was able to start picking my way through the field fairly quickly.

The rain meant that Stirling, in one of the better-handling Sprites, was racing away from the field, but his advantage didn't last long when it stopped raining, the circuit started to dry, and we were able to use the Abarths' power, which had made them dicey in the damp.

After a couple of hours' hard motoring and managing to keep the car right side up, I found Walt just ahead of me in his Abarth, with Stirling's Sprite about a quarter of a mile ahead. We were gradually catching him. Walt could see him, too, and we set off in pursuit.

Through the fast "esses", where the Abarths were really a handful, it was a matter of holding the steering wheel with fingertips and easing it gently into the corner. Flinging it in, as we had done with the Sprites a year earlier, would probably have taken us to the Cunningham hangar on the back of the circuit! Walt's car suddenly took charge and spun off, bouncing into the long grass, and I was left to chase the fleeing Sprite on my own. I pulled out a couple of extra stops and in a few laps was on his tail and past. Walt was soon mobile again after his excursion and when Stirling ran out of fuel moved up to finish second.

I had won a race that I almost talked myself out of contesting.

The Cooper-Monaco Maserati was encouraging in practice and after comparing our lap times with the Ferraris, Roger and I were looking forward to a good race. I didn't make a very brilliant job of the Le Mans start, but after six laps was up in fourth place. Walt was flying in the Type-64 V12 Maserati, lying second, but his hurricane progress was checked when he stopped after only 15 laps of the 5·2 mile track for new rear tyres. A few laps later he had to retire with some of the lattice-like tubes in the "birdcage" chassis broken.

Our car was using far less fuel than the Ferraris, which had to stop every one and a half hours for replenishment whereas we could run for an extra hour before making a fuel stop, and I was well in the lead when John Cooper signalled me in to refuel.

Roger took over, but made an early stop to fit new brake pads. Everything seemed to go wrong and it was an impossible $26\frac{1}{2}$ minutes before the car was back on the track. On my second spell a brakeless Corvette had brushed me into the hay bales and I had slightly dented one of the front guards. After seven and a half hours, we had another long stop to repair a chain reaction of electrical troubles caused by my brush with the bales. The generator had apparently been dislodged, the battery had gone flat, fuses had blown and one of the headlights was pointing at the sky. By the time all these bothers had been repaired, we were an extra quarter of an hour in arrears.

When the car was mobile, however, it proved a flier and both Roger and I were turning in laps close to the record. As John Cooper commented later, it was no wonder we could lap fast when we were on the track, as we had a quarter-hour break every two hours!

Another problem came to light—or rather failed to light—when darkness fell and we discovered the tail lamps refused to work.

We hoped to hold off calling Roger in to mend the faulty tail lights until we were due to stop for fuel and it wasn't until an irate official came down to the Cunningham private pit to see why Penske wasn't stopping, after several reprimanding notes had been sent down, that John Cooper climbed over the pit wall and held out a huge IN sign.

Briggs was upset that John, who had been riled by the tone of the official, was holding the huge signal board out until Penske came past, despite the fact that a lot of others were reading it.

John thought it a huge joke. "What are you worrying

about," he shouted, "I've already brought in a couple of red ones!" Red was the colour of the Ferraris.

Roger eventually stopped and we lost another 15 minutes while the tail lights were re-wired. He set off in a hurry and, when he handed over to me again a few laps later, the car was fourth. It also had no brakes. And when I took off again I found the lights were little better than a pair of candles (due to the flattened battery), so with neither lights nor brakes had to try and improve or at least maintain our position.

I groped round in the darkness as long as I dared and, with only 35 minutes to go, pitted again with the lights threatening to snuff completely. This stop was a rather more comprehensive one and it was 18½ minutes before I took off again, to finish fifth behind three Ferraris and a Porsche.

John Cooper was the only bright spark during our maddening series of stops. One of the Corvettes seemed to be covered with flashing identification lights, in addition to its four powerful headlights, and John was heard to shout, "Look at that—lit up like a Christmas tree and we haven't even got tail lights!"

After Sebring I was excited about the potential of the Monaco sports cars. Mechanically the car had been fine for the full 12 hours. The transmission had run through without a hitch. The suspension and brakes had given no trouble that couldn't have been cured in infancy with any sort of reasonable testing programme. Our Monaco actually had too much braking on the rear wheels, which was largely responsible for wearing the pads out so quickly.

The other problems with the generator and lights falling off were because normally none of this equipment is used in the short sports car races for which the car was originally designed.

I thought the car would have great potential for the longer sports car races like Le Mans, the 1,000 Kilometres at the Nürburgring and Sebring.

I put this to Charles Cooper as soon as I got back to England, but he was unimpressed. The fact that Jack Brabham was now building his own car had made Charles feel that drivers employed by him should be kept purely as drivers and not involved in development, or more particularly design.

In my opinion, for Charles to feel they had taught Jack all he knew was unfair. It is similarly unreasonable for anyone to suggest that without Brabham, Coopers would never have developed their successful Grand Prix cars. John and Jack were a terrific combination, one supplementing the other, but it appeared things would now be a little different.

But I had another project to interest me. Tommy Atkins had arranged to borrow my 1961 works four-cylinder Cooper and was having the engine extensively modified by Bill Lacey, one of the top tuners in England. On the chassis side, Harry Pearce, Wally Willmott and I pooled ideas, and in Tommy Atkins' quiet little racing workshop in Chessington started making some alterations, lowering the car, then widening the track by making and fitting longer suspension wishbones.

The Easter Goodwood meeting was a week and a half away and we wanted to have two or three days' testing to make the car as perfect as possible. We used an old engine while we altered the wheel angles, tyre pressures, springs and anti-roll bars, until the car stuck to the road through corners like a limpet.

We had entered the car for two races at Goodwood, the Lavant Cup for four-cylinder cars and the main event for Formula One cars, which meant we were running against the V8s.

I was comfortably on pole position in the Lavant Cup race, with fellow New Zealander Tony Shelly beside me on the grid in the black four-cylinder F1 Lotus he had just acquired. There had been no official "Driver to Europe" for 1962, so Tony was trying European racing at his own expense.

I led into the first corner, with John Surtees close behind in the new Lola and for the first couple of laps he and I were virtually neck and neck. At the end of the second lap, as we shot down into Woodcote Corner, John nipped past and saw what looked an opportunity to make ground by passing a slower car at the entrance to the chicane. But this didn't quite work and his Lola and the dawdling Lotus got well and truly tangled with each other and the chicane walls. I was only a few feet away, but with brakes hard on, just managed to creep through a narrow gap and motor on to win.

The real excitement came in the Glover Trophy race for F1 cars, however. My Cooper was on the front row of the grid with Grahan Hill's BRM V8 and Stirling's Lotus V8. I made a tremendous start and for two glorious laps led all the F1 cars with the old four-cylinder!

The extra power of Graham's BRM V8 brought him by on the straight, but I found that I could almost hold him, using the slipstream to advantage. I hung on to his tail for three laps and it wasn't until we caught Richie Ginther in the second works BRM, who had stalled on the line, that I lost the tow. Richie, as a good team-mate, didn't baulk me, but made it difficult for a lap. John Surtees drew alongside in the Lola V8 going into Woodcote, but I was on the inside. We apparently both thought it was our corner and tangled wheels, John coming off worst and spinning.

With a few laps to go, I saw a flurry of spectators and marshals at St Mary's. There was a green Lotus with its nose half buried in the bank. Moss!

Two laps. Three laps. Four laps. Five laps. Each time we went past he was still there in the car. What were they doing?

When the race finished I went straight to the pits. "What's happening over the back? . . . Why can't they get him out?" were my first worried questions.

"They're having to cut the car apart," someone said, "it's folded up around him." Rumours came thick and fast, but it appeared he was still alive and in the circumstances reasonably all right, though still unconscious.

Earlier in the race Stirling had made a pit stop. When the

bonnet was clipped down and he started the engine, the throttle stuck open and the bonnet had to be removed again to free it.

The throttle linkage on the Climax V8s at that time was complicated and a little messy. Had the throttle stuck open at that particular part of the circuit, the car would have gone straight off, or if anything broke in the steering, which is not impossible, a similar accident would have been inevitable.

On the third lap, when I was following Graham round Fordwater I was within inches of his tail-pipes. He pulled over to the right to brake in a straight line for the right-hander at St Mary's and I thought for a split second he was giving me a chance to get by, as I normally stay out to the left and brake in a slight curve for this corner.

In fact he was taking a slightly different line for St Mary's. Perhaps Stirling found himself in a similar position, started to go outside Graham, then realized his mistake.

The trouble with an accident like this, however, is that definite conclusions afterwards are almost impossible. Even reliable eye-witness reports vary. The evidence left in the wreckage of the car is also liable to be inconclusive.

Graham, one of Stirling's closer friends, won his first major race that day. He had achieved a string of thirds, just as I had a series of seconds behind Jack, but he never quite managed to pull off a big race. He came close to it at Silverstone a year earlier and missed, but this win at Goodwood was to set off a run of successes that were to earn him the 1962 world championship.

I had no reason to feel despondent, as my four-cylinder Cooper seemed satisfyingly fast. At Aintree a few weeks later I again finished second, this time behind Jimmy Clark, beating the Ferrari and the rest of the factory opposition and at Silverstone I finished only a few seconds behind Innes Ireland in one of the works Ferraris.

If we could keep that handling and add the V8's extra steam

—our first new V8 car was nearly ready—Coopers looked like being hard to beat.

Extreme degrees of good handling are obtained only by very careful chassis tuning—there isn't any other word for it. Improvements are made in the same way that extra power can often be obtained from an engine by painstaking intelligent trial and error. One has to work hard for every fraction over the ordinary.

Twelve months earlier at Aintree the Ferraris had romped away from us. Now, with virtually the same Cooper, I was able to stay with them. Why hadn't we made the improvements to our car the previous year and why hadn't we found the extra power earlier?

The reasons are subtle and not everyone will accept them. Why does one violin give a better tune than another? They both look the same—at least to my musically ignorant eyes. It takes an expert touch to achieve perfection in violins and in motor cars.

While we are asking questions, why did Enzo Ferrari send one of his F1 cars to Silverstone for a top English driver to try? People said he wanted a comparison between his own drivers (Phil Hill, Baghetti and Bandini) and the Englishmen. This was certainly no way to inspire his drivers with confidence and without confidence in a car and team one loses half a second a lap before even stepping into the cockpit.

Ferrari found out what any of us would have been able to tell him—that Phil Hill was as good a driver as he could get. Phil can boast the determination and ability to match anyone, but he has had to handle some poor cars.

Motor racing isn't only drivers *or* cars, it's car-driver combinations. More than that, it's car-driver-team combinations and driving a racing car on or over the limit is a special art. Nerve has nothing to do with it.

Skill is certainly needed, but if I made fastest lap in a race, or reached pole position on a starting grid against the top-liners

14

in F1 racing today, those laps would not have felt excessively fast or dangerous. I wouldn't have wrestled with the wheel or thrown the car into corners. I *would* have balanced the power, steering and brakes as near perfection as possible. Like executing the perfect slalom run in ski-ing, it takes more timing and grace than strength or nerve. . . .

The new F1 Cooper was a good solid car, fairly clean in its lines. The new six-speed gearbox looked good and was reasonably light at 100 lbs for complete transmission unit and bell-housing. There was a last-minute panic when the gearbox, which had been designed to take inboard rear brakes, refused to fit in the chassis. Only a few days before the first race at Zandvoort the gearbox casing was hastily modified and the brakes re-fitted outboard.

A distinctive feature of the new Cooper was the howl from the downward-swept exhaust pipes, which converged from the tangled cross-over system that Coventry-Climax had devised for us.

The Press showed mild interest, but the night after the first practice session the new Lotus 25 was rolled out of the transporter to "Oohs" and "Aahs". Lotus fans were saying "Aah" —Cooper supporters "Ooh!"

Here was a remarkable racing car, small in the extreme at that stage and inches smaller in cross-section than any other F1 model. Gone was the tubular framework of the chassis. Instead, the basic construction was sheet metal in the form of two long D-shaped sections on each side of the driver, joined together by bulkheads. Clearly much meticulous work had gone into this new Lotus.

Jimmy Clark had been getting gradually faster during the previous season and it was easy to foresee that he and this new Lotus 25 would be a formidable combination. We were relying again on our reliability and there were many new techniques in the Lotus—perhaps their inboard front shock-absorbers would get too hot (we hoped!) and remembering our overheating problems with the V8s we felt sure the Lotus would boil with such a small air intake to cool the radiator.

But Coopers were the first to be struck by unreliability and in practice we had a quill shaft break. Part of the transmission, this is a long spring-steel shaft with a small cross-section, meant to absorb vibration, but it wasn't strong enough. It always looks wrong to put high horse-power through a spindly shaft, although if the design calculations are correct and the machining good, it must be correct. This one broke.

As our only replacement was an identical shaft, we weren't confident about what would happen in the race. On the warm-up lap, fourth gear refused to drive at all, so I was committed to ignore it for the race. Despite several small teething troubles, I was on the second row of the grid with Jack, who was running a Lotus until his own new F1 car was finished. I took off very smoothly and slowly, to safeguard the precious quill shaft, but within a few laps lay second to Graham's BRM.

The car was handling well and I was picking up half a second or so on Graham, but on lap 15 another gear failed to report for duty and on the following round the quill shaft broke and I was a spectator. A little development testing at the right time of the year and we might have won.

The next race on our Continental calendar was the 1,000 km sports car event on the Nürburgring. Patty and I in my E-type Jaguar; Trevor Taylor and Jimmy Clark in their Lotus-Elite, and Tony Maggs in a little Ogle Mini-Cooper set off in convoy. We were all driving for John Ogier's Essex Racing Team—Jimmy and Trevor in a Lotus 23, with the first-ever twin-cam 1½-litre Ford engine; Tony and I in the veteran Aston Martin DRB1, reputedly borrowed from Lord Montague's motor museum specially for the occasion!

On the way through to Germany we stopped off for Count Carel de Beaufort's cocktail party, held in the family castle, complete with a moat, drawbridge and suits of armour in the hall ways. The party was hilarious, featuring a mock battle with mediaeval weapons between Jimmy, Phil Hill and Dan Gurney.

Tony and I weren't very optimistic about our chances in a five-year-old car against the latest Ferraris. Jimmy and Trevor were looking hard at the light tubes that made up the chassis of the little Lotus.

A sudden shower as we lined up for the Le Mans start threw Ferrari and Porsche teams into panic, as they scrambled to fit rain tyres—Bandini's Ferrari was still on the jack when the flag fell.

I started well in the big Aston and surprised myself by leading the field into the South Curve.

We had made a joking arrangement before the race that Jimmy would come alongside the Aston and knock when he wanted to pass, but he had no time for games as he pulled ahead on the wet track coming out of the South Curve and disappeared down through the woods. The Ferraris and Porsches were no match for the agility of the knee-high Lotus and before a leaking exhaust spread fumes into the cockpit and Jimmy spun off after missing a gear, he had built a long 100 sec lead on the field.

It wasn't long before the modern metal went thundering past me in the opening laps and I settled down in eighth position, lapping at an agreed speed and waiting for the opposition to eliminate themselves, as they obligingly proceeded to do. Two Ferraris finished up in trees and the starter failed on another, bringing the Aston up to fifth, but according to the complicated classification system we were actually second behind Hill and Gendebien in the winning Ferrari.

We were all staying at the Lochmuler Hotel in Altenahr, where some of the best food in Europe is served. The Essex Racing Team was paying the bill, or so we thought, and each evening after practice we ate at a large table. Most of us stuck to four large courses. Such as lobster, or that delicious oxtail soup; a quick chicken and mushroom entrée, or pâté; then an exotic steak, grilled with oranges and tomatoes or a wine sauce. Jimmy generally managed to fit in a grilled trout, probably caught an hour earlier in the river beside the hotel. For a small man it was amazing how much he could stow away! We lived particularly well until John Ogier glanced at the bill and decided that he'd pay bed and breakfast only!

He was a grander gourmet than any of us. The first time we sat down to dinner, he ordered a bottle of red and a bottle of the local white wine. He sampled them, expressed himself satisfied, then spluttered with indignation as the waiter began to serve round the wine, "Fool, those are for me! Bring some more!"

The prize-giving dinner at the Sport Hotel on the night of the race was a riot. The next morning out at the Lochmuler Hotel, the staff gazed in wonderment at two gigantic urns adorning their front steps. At the same time the staff of the Sport Hotel were wondering where their own urns had gone!

While Tony and I were in Germany, the Cooper mechanics had been hard at work fitting a guaranteed-not-to-break quill shaft. Six speeds had been an asset at Zandvoort, with its fast corners, but with 100 laps round the tight Monaco circuit only a week away, we decided to try something new and convert the box to four speeds by removing two gears.

Monaco produced some weird-looking cars. Both BRMs and Lolas arrived with chopped noses to improve the cooling on the short circuit—it was also rumoured that this made them far less prone to shunting!

I was very glad of a good start in the Grand Prix. I led the field away and glimpsed the beginning of confusion in my mirrors, as Willy Mairesse jumped his Ferrari between front-row men Hill and Clark to follow me. When I slowed for the Gasworks Hairpin second time round, I saw marshals busily sweeping debris off the track from the multiple pile-up that resulted when the throttle jammed wide open on Richie Ginther's BRM. There was little the American could do but plough through the group in front of him. He hit the wall, tearing wheels off, after shunting Taylor's Lotus, Ireland's Lotus, Gurney's Porsche and Trintignant's Lotus, putting the last two out of the race. Ireland and Taylor continued, only to retire later from the effects of the crash.

For five or six laps I pounded round in the afternoon sun, enjoying leading a Grand Epreuve so early in the season. Then my signal board told me Graham was beginning to pick up time and before long he was on my tail. Monaco was a long race and if he had been able to regain ground so quickly, I would be better off to let him set the pace.

Clark's Lotus had left the line with an oiled plug, but when this cleared the Scot began motoring in earnest, passing me in his pursuit of Graham and the lead. He never passed the BRM, but broke the lap record several times in his attempt before the Lotus went sick and I left Jimmy at the side of the road.

The crowds at the corners suddenly started waving and I realized they were trying to tell me I was catching Graham and could win. Two laps later the BRM was stopped with a broken engine.

All I had to do was hold the lead for the five remaining laps. Phil Hill was 17 sec back, so I could slow a little and make absolutely sure of not spinning, making any last-minute mistakes, or over-stressing brakes, gearbox, or clutch. They had already withstood more than 90 laps, with some 30 gear-changes on each one. Anything could break in those last laps. It had happened to Jimmy and Graham and could just as easily happen to me.

There seemed a terrific amount of oil on the Station Hairpin and the right-hander before it. A moment's respite there to imagine the chequered flag, or worse, an extra effort to make sure of it, and the tail could come round in a flash and the lead would be lost.

With three laps left Mike and John began feverishly hanging signals on the pit board. They had been timing the gap between the Cooper and the Ferrari on one side of the pits and hurriedly putting it on the board for me to read as I went past on the other. They were working fast, with only seconds to get the figures from the watch to the board and on one lap they dropped the numbers. As I accelerated past, John was frantically trying to pick them up and hold them on the board. I had time to chuckle.

Phil was still five seconds away. I didn't think he could pick that up in two laps and by holding my pace was sure he would be a couple of seconds away at the finish.

Even if he were on my tail, there was nowhere to pass on that last half-lap. Especially if I didn't want to let him!

As I braked into the chicane for the last time I couldn't see the Ferrari in my mirror, but on entering the left-hander at the Tobacconists there was a red dot about 200 yards behind. I had won.

"This is a terrific car," were my first words to John on stopping at the pits. It was a well thought-out car, with nothing liable to fall off . . . not particularly light, or particularly original, but I had proved it was a winner.

FIFTEEN

On Fire at Oulton Park

FROM THE TIGHT twists and turns of Monaco, the championship scene turned to the fast climbs and swoops of Spa in Belgium. Coopers had the second V8 ready for Tony Maggs and we were looking forward to a good race. My car was going well and I made the front row of the grid with Graham Hill and Trevor Taylor, who was going very quickly in his first F1 season, especially at Spa.

Graham shot into the lead with Trevor and me on his tail, then Trevor moved in front, closely followed by Willy Mairesse in the Ferrari, obviously out to do well on his home circuit. The pair were dicing wheel-to-wheel and at 140-plus swooped up the hill after the pits side by side. Going into the first left-hander I was sure one would back off and let the other through. I braked, because it looked as though they were going to take the corner abreast—and they did. They couldn't get around the next right-hander together, however, and Willy went through just in front of Trevor, with his back wheel missing the Lotus front by inches. On the uphill straight Trevor drew alongside and at the next right-hander pulled in front of the Ferrari.

If there was going to be an accident I had no intention of being in it, so I sat back a safe 20 feet. Jimmy was motoring as though he meant business in the monocoque and had passed the three of us for a lead he never lost, but my race ended abruptly when a big end bearing let go.

Walking back to the pits I watched the battle for second place which was still raging. Then it happened. As I reached the brow of the hill after the pits I was shocked to see a column of smoke a mile away across the circuit. Walking down the hill, I heard photographers describing what they had seen.

"The two cars went behind a clump of trees and only one came out—in a ball of flame," said one. This sounded bad.

But Trevor had beaten me back to the pits and was surrounded by a crowd, wanting to know what had happened and expressing their delight that he was still with us. Apart from a graze on his wrist, where he had snagged his watch-strap, he was completely unhurt. The Lotus had felled a pole and was a complete wreck. Mairesse, whose car had been the ball of flame, was in hospital but all right apart from burns and bruises. What appeared to be a catastrophe had amazingly resulted only in the loss of two cars. They had eventually touched—and I wasn't surprised.

After Spa we faced the long grind at Le Mans, where I was to share a brutish 4-litre front-engined Cunningham-entered Maserati coupé with Walt Hansgen. Jimmy and Trevor were to have driven a Lotus 23, powered by the twin-cam Ford engine which Jimmy had driven so fast at the 'Ring. It looked a certainty to win the Index of Performance if it kept going, but after a petty wangle over minor regulations, the Team Lotus entry was rejected and the boys spent the week-end in the hotel swimming pool, while we slogged around the Sarthe circuit in our big banger. It was tremendously fast—I threw a tread at 180 mph during the race—but a piston went in the early hours of the morning and yet another tiring Le Mans was over for me before dawn.

The Rheims Grand Prix (the French Grand Prix had been moved to Rouen a week later) followed Le Mans. I had a feeling about this race. On the first day of practice the Cooper was fast

—not so fast as Clark's Lotus, but fast nevertheless. Team Lotus were out to win all the fastest-lap champagne and while Jimmy pounded round we quietly took the Cooper back to the garage.

Rheims is always hard on cars, with the engine screaming on full throttle for nearly four miles out of five and two slow hairpins to give the brakes and gearbox a good work-out.

With Jimmy directly in front of me on the starting grid I couldn't have been better placed, as I was in an ideal spot to latch on the tail of the Lotus, which looked like being the pace-setter. The more carefully you lay plans, the more easily they go wrong. Jimmy made a bad start. Assuming he would make a good one and to ensure I would be right on his tail, I had jumped the start a fraction. With the Lotus almost stationary in front of me and my back wheels smoking I had a busy moment with the steering wheel to swing out past Jimmy and howl off with the pack. One of the local newspapers the next morning carried a front-page picture of the start, with my Cooper almost sideways on the second row.

When Jimmy went by as we accelerated up the long hill, before the downhill run where we reach nearly 160 mph (tame after the old $2\frac{1}{2}$-litre cars at 180 mph) I ducked in behind him. Within a lap he had drawn me well clear of the pack, but one thing was upsetting both our calculations—John Surtees lay a couple of hundred yards ahead of the pair of us with his Lola, pulling out half a second or so every lap.

To my surprise after a couple of laps Jimmy's arm shot up and he swerved off to whistle into the pits with a burst header tank. First Surtees had drawn away from any hope of slipstreaming, now Jimmy was in the pits. Most unthoughtful of him, so far as I was concerned, as it left me on my own. Two hundred yards back I could make out a gaggle of cars— Graham's BRM, Jack in his Lotus and behind them Innes Ireland in the light-green UDT Lotus V8.

I was sure these three would pick me up in a lap or so, as I had made a break on them by slipstreaming the Lotus, but Jack, Graham and Innes, by passing each other once or twice a lap, would be able to work their speed up fractionally higher than mine, so I maintained my solo pace and they soon joined me. What a wonderful race followed, as the four of us combined in a 140 mph square dance, continually swapping positions to gain maximum assistance from the slipstream.

The six-speed gearbox on the Cooper seemed to be giving me an advantage. While the others changed into top in their five-speed boxes, I could hang on to my fifth gear, which gave me a definite pull to the top of the rise on the straight. My engine was running sweetly and I hadn't revved over 8500 rpm. Three or four times we passed the pits side by side before barrelling into the long fast right-hander. At least twice Graham and I went into this corner abreast. I thought he would back off for an instant and tuck in behind, but he stayed on the outside all the way round. Graham was certainly putting faith in my judgment.

Surtees fell by the wayside after 26 laps and our high-speed argument over second place developed into a tussle for the lead. With about eight laps left I decided to test whether it was possible to get away from Graham and Jack. I started experimenting with braking distances, running further into the corners, and managed to pull out a slight lead. Going into the hairpin on the back of the circuit I left it really late, squeezing the brake pedal hard, but when I arrived at the part of the track where I normally locked over into the corner was still a fraction too fast. I squeezed the pedal harder and the right front wheel locked, with a puff of smoke from the tyre. Rather than risk a spin by trying to get round, I put the wheel straight again and shot down the escape road.

Fortunately there was another way around the back of the corner, which was simply a rounded-off section of a road junction. This was a handy unorthodox dodge if one was in trouble, but Graham and Jack had picked up a 100 yard lead by the time I got under way again. Next time past the pits I could see the despondency among the Cooper crew. They looked at me as though to say, "Oh no, what have you done?"

Now the car was really going. With only five laps left, I pulled out all the stops. It was worth extending things a bit and I started using an extra 300 revs, taking the engine up to 8800 rpm between gear changes. Within a lap I was back on the tail of Graham and Jack and soon I was in front. With those extra few revs I could pull out a second a lap and I cruised across the finishing line with a five-second lead.

That night there was plenty of champagne and a noisy dinner at the Café de la Paix, with a battle of bread rolls and sugar lumps between the Cooper and Brabham tables. The next morning John Cooper found his little Mini van on the footpath between two trees and it took the help of several French passers-by, who couldn't quite make out what was happening, to bump the van back on the street.

Bob Jane, an Australian who races Jaguars with great verve, was travelling to several of the Continental races with his wife Beverley in their E-type Jaguar and they accompanied us down to Rouen for the French Grand Prix the following week-end.

I was an early casualty at Rouen, when fourth gear sheared going into the uphill hairpin. I spun and hit the kerb, which broke the chassis. Fourth gear had gone, but cars were retiring one after the other, so I set off again, with the car handling a little oddly, and to my surprise and delight finished fourth.

Dan Gurney had given Porsche their first F1 win and was also celebrating his own first GP victory. That big grin was broader than ever!

Rouen was the scene of an after-race crash that could easily have been far more serious. For some obscure reason a long line of police formed up shoulder to shoulder between the track and pits, not letting anyone on the track and, worse, not letting anyone from the track into the pits. John Surtees limped across the line in a Lola that was barely mobile to be refused entry to the pits and had to swing on the track again, just as Trintignant crossed the line. Trint swerved to dodge the Lola, but as he did so Trevor Taylor's Lotus came whistling over the brow of the hill and the two cars collided in a huge cloud of dust. Miraculously neither driver was hurt, though each car lost a wheel.

Back in England the British GP at Aintree was another third-place race for me. Bob Jane had a drive in one of John Coombs' 3·8 Jaguars and, despite polite warnings at the start not to tangle with the "big boys", he blasted off the line and led the field in the opening laps, until a spot of bumper-tapping sent him spinning through Melling Crossing. Bob isn't the sort of driver to take tips from anyone and it was a pity he didn't have another race in a Jaguar before returning to Australia, where he cleaned up the series in his own 3·8 Jaguar, which he had bored out to just over 4 litres.

Patty and I motored to the German GP with Tony Shelly and his wife, Sylvienne, in their new 3·8 Jaguar. Tony had never been to the 'Ring before, so I took him round for a few laps just after we arrived. He was visibly impressed.

First official practice for the Grand Prix was on the Friday morning and all the teams were hard at work sorting out their respective cars—checking how much lower the bump stops could be set and how long the springs should be to avoid bottoming on the bumpy sections.

I started my first run a few seconds after Graham Hill had taken off in the BRM. The Cooper V8 sounded crisp and was handling nicely. I was swooping down into the Fuchsrohre, when a cloud of dust spelt trouble and I jammed on the brakes, stopping a little further up the hill to glimpse Graham and the BRM virtually out of sight behind a belt of trees.

Graham had come scorching down through the curves to find a large 16 mm movie camera lying in the middle of the track. He must have been doing 140 mph and straddled the camera, rather than run a wheel over it. Unfortunately BRM ground clearances weren't designed to cope with movie cameras and it ripped the bottom out of the oil tank.

Graham said later, "We turned sharp left." The car left the road and went ricocheting down a ditch for about 200 yards, getting farther and farther into the scrub. If I'd been any closer to Graham, I would probably have missed the warning cloud of dust, hit the oil and joined him in the ditch.

As it was Tony Maggs came down the hill flat out in the other Cooper V8, just as the flag marshal had "taken five" from the oil-warning flag to phone control. Tony arrived at speed to hit the contents of the BRM oil tank and revolve the Cooper. He said he tried to steer the car backwards, but it was difficult because of the bend!

Race day was terrible. Fog and rain reduced visibility to a few yards and a small avalanche on the back of the circuit held up the start. By the time we were called to the grid, most of the fog had lifted, but it was still teeming. I missed second gear off the line and this let half the field between my car and the leading trio, who left everyone standing.

Porsches had spent a lot of testing time at the Nürburgring and it wasn't surprising in these adverse conditions that Dan Gurney led for the first three laps. Graham and John Surtees then nipped past and the three cars circulated the streaming $14\frac{1}{2}$-mile circuit nose-to-tail for the rest of the race, to finish in that order. I placed a very damp fifth, having driven in borrowed kit as my racing bag had been stolen from the boot of the Jaguar, while it was in the paddock. I also lost my wallet, with all my racing documents, and was surprised a few months later when this arrived looking very much the worse for wear, having spent some time at the bottom of a river. It had been found and returned to the German race organizers, who mailed it to me.

There was plenty happening back in Surbiton. Coopers were busy building a new Cooper-Monaco sports car for me to race in California and down in Tommy Atkins' little workshop at

Chessington, Harry and Wally were working on a new Cooper for the "down under" season.

Earlier in the year Tommy had arranged with Coopers to buy a F1 chassis with suspension parts and fit it with a BRM V8 engine, for me to drive in races the works team were missing. By the end of June it was obvious the BRM engine would not be ready in time, so I asked Tommy to sell me the chassis, so that I could fit it with a 2½-litre engine. Prompting this was a letter from the organizers of the Australian GP to be held at Perth in conjunction with the Commonwealth Games in November. Tommy's offer suited me perfectly:

"Harry and Wally can put it together in the workshop as you want it," he said, "we'll try and keep the charges reasonable and you can have Harry to help you look after it again." By mid-September we had the car running and down at Goodwood.

On the first day the chassis was flexing and the car rolling too much in the corners, so we took it back to the workshop and set it up on stands, applying some twist to the chassis to find where it might be flexing. The large engine bay was the main trouble-spot, so we braced this area and also strengthened the front wishbone points. We also fitted larger steering arms.

To stop the car rolling we borrowed some stiffer springs from the Cooper works and cut off a couple of coils to get the chassis sitting at the right height. We brought the ends of the springs back flat and square, by standing all but the top coil of the spring in a bucket of water, heating the top coil, then flattening and grinding it off so that our modification looked quite professional.

The second day at Goodwood was much better. With adjustments to camber and tyre pressures I soon had my times down to a fraction over 1 min 20 sec and managed a flier late in the day at 1 min 19·8 sec, faster than anyone had ever been round the circuit.

Earlier we had been to Monza for the Italian GP and after a race-long slipstreaming dice, which ended with an outfumbling match against Willy Mairesse's Ferrari on the last lap, I was pleased to place third behind Graham and Richie in the BRMs.

The Gold Cup race at Oulton Park was exciting and could easily have had dangerous consequences for me. It had been my birthday on the day before practice, so I suggested to John that we should have a day testing at the circuit. I was even rash enough to promise I would put the Cooper on the front row of the grid.

In view of what followed, it was ironical that a salesman had spent most of his lunchtime trying to sell us fire extinguishers. He lit a couple of petrol fires and put them out very smartly. Just the job, we said, but we're fairly well off for fire extinguishers at the moment, thank you.

As promised, I managed a position on the front row and the race soon settled down into the pattern of so many in 1962: Jimmy, Graham, then myself. I was about five seconds behind Graham, having a dice with Richie, who had surprised everybody by being faster than Graham in practice.

I thought I had a fighting chance of catching Graham, especially when there was a strong smell of burning. Surely this was the BRM clutch starting to slip.

Then my engine cut, picked up and cut out again, as though the ignition had been switched off. I glanced at the fuel pressure gauge and saw that it was flickering. It had all the symptoms of a loose wire on the fuel pump, so I coasted into Lodge Corner heading for the pits. The smell of burning was suddenly stronger and I suddenly realized it wasn't the BRM clutch—it was the Cooper on fire!

Smoke started drifting through the cockpit and I was glad to be near the pits. Then a tongue of flame licked up and I changed my mind, steering for the grass verge and hauling myself up to stand on the seat. Then I remembered there was no one near with an extinguisher and the £7,000 car stood a good chance of going up in smoke if I abandoned it there. Looking a lot braver than I felt, I steered back on to the track and coasted the hundred yards to the pits, before slipping it into gear and hopping overboard.

After lapping a circuit at speed one becomes velocitized and instead of moving at about 5 mph, as I thought, it was probably nearer 15. I almost went a header and John and the mechanics had a job to stop the car. One of the boys pushed a small CO_2 extinguisher into the cockpit and put out the blaze, which centred on the battery box, then some valiant fire-fighter triggered off a huge extinguisher and foam was spraying everywhere.

The gravity of the situation was lessened by the gentleman in question trying to hold his thumb over the nozzle of the extinguisher and wrestle it into submission, while it continued to spray everything in range with clinging white foam. The Cooper looked like a runaway advertisement for soap powder.

The Monaco sports car was already on its way to California when we left for the American GP at Watkins Glen. Patty and I were to fly from Watkins Glen to California for two sports car races there, on to Mexico City for their Grand Prix, then globe-hopping to Perth. My secretary, Eoin Young, was travelling with us, then flying from California direct to Perth, to meet Wally, who was flying from England. Eoin, also a New Zealander, had been working with me for a year, having returned from Australia with us at the end of the previous season. He had already spent a year in Europe during 1961, covering the races as a free-lance journalist.

The Ford Motor Company looked after us well in America. On arrival at Idlewild international airport we had our choice from a long line of new Thunderbirds and Galaxies for the 200-mile drive to the top of New York State. We chose one of the monster Galaxies, threaded our way through the outskirts of New York, and arrived at Watkins Glen late that night.

The weather was bleak, cold and uninspiring for the race, in which I finished third once again, this time behind Jimmy and Graham. Clark's win made him the only driver with a chance of pipping Graham Hill for the 1962 championship, but he had to win the South African race to do so.

Fog at the local airport meant taxis to the next 'drome, and a series of near-misses, which ended with us climbing into a Boeing just before the telescopic gangway was drawn in. For a moment we thought we had rushed to catch an empty plane. There were only three other people in the tourist section and we had royal attention from the almost out-of-work hostesses on the trip across America.

I was worried that the new Monaco would be too heavy, because it had been designed to take either a large American V8 engine, or the 2·7 Coventry-Climax.

Roger Penske proved the star of the series in his FUBAR (Fouled Up Beyond All Recognition) special, as his highly-modified, trim little central-seater sports car, based on a 1961 F1 Cooper, had been christened. Dan Gurney and Indianapolis driver Lloyd Ruby were fast in their Lotus 19s, but they failed to last the distance and Penske cleaned up both the Riverside and Laguna Seca races.

At dinner on the night before the Riverside race we had jokingly suggested that whoever won should stand the others a trip to Las Vegas. After winning both races, Roger could afford the trip and we all enjoyed a few days in the gay, garish, gambling capital of the world. Roger topped off his race wins by collecting 500 dollars on the tables.

After Laguna Seca, Mike Barney went straight to Mexico City to prepare the F1 car. The autodrome circuit there is 7,000 feet above sea level and for the first few days we all felt weak. After walking any distance we had to take a rest to regain our breath. The Climax V8s had the same trouble and it took quite a bit of tinkering with carburation to get them running right.

Mexico City was the home-town of the Rodriguez brothers and they were tremendous favourites with the crowds at both practice and the race. It was tragic that Ricardo, while trying hard to improve his qualifying time in the Rob Walker Lotus V8, lost control on the bumpy banking and was killed. The new autodrome was later named after him as a tribute.

The start of the Grand Prix was a shambles. We all sat on the grid with motors revving, waiting for the man with the flag to do something, when there was frantic activity round Jimmy Clark's Lotus. It wouldn't start and the race was held up while mechanics tried desperately to trace the trouble.

It was a hot day and engines soon began to overheat, the temperatures rising as fast as the drivers' tempers. Then there was a puff of smoke from John Surtees' Lola. The transistor ignition "black box" had exploded! A car on the other side of the grid was on fire. An oil line had melted.

Minutes later the race started with the stricken cars being rushed to one side. I soon found myself in the lead and, as the Cooper sang along with all the gauges reading favourably, I seemed set fair for a Mexican win. Jimmy had taken over Trevor Taylor's Lotus and he was really flying through the pack, however. He would probably have passed me before the end of the race anyway, but my engine didn't give him the chance, expiring with a clatter. I watched Jimmy rocketing on to win, despite all his starting bothers, as I walked back to the pits.

A fortnight later I was due on the starting line in my own 2·7-litre Intercontinental Cooper half-way across the world in Perth and looked forward to the race. The Cooper had shown promise of things to come during testing and I was keen to see how it would perform in its first competition.

We reached Perth with a few days to spare and booked in at a brand-new, American-style motel, just completed for the Commonwealth Games, which were due to start a few days after the Grand Prix.

The Cooper had been shipped out and Wally and I collected it from the docks. Jack had been short of time building his Intercontinental Brabham and flew it out in the hold of a Boeing.

A few days before the race, we discovered the chest containing all our racing tools had been stolen from the boot of our tender car, parked outside the motel. We called the police, also the local television and radio stations, asking them to help recover the tools. Their news-flashes throughout the day brought a phone call to the motel proprietor by an unidentified caller, who said he had hidden the tool box under a tree in one of the local parks. A police squad rushed to the park and combed it unsuccessfully, apparently watched by the culprit. When the search was called off, he phoned the police station and told them exactly where the tools were hidden.

The 2½-mile Caversham circuit near Perth had just been re-surfaced and there was still plenty of loose metal on the track, as I discovered early on the first practice day. The Cooper went a little wide on one corner, and as I tried to correct it, the tail went on to a patch of pebbles and I lost it. A large rock hidden in the grass stove in the nose, fortunately without damaging the radiator. The car looked a sorry sight as I drove slowly back to the pits and understandably no one in my little team looked impressed at my efforts. We soon found a couple of local panel-beaters willing to work late that night to repair the damage and next morning the Cooper looked like new.

Brabham and I were easily the fastest in practice, but Jack was having his troubles and blew up a couple of engines during the sessions. I lent him my spare 2·5-litre Climax, so that he could start in the race.

Caversham was the sort of circuit to even out the 200 cc capacity advantage, as the extra permissible revs with the 2·5 unit almost made up the difference.

I had my handling problems, too. The special springs from the Atkins workshop improved my car so much that we had decided to try them on the F1 car at Monza and my Inter-continental Cooper had been sent to Perth fitted with the original unsuitable springs. Coopers had ordered duplicates of our modified springs and Wally flew to Perth with a set crammed in a grossly overweight overnight bag, but someone had mixed things up, for when we put them on the car we found that they would have suspended a truck. They were the stronger springs made for the Monaco sports car, but we were committed to using them at Perth and the Cooper was very twitchy.

I leapt into the lead with tyres smoking and held an advantage Jack couldn't do much about, though he was certainly trying. Making a determined effort in the closing laps, he nipped through on the inside of a slower driver, who thought he was going on the outside. Jack was forced into a marker fence, ripping the nose off his car and damaging the radiator. This left me untroubled, to enjoy a win first time out with my new car.

The local BMC agents had imported one of the first Mini-Coopers in Western Australia and were keen for me to race it. We had prepared one of these cars for the New Zealand races before leaving England, so we soon converted the little Mini-Cooper to a real racer, using a special Downton exhaust system that Wally had managed to disguise as a toothbrush in his suitcase, for the benefit of the Customs Department.

With the time and materials available we weren't able to make it as potent as the Mini-Cooper we had sent to New Zealand, but the little car was still capable of seeing off most of the local opposition, though many of them refused to believe it until the race was over. I finished sixth in the touring car event behind an E-type Jaguar, a Ford Galaxie, a Lotus-Elite and a couple of stove-hot Holdens. The BMC agents were delighted.

We all flew to New Zealand after the Perth race and a week after we arrived there, while Patricia went home to Christchurch, and Wally and Eoin paid annual visits to their parents in Timaru, I boarded a plane for South Africa and the final Grand Prix in the world championship series. If Jimmy won the race at East London, he was champion, but if Graham did so, it was his title—things were that close.

I drove to East London with Tony and Gaile Maggs from their home in Pretoria and was looking forward to arriving after their tales of the surfing there. It was an 800-mile trip, but Tony said if we took turns at driving his Alfa Romeo, we could manage it in one night.

Soon after we started I began to feel ill and on taking over the wheel I felt worse. I couldn't concentrate, was seeing double and soon wandered over the road. Tony hurriedly said that he couldn't sleep and perhaps ought to drive again. I was grateful to let him.

We arrived in East London early in the morning, with the sun beating down and the surf roaring. But it was bed for me. The kindly hotel proprietors called a doctor, who diagnosed a bad attack of influenza. While everyone else was living it up in the surf and sun, I had three days in bed, just making the first practice session, still a little off colour.

Cooper and Lotus both had a new fuel-injected Coventry-Climax V8 to try and my car had been fitted with a new V-shaped nose that was far from beautiful, but we were experimenting with a special V-shaped radiator. Apart from spending time in the pits getting the fuel injection sorted out, I was having bother with a leaking water pump and the new radiator didn't seem to be handling the cooling very well. With the after-effects of my 'flu added, I was well down the list on the first practice. On the following day, however, I felt better and managed to equal the time Tony had set the day before with the carburettor Cooper.

Jimmy had been trying his new fuel injection engine, but as he turned in fastest lap with the carburettor Lotus he decided to use the latter for the race.

Tony made a great start and was away on the exhausts of Clark and Hill, but couldn't hold the pace of the championship contenders and dropped back to battle with John Surtees and me. Jimmy was drawing away from Graham, who could do little but hope something would happen to the flying Lotus. Surtees' Lola dropped out with a broken gearbox, leaving our Coopers third and fourth, running nose to tail.

By half-distance Jimmy had a full half-minute lead, but a few laps later wisps of smoke from the tail of the Lotus hinted of unpleasant things to come and soon he was laying a smoke-screen. It meant throwing away the championship, but there was nothing Colin Chapman could do but call Jimmy in before the engine blew up. Mechanics fell on the car almost before it stopped rolling and discovered a small bolt, plugging the housing for the distributor jackshaft, had unscrewed itself and oil was spraying out. Rules forbid adding oil during a race, so Jimmy's valiant championship challenge was over.

This left Graham almost a minute ahead of our Coopers, so he could afford to relax and make sure of his title. We couldn't afford to take time off, as Jack was flying behind us in the Brabham and had closed to within three seconds of Tony when the flag fell.

Graham Hill's title was due reward for hard work. His climb to the top had been almost too difficult to credit. Only seven years earlier he was unable to drive a car of any description and had taken a job as a racing mechanic to gain experience.

My second placing was a fitting climax to a successful season and I finished third in the championship, three points behind Jimmy.

Graham had little time to enjoy his win, as we had to leave on the following day for the New Zealand GP, which was less than a week away. Graham, Tony and Gaile, John Surtees, Jack, Innes, Reg Parnell, a few of the mechanics and myself set off on the long trip half-way across the world, but were held up in Karachi waiting for a jet that had been snowed in at London Airport. Most of us had yellow fever vaccinations, but those who didn't, Graham among them, were confined under quarantine in the airport jail. Not the most pleasant New Year's Eve for a world champion.

We were eventually bundled on another plane bound for Sydney and a group of very weary travellers eventually stepped off in Auckland, on the eve of first practice for the Grand Prix.

SIXTEEN

A Successful "Down Under" Season

MOTOR RACING IN New Zealand has progressed since the days of the stripped-down specials on the beach. The 1963 GP was to be held on a new circuit, finished a few days before the race. It was built round a horse-racing track at Pukekohe about 30 miles from Auckland and the new venue was a credit to the club.

For the '63 season, Jack had signed with the Brabham he shunted at Perth; John Surtees and Tony Maggs formed the Bowmaker racing team of two 2·7 Lolas; Graham Hill was driving the front-engined, four-wheel-drive 2·5 Ferguson, while Innes was actively engaged in being a spectator. He was to drive the Ferguson in the other three New Zealand races, while Graham took over again in Australia.

The Cooper was flying in practice and I had little trouble making pole position on the grid. I think everyone has a sense of patriotic pride when it comes to doing well on one's home ground. Footballers generally do better in home games and after practice I felt more confident than ever before that I could realize an ambition by winning the Grand Prix. Everything seemed to be going right. Even the little Mini-Cooper had proved only a fraction slower than the fastest 3·8 Jaguar.

I had suggested to the organizers that it might be a good idea to enter the Mini-Cooper in the class for saloons over 2000 cc, to provide a "David and Goliath" spectacle for added excitement. Some agreed, others opposed it, but it was fixed that I should run with the bigger cars. On race day officialdom changed its mind three times, however, and eventually I was allowed to start with the bigger cars—providing I started from the back row! I was furious, as my practice times placed me beside McBeth's 3·8 Jaguar on the front row.

Apparently some of the drivers with big American coupés had protested that they didn't want the Mini under their front wheels as they accelerated away. I passed most of these monsters before the first corner, within a couple of laps was running with the first three and a lap later led the field. The crowd thought it was wonderful. So did I and the BMC agents were thrilled. For three laps I kept my nearest opponents, McBeth in the Jaguar and Ernie Sprague in his red-hot Zephyr, behind me, but the temperature started to rise, forcing me to ease off slightly. The Jaguar went by in the closing laps, but I was able to sit on his tail and the three of us crossed the line only inches apart.

As we took the grid for the Grand Prix I felt tremendous. I had resolved to make a good start, without too much wheel-spin, and hadn't quite enough revs up when I dropped the clutch. John Surtees streaked ahead of me as we went underneath the India Bridge and into a tight hairpin. We had already made a break on the field and though John was driving the Lola fast, I knew I could pick him up. Within seven laps I headed him, moving away at a second a lap. The field was starting to dissolve. Tony's Lola had jumped out of gear at the start and he was in the pits with a bent valve. Jack's Brabham went out with a blown head gasket after nine laps. Behind John and me came Graham in the Ferguson, feeling his way cautiously. The sun was giving Graham a roasting behind the engine.

Racing never seemed better as my lead increased with each

lap, but suddenly I felt the engine falter for a second. It must have been imagination? But a few minutes later it ran ragged again for a second or two. Soon it sounded right off song and the Lola began drawing nearer. Diagnosing a faulty spark plug, I whistled into the pits where Wally and Harry waited apprehensively. They whipped back the tail and, while one checked and changed the plugs, the other quickly checked the car. With the tail slammed down again I was off with wheels spinning, but it took only another couple of laps to realize that plugs weren't at fault. This time we discovered one of the petrol tanks had split as well. This clearly must be a race I wasn't meant to win.

I sat dejectedly on the pit counter and watched Surtees, now minutes ahead of Graham in the Ferguson, strolling on to take the chequered flag in "my" race. Behind him cars were still dropping out. Shelly blew his engine trying to catch Hyslop's Cooper; Amon, in the Cooper I had raced the previous season, was hit with ignition trouble. On the last lap a gearbox shaft broke in the Ferguson and a very hot and angry world champion stormed back to the pits on foot, while Angus Hyslop took second spot and Jimmy Palmer was third, in a 2·7 Cooper loaned to him by the Bowmaker team. It was Jimmy's 21st birthday and he couldn't have wanted a better present. I was fed up.

As things couldn't get worse, I consoled myself, they had to get better. Once again I was wrong. It looked like being a close race at Levin, but the Cooper refused to fire as we push-started it for the first heat. We had discovered by this time that the magneto was at fault. It had caused the engine to misfire twice towards the end of the Perth race, though I had thought nothing of it at the time, but the trouble made its presence decisively felt at Pukekohe. We had the magneto thoroughly checked and were assured our troubles had ended. At Levin they seemed to be starting again.

With a new magneto hurriedly fitted, I thought we were

ready for racing, but our next attempt at starting revealed something amiss in the clutch. Harry and Wally set some sort of record pulling off the Colotti gearbox, finding and fixing the trouble and bolting everything together again, but by this time the heat was over.

Innes had roared into the lead with the Ferguson, using the four-wheel-drive to advantage. "It seemed as though Brabham had been tied to a tree," he commented afterwards. The car was a little unsteady on a trailing throttle going into corners, however, and gear selection troubles dropped Innes down the field as Jack took over the lead.

Missing the heat meant I was placed well back on the grid, a real handicap on a short, tight circuit like Levin, but I was determined to catch Jack and in a few hectic laps reached his tail. We were both shattering the lap record and I'm not sure what the outcome would have been because after 18 laps, when just two seconds behind the sliding Brabham tail, I hung the Cooper way out on the bumpy Cabbage Tree bend, clouting a pile of marker tyres with the nose, spinning the car and altering the camber of the front wheel.

So for the second time in a week I was a spectator before a race was half over and didn't feel particularly interested in the fact that Jack had won his first international race with the Brabham.

Between races we had been touring the Mini-Cooper, show-ing Tony and Gaile Maggs the beauty spots of the North Island.

While in Hamilton Lenny Gilbert took us water ski-ing on a nearby lake and introduced me to tobogganing on water. A light plywood toboggan with handrails was tied on behind a speedboat and, with two aboard, set off in the wake. This part was easy, the art of riding the toboggan was to rock it clear of the wake, at which point the driver of the boat started to turn, so that the toboggan began to orbit the boat outside the wake. Centrifugal force threatened to throw off the riders at any minute and the flat-bottomed toboggan bounced and scudded sideways across the water at nearly 60 mph.

Eoin and I were doing well until we came round on the wake of another boat. The toboggan and the pair of us bounced high in the air—still at about 60 mph—and we bounded head over heels on the surface before going under. The fun lasted until, in one memorable shunt, the toboggan broke in half.

After a frustrating season, my luck changed when we went south. During practice for the Lady Wigram Trophy race on the airfield circuit, we found D12 tyres might not last the distance if it were a hot day and the going hard. To be sure of having enough rubber for the race in the event of a lengthy dice, D9s were advisable, but as these were about two seconds a lap slower than the D12s round Wigram, they would have involved playing a cautious, waiting game. This was not the style of racing Surtees, Brabham and I were using at the time. So there we were, all on the front row of the grid with D12s when the flag went up, feeling a little insecure in the knowledge that if we had a ding-dong scrap for the whole race, we would probably end up with blow-outs.

John made the best start and I followed him into the Hangar Bend, with Jack on my tail.

We kept this close order for a lap, but entering the tight hairpin next time round found the contents of an Aston Martin's oil tank spread across the road. John went one side of the pool and I went the other, managing to sneak into the lead by finding a slightly better path. On the left-hander into the pit straight there was another flood of oil—those old Astons must have held an awful lot of it!

It was a relief in one sense, as with two out of the seven corners very slippery and a third getting that way, we knew tyre wear would be kept down.

Things were settling down nicely after about 20 laps. I'd been keeping a close watch on the red nose of the Lola in my mirrors and noticed that Surtees appeared to be in a haze of oil smoke. But if it was his smoke, the haze should have been behind him, not in front, and I realized my car must be laying the screen.

Normally the 2·7 Climax burned little oil and I began to get worried. I eased up slightly, paying close attention to the oil pressure and temperature gauges, and thought I'd better check pit signals next time round to see how far Jack was behind.

As I was about to lock over into the hairpin, however, the Brabham arrived beside me with wheels locked and tyres smoking. I'd forgotten Jack had been on the tail of the Lola. Now he had nipped into the lead and as I wasn't keen on playing follow-my-leader with him, we really started to fly, using all the track out of the corners. We had wheels on the grass, and must have been using our tyres at an alarming rate.

Jack's car started to puff oil smoke and I heaved a sigh of relief as he pulled into the pits to take on more oil. Now I had a lead of about 80 sec, but needed it. Jack and I had different types of pistons in our 2·7 engines. He was using a type which didn't break but used a lot of oil because they had only two piston rings. Mine had three rings and didn't use very much oil, but the rings had a tendency to break occasionally and this was what had happened. Two of the piston ring lands had broken. This caused a slight loss of power, but it was also pressurizing the crankcase and blowing oil out of every joint and seal in the engine.

With 25 laps to go I was running dangerously low on oil. Going round corners the oil would surge away from the pick-up in the tank and the pressure was dropping to zero. A quick calculation showed I still had 80 sec on Jack with 25 laps to go, which meant I could afford to let him catch up nearly three seconds a lap. There was just a chance.

The last 10 laps of that Wigram race were the longest I've ever done. I was expecting the oil pressure to drop to zero and stay there and had signalled the position to my crew, who were ready for a quick pit stop. But stops are always dangerous and I didn't particularly want one.

When the chequered flag at last came out, I had barely two quarts of oil left in a tank that normally holds three and a half gallons and, although I had cruised the last 20 laps, my outside rear tyre had only half a millimetre of usable rubber on it. Jack had pressed on in the closing stages and had completely bald rear tyres. Had we kept up our mid-race pace, we would certainly have worn out our tyres. Tony Maggs took third place in the Lola, but didn't know how close he came to winning.

Harry and Wally stripped the engine after the Wigram race and fitted new pistons, before setting off for Invercargill. Fortunately we decided to trundle round on the day before the first official practice, to run in the new pistons, as the following day was cold and showery, with strong gusts of wind dissuading anyone from breaking records. Jack was lapping fairly rapidly, but when his car was tossed sideways at the end of the straight by a sudden gust, he changed his mind and went back to his hotel.

This race also featured a couple of crowd-pleasing short heats to sort out grid positions and give the spectators value for money. They had their fill in our heat. Innes now had the measure of the Ferguson and left the line in a shower of small stones and rubber smoke. It took me several laps to work out where I would be able to pass him, but I was leading well before the finish.

Jack and John Surtees were paired in the second heat and the verdict went to the Brabham by a short head, but I was worried by the fact that both had been lapping nearly a second quicker than my fastest. Resolving to make an exemplary start, I covered the first 20 yards in low gear, botched the change to second and half the field had streamed by before I sorted out the right slot and got under way. The two Lolas had started well, John leading Tony on the first lap, but Jack was soon in front. John spun in a patch of oil on one of the tight left-handers and, though he battled his way back to third place, a couple of pit stops with a faulty fuel pump dropped him from the running.

I passed Tony to get on Jack's tail and for 19 laps raced in his wheel-tracks. Just as I was beginning to think the Brabham wall was impenetrable, he "opened the gate" inadvertently at the end of the straight and I was through.

But I was well aware my first mistake would find me staring down the Brabham exhaust pipe again. About 10 laps later, when I had managed to pull out a few seconds on Jack, he realized pieces of rubber were flying past his ears. With oil on the inside of some of the corners, we had been forced to use the coarser surface on the outside, which had torn the rubber off our tyres and Jack finally wore his right rear through to the air with a lap to go—and clanked home on the rim in fourth place behind Tony and Innes.

Angus Hyslop had made a brief pit stop to change his goggles after a stone had shattered a lens and cut his face, but he set off again in his Cooper and crossed the line side by side with Tony Shelly's Lotus. His consistent performances that season won Angus the New Zealand Gold Star.

Tony and I were lifted up through the sunroof of a Bentley to perch there for the victory lap and Innes, not to be outdone, opened the boot-lid and sat on it for half the lap, before climbing up over the roof to join us.

The Australian GP was a fortnight away, giving ample time to ship our cars from Wellington to Sydney. Jack had sold his car to Sydney journalist David McKay and was waiting to collect a new Brabham from the docks in time for the race. The ship had made a detour to aid another vessel in distress, however, and the Brabham was late arriving. At Melbourne Jack found his car was buried beneath the huge crates containing Donald Campbell's *Bluebird* and tons of spares. The Brabham patience must have run very thin on the wharf and I doubt if he shared in the general consternation when Bluebird almost rolled into the sea. He and Tim Wall were at the circuit for the second day of practice, looking very weary as they put the finishing touches to the new car.

John Surtees, aiming at a Grand Prix double for the series, was sitting on a pole position with the Lola. My Cooper and McKay, who had settled in very quickly with his Brabham, completed the front row. The surprise of the practice session was Sydney driver Frank Matich, in a little locally-built Formula Junior Elfin. This pretty little machine had been fitted with a 1500 cc Ford engine and Matich must have impressed even himself when he equalled the times of Maggs and Amon in their 2·7-litre cars. He was little more than a second behind John and me.

Jack had his hands full with teething troubles, and was on the last row but one. I think both Surtees and I had crossed him off our danger list and resolved to concentrate on each other.

Race day was roastingly hot. We packed dry ice round our fuel and just before climbing aboard I filled my pockets with ice and emptied a watering can into the seat. This tremendous heat was to have a profound effect on the results.

Surtees made a good start and McKay followed him into the first corner. I knew I had to latch on to the Lola before Surtees made a break, so nipped past McKay on the second lap—and promptly spun, dropping myself to the middle of the field.

The huge crowd had been roaring encouragement to Jack at the start and he had soon carved his way through the pack to second place. But even Jack on top form—as he undoubtedly was that day—could not have reeled in the lead Surtees had built up. I was back in third place again, but well out of arguing distance. The heat was merciless and several exhausted drivers were stopping to have a bucket of water doused over them. What a luxury that would have been. In such heat one's feet and legs blister and one longs for a drink.

Surtees was feeling the effect of the heat and a momentary lapse caused a spin. He recovered immediately, but the Lola was in the Brabham sights and the race was all over bar the shouting. There was plenty of that. Jack, using more grass than road, closed in and passed the Lola, carrying on to win his first-ever Australian GP in his own car, that had still been on the drawing-board 12 months previously. McKay and Bib Stillwell brought their Brabhams home fourth and fifth behind me, so it was a real day of triumph for Jack.

He unwisely called at our motel on his way home and my crew showed their appreciation by tossing him fully-dressed into the swimming pool. Jack probably expected it, anyway.

Patricia and I motored up to Surfers Paradise with Bob and Beverley Jane, to fit in some water ski-ing before the race at Lakeside. This was disastrous. Bob's speedboat, with Patricia, Beverley, myself and a driver aboard, capsized in freak conditions while Bob was ski-ing behind and threw us all into the water. Patricia is a strong swimmer, but she was run over by the propellor, which smashed one ankle and lacerated the other. The boat had righted itself and was starting to circle our struggling group on the water, dragging a rope which was starting to wind itself round Beverley. While I supported Patricia, the boat was brought under control and we made a dash for shore where an alerted ambulance was waiting to rush Patricia to the local hospital. The bones in her left ankle and heel were badly smashed and she had a lengthy and painful session in a thigh-high plaster cast ahead.

I stayed at a motel near the hospital, commuting the 30 miles to the circuit. During practice and the race heats it was tropically hot and humid, but the following day a thunderstorm deluged the circuit.

John Youl and Bib Stillwell dashed into the lead before the storm broke and within a couple of laps I was backwards in the long grass, having dodged a spinning car. I set off again as fast as I dared, but a few laps later scudded straight off the track on a huge pool of water that had formed on the pit straight. I must have been doing about 110 mph when I hit the water, but

16

fortunately the car wasn't damaged and came to rest a few feet from one of the lakes.

John Surtees sorted out the opposition in his Lola, specially fitted with one of the Monaco snub-noses, and Graham Hill, who had at last come to grips with the Ferguson, took second place half a minute behind. Altogether 15 of the 22 starters spun off the road while the storm raged.

Patricia recovered sufficiently to leave hospital and fly down to Melbourne, where she stayed with Beverley Jane, while Bob and I went across to Longford in Tasmania. It was the first time I had seen this 4½-mile road circuit and it impressed me. The average lap speed is over 115 mph; one straight gives speeds of over 170 mph, another something over 160 mph. The flavour of true road racing is captured on the Longford circuit, which has a pub corner where the regulars lean on the bar and watch the cars flashing past the window, a railway crossing with trains that sometimes interrupt practice—one handicap race was stopped a couple of laps short to let the "local" through—a very solid looking brick viaduct and a long and bumpy wooden bridge.

Ferrari had called Surtees back to Italy for testing, and only three of the "internationals"—Jack, Tony and myself—were at Longford. Jack was cutting things fine, as he had flown back to England after Warwick Farm and didn't arrive at Longford until the second practice day. This soon ended for Jack, when a piston broke and he and Tim Wall dashed off to change engines before the afternoon's heats. They were still working on the car when the first heat started. I was too miserly with revs at the start and stalled, feeling very relieved when everyone managed to scrape past without coming over the top or taking one of my rear wheels with them. In a few laps I was back in the scrap the Aussie boys were having—a crowd-pleaser with positions changing several times a lap—and had established a short lead when, coming out of a low-gear corner, a drive-shaft yoke burst. Fortunately the shaft dropped neatly down on the bottom wishbone and lay there without flailing around. Now we were in real trouble. We hadn't foreseen breaking this part and had no spare.

The Repco branch in nearby Launceston and Merv Gray's little engineering shop probably did a better trade that Sunday than during the entire previous week. Jack had arrived in time for the second heat, but further engine trouble dropped him from the lead. Merv managed to make a new drive-shaft yoke for us and we installed it with suitable prayers that it would stay together for the race.

We rose on race morning to find the wind had turned. In practice we had been slowed on the straight by a 10 mph wind, but now a similar breeze was behind us. To avoid over-revving on the long straight, we decided to make a last-minute ratio change. This was fortunate, as we discovered a cracked ball-race in the gearbox.

The pace was a cracker, at least for the first 15 laps of the race. I had decided to use the harder D9 tyres, which gave me a little more speed down the straights, while Jack was using the softer D12s, which gave him an advantage on the slower corners. We were racing nose to tail and I was disappointed—and relieved—when the Brabham suddenly and spectacularly enveloped itself in smoke and dropped most of its oil on the track. I felt sorry for Jack, as I know what it is like to have made such a great effort to prepare a car, then fail to finish. A small oil pipe had broken.

His misfortune left me with an 80 sec lead over Stillwell in his Brabham and I was able to cruise to the finish. Tony's Lola seemed to be falling to pieces round him. One of the oil-carrying chassis tubes had fractured and was spraying him with oil and one of the rear radius rods had come adrift.

The Sandown Park meeting was largely a repetition of the Tasmanian race. Practice times had shown Jack and I were comfortably faster than the field and we set off for the first few laps swapping places for the fun of it, to see who could get away. We soon convinced ourselves we were stuck with each other in a race we both badly wanted to win. We passed each other repeatedly and our race times were dropping two seconds under our best in practice. Both of us were revving over the limit, but after all it was the last race in the series!

I had taken the precaution of asking Wally to change big-end bolts after the engine-punishing Tasmanian meeting and had reason to be glad of this. With a lap and a half left Jack had a lead I didn't think I could break and I was settling down to second place when he slowed suddenly right in front of me, with smoke billowing out under the engine cover. I swerved to miss him and looked round to see Jack hopping over the side and start pushing to the finishing line. A big-end bolt had let go in his engine.

This was a triumphant climax to my most successful season, in my own car. Of the nine races in the international series which started at Perth, I had won five. Luck had been with me and but for Jack's engine trouble I might not have won so many. But luck is part of motor racing and winning is what matters.

One must be able to finish a motor race before one can win it and to do this one needs a fast, reliable, well-prepared car and a competent crew. For that 1963 season "down under" I had both.

SEVENTEEN

The Road to Success

No MATTER WHERE you go, people will ask for the secret of success in motor racing and why some drivers are better than others. The answer is the same as for nine out of ten other sports: the first essential is enthusiasm. Not just mild, but burning enthusiasm. To succeed in motor racing or in any sport, it must be the most important thing in your life.

This goes for many things other than motor racing in particular or sport in general, because if it isn't the most important thing to you, there are a dozen other people for whom it is. Those are the people you have to beat.

You must eat, live and think motor racing. The more you think about it and plan, the better you will do. "Scheme" is probably a better word than "think". Stirling Moss used to think about racing more than anyone else I know and John Surtees comes a close second. Jack Brabham is another for whom his sport is everything.

When I get wound up in a project, whether it is one of Cooper's new F1 cars or building my own cars for New Zealand and Australia, everything else is made secondary to it. Everything. I often force myself to go to sleep when trying to worry out a problem, or I am stuck with it all night. I decided long since that solid sleep is one of the first essentials when trying to work hard. It is more a question of attitude of mind than anything else. The people who succeed in racing are those who would do so in any walk of life.

First comes natural ability—and there are hundreds with it—but there must always be the dedication to want to apply it, continue applying it and keep improving it.

Motor racing is unlike some other sports, in fact it is sometimes argued that it isn't a sport at all because one uses machinery and its efficiency is the important thing. This is true, of course, but it is common knowledge that with any piece of equipment, be it a good gun, a good yacht, or a good racing car, one person or one crew will do better with it than the others—and here lies the big difference between one competitor and the next.

Grand Prix drivers all have considerable ability, otherwise they wouldn't get to the stage of driving GP cars. It usually involves a pretty selective apprenticeship, but once having reached the GP driver stage, there can be two types of person. One is the pure, natural driver, who wants to go fast and win in any car or anybody's car; the other loves the machinery as much as the race itself. Going through a list of drivers, one can generally put them in one category or the other. Sometimes mechanical knowledge will compensate for the other's slightly better driving ability—sometimes the latter will exceed the former—or vice-versa.

Among the top three drivers there are generally one of each of these types and even those who say they know nothing about cars can surprise you with their knowledge. I like to feel a combination of driver and car is important. I'm sure Jack Brabham feels the same way and that's why he is building his own car. By winning with one's own car, both the other drivers and the other cars have been beaten.

The usual ambition once a person becomes serious about motor racing is to be a works driver. This is the pinnacle of GP racing, but one can go beyond it, full circle. The normal beginning is driving one's own car . . . when driving my F2 car in 1958, my big ambition was to become a works driver for the Cooper factory. Now I enjoy nothing better than running my own cars again.

One can't always do as well as the works, but there is often far more satisfaction in it and one can do as one wants. Sometimes much quicker—especially when it comes to testing and organization. Say you feel you ought to change the gear ratio, there isn't a half-hour discussion to convince the team manager of the need to do so, followed by another half hour while he convinces the mechanics. By then it's probably lunch time, so the half-hour job can easily take three hours. That is, of course, if you are able to convince anyone that the ratio should be changed. And woe betide you if you are wrong, and it has to be changed back again.

All this doesn't happen if you own the car, drive it and manage the team yourself—you just change the gear ratio. This may be one reason why Jack Brabham is getting on so well. Although his car may not be one of the best-designed in GP racing, it does appear to be one of the best handling cars—and handling depends about 50-50 on design and development-testing, in which Jack has been able to make considerable refinements. He has been able to make adjustments and try them with very little fuss. This is sometimes why small manufacturers—perhaps like Lotus and Cooper at the outset—defeat the larger teams. The big organization can get well and truly tied down with red tape and protocol.

How fit must one be to drive a racing car? I've personally always been interested in physical fitness. When very young I used to play rugby, cricket and all the usual schoolboy games. I seemed to get entangled in the odd fights and there were only a couple of characters I couldn't beat—but they were a lot bigger than I.

All this went by the board when I had my spell in hospital. In my late 'teens I did a fair amount of club rowing and was definitely at my fittest at that time. Since then, in the five years I've been motor racing, the amount of time I've been able to devote to physical fitness has depended on how much has been left from that activity.

There is no point in being 100 per cent physically fit, or going to bed early the night before the race, if the car is not capable of winning. Far better to spend one's time ensuring that the car would be more competitive.

In 1958 with the F2 Cooper I never had a moment to spare for exercise, but being fairly young and not smoking or drinking, this didn't matter too much. During the next couple of years as a works driver, with a little more free time at the height of the season, I used to cover a little over a mile a day jogging round a local football field. This really makes a difference if done consistently. You soon feel really fit.

My pattern over the last two years has been to rely on a steady two months' water ski-ing in New Zealand and Australia, going hard at it as often as I can over a slalom course, or just zipping backwards and forwards across the wake of a fast speedboat. This does wonders for general fitness, and improves co-ordination and timing. It's also a lot of fun!

Before one of my better drives, the British GP in 1959, I was feeling particularly fit. I'd been racing each week-end, but had been able to spend time swimming on the Continent and I was at peak condition. On the morning of the race there was a compulsory medical check. Being a bit late, I ran the half mile from the pits to the medical hut and arrived thinking it might give some peculiar results. But the doctor told me I was pretty fit. He said an extremely slow pulse and a nice low blood pressure were two good qualities for anything physically exhausting.

Grand Prix racing is unquestionably tough. If the weather is cold, the actual physical effort involved in sliding or drifting a car about is slight and there is no reason why a stronger man should be better at driving a racing car than a smaller, weaker man. But 300 miles of gruelling concentration, noise, buffeting and extreme heat, soon find any flaws in fitness. I have seen drivers lifted from their cars exhausted after a race where the sun was beating down. Brake and clutch pedals sometimes get almost too hot for one's feet . . . hands become sore and blistered from holding the steering wheel . . . one's face feels hot and dry and it seems worth £1,000 for the race to be stopped to give the chance for a long drink of cold water. If you are not fit, you cannot keep going at maximum pace in these conditions.

EIGHTEEN

Full Circle — Victory at Home

FRANK FALKNER HAD contacted me in Australia, asking if I would drive one of the new Cunningham-entered lightweight, fuel-injected competition E-type Jaguars with Walt Hansgen at Sebring. The race was only a week after Sandown Park, so Patricia and I set off for America while the boys drove back up to Sydney with the hard-worked Austin-Freeway that had been loaned to us by BMC Australia.

The E-type was faster than most of the GTO Ferraris. At one stage we were running second to Penske's Ferrari in the GT classification at Sebring, but the four-speed gearbox of the Jaguar was no match for the five-speed Italian car. Walt and I eventually placed eighth, when a very groggy John Surtees took the winning Ferrari across the line after 12 hours' racing. John was ill from the fumes, brake-pad dust and smoke sucked back into the Ferrari cockpit and I understood this. There is no chance to eat properly during the 12 hours and the heat makes one terribly thirsty. To quench the thirst one drinks too many cokes and orange juices. The more one drinks, the thirstier one gets. I'm not speaking from experience, but it's probably like having a hangover and being exhausted at one and the same time.

I was due back in England for a race at Snetterton the following Saturday. After months of sunbathing and water ski-ing in New Zealand and Australia, England was chilling. Following that super-severe winter, we were told it was warm again, but I wasn't convinced. The paddock at Snetterton was ankle-deep in freezing mud and it was hard to believe we had been troubled by the heat a few days earlier at Sebring.

Coopers' new F1 car wasn't quite ready, so I drove one of the '62 cars. We also hoped to have one of the new fuel-injected Climax V8s, which had been considerably modified and refined since the South African GP, but these, too, were just short of completion.

Jimmy Clark rushed into the lead while Graham Hill was trying to make his BRM fire on eight cylinders. When the recalcitrant plug finally sparked, he set off through the field and, as Jimmy made one of his rare off-course excursions with the Lotus, Graham closed up, took the lead and was never headed. I was having a fine dice with Richie's BRM and Innes in the British Racing Partnership Lotus-BRM. Their fuel-injected V8s had the edge on the Cooper along the straights and I was trying hard to finish within sight of them.

Aston Martins had made a comeback to Grand Touring racing with a team of 3·7-litre cars and a 4-litre prototype with independent rear suspension. Innes, myself and Bill Kimberley were to be team drivers and John Wyer asked me to fly with them to Le Mans for the test week-end. This was my first experience of the legendary Aston Martin efficiency. We touched down at Le Mans airfield in the Aston Martin private executive aircraft at 5.55 pm and our ground transport—a Lagonda shooting-brake and a DB4 Aston Martin—pulled up alongside at 6.03 pm, the drivers apologetic for being three minutes late.

Later that evening a transporter drove into the little square in the village of La Chartre and, while half the townsfolk looked on, three dull-green and purposeful Aston Martins were rolled down on the cobbles. Breakfast was at 7.30 the next morning (no one more than a minute late) and at 8.15 precisely the three works Astons set off for the circuit in line astern, bellowing and coughing in the cold, misty morning air.

I did a few laps in the two new 3·7-litre DB4 GT Astons, one of them set up with slightly heavier springs than the other, so that an optimum spring rate for the Le Mans circuit could be arrived at as quickly as possible. The Aston team had a very comprehensive range of springs, anti-roll bars and shock absorbers. To the uninitiated that might wrongly indicate they were not too sure of their design settings. After lunch at the restaurant beside the Mulsanne straight, with Ferraris and such-like flashing by at 150 mph-plus, I took out the Aston on a drying circuit and found it one of the best-handling cars I have ever driven.

Aston Martins feel as I do, that a racing-car chassis is a little like a piano. One can build something that looks fine with all the wires the correct length and size and pretty close to the right settings, but it won't play until it has been tuned. The Aston was a delight, particularly on the fast corners, and late that afternoon we began reeling off laps substantially faster than the best GTO Ferrari times. I liked the cars, and the confident, precise organization of the team under John Wyer made a driver want to try hard and do well.

Back at the Surbiton workshop, Wally had joined Coopers' works team and he was helping Mike, Ray and Hughie to get the new F1 car ready for the Easter Goodwood meeting. The car was slimmer, as the chassis had been narrowed slightly. Size and weight had also been saved by having a special petrol tank built in the shape of a seat. It was like riding in a bath! Suspension was still wishbones all round, but the wishbone angles had been altered to stop the nose of the car diving under braking. The nose was slimmer and the tail little more than a curved cover over the engine, ending in a turn-up above the gearbox.

The first of the new Climax V8 engines, with a shorter stroke and revised fuel-injection system, arrived a couple of days before the race and the mechanics worked late to make the new car a runner in time for the race. The shorter stroke of the new engine meant we could now rev to 9500 compared with a 8800 rpm limit the previous season.

Practice times were very close. Graham was fastest in the works BRM with a comfortable one-second advantage, but my Cooper (still unpainted), Jack's new Brabham, Ireland's Lotus-BRM and Ginther's BRM were blanketed by 0·8 sec.

I led on the opening lap, then had a fine dice with the two works BRMs and Jack, until he dropped out with a loose ignition wire. Richie slowed, leaving Graham, Innes and me in front. When Innes is in the mood, any circuit is his favourite and I couldn't hold the apple-green Lotus-BRM. Graham was playing the world champion out in front, however, and looked like winning until five laps from the end, when the BRM started to splutter and he shot into the pits. A piece of rubber lining the fuel tank had come adrift and blocked the outlet pipe. This left Innes in the lead and, although I put everything into a last-minute bid, he took the flag five seconds in front of me.

The New Zealand Grand Prix Association had apparently decided there had been no promising racing drivers in the country since Angus Hyslop went to Europe in 1961, but Tony Shelly came over in 1962 at his own expense and in 1963 two more young New Zealanders were trying their hands. Chris Amon had shown potential in his drives with my old Cooper and Reg Parnell had signed him to drive one of his Lolas in championship events. Chris arrived from New Zealand almost on the morning of the Goodwood practice and placed a creditable fifth in the race. Ross Greenville, another Kiwi, was having his first try-out in a Gemini Formula Junior car and also showed promise of things to come before he crashed at Aintree later in the season and had a foot amputated.

Denis Hulme had been taken on as Brabham works Formula Junior driver and did much towards putting the smaller Brabhams on the map as he won race after race, eventually placing second in the championship, only a point behind Peter Arundell. It looked like a vintage year for New Zealanders, but things didn't work out that way for me.

The previous season Jimmy Clark had been motoring very quickly and Graham Hill, for one, must have been greatly relieved when his signal board told him the Lotus had retired at East London. If (that word again!) Jimmy hadn't broken down, he would have won the '62 world championship, but at the Aintree "200" he showed he was going to let nothing stand in his way for the '63 title. Graham won in the BRM, but Clark had lost a lap with ignition trouble at the start, carried on for 18 laps, was called in to change cars with Trevor Taylor—and roared off to reel in the leaders and place third.

Jimmy was now taking over the Moss role. After practice sessions, a well-known driver said to me, "I'm very pleased with my car—very pleased indeed. I'm only half a second slower than Clark." There was a time when the proud phrase "only just slower than . . ." could only refer to Stirling.

I scraped home fifth at Aintree, but the Cooper didn't seem to be handling right. A proper testing session was the only way to sort things out, so we decided to take the Cooper to Silverstone a few days before practice for the international meeting.

Accidents seemed to haunt the Cooper equipe during 1963. First had been Patricia's accident with the speedboat in Australia, then the week-end before Silverstone John Cooper crashed in an experimental twin-engined Mini on the Kingston By-pass.

Roy Salvadori had invited John and Paula Cooper, Patricia and me, and Jim and Sandy Hall to dinner at his new home in Esher and we were waiting for the Coopers to arrive when their housekeeper phoned to tell us of John's accident. We rushed to the hospital and were allowed to see him for a few minutes. He spoke to us, although later he couldn't remember having seen us. The car had rolled several times and was a complete wreck, but John had escaped with abrasions, lacerations and a few cracked ribs. The crash had shaken him up, however, and it was obvious that he would have to stay away from the circuits for a while.

The crash was a mystery. John had always struck me as being a very safe driver on the road. He wasn't particularly smooth, but always gave the impression of knowing what he was doing and having the situation well under control. I am convinced some part of the prototype twin-engined car must have broken to cause the crash.

Ken Tyrrell stepped in to assist Charles Cooper in looking after the racing team and went up with us to the testing session at Silverstone. There we were able to try various suspension settings and experiment with different combinations, until the car handled really well.

In practice I proved the worth of our testing by scoring a front-row grid position with Ireland, Hill and Brabham. That Saturday was quite a day for me. In the morning Princess Margaret and Lord Snowdon stopped to inspect the Coopers on their tour of the paddock. She asked how John was progressing and said that she noticed a considerable change in the cars since watching her last race in 1951. Presumably in 1951 they were mainly Italian racing red, much bigger and higher, with the driver sitting straight up. The Royal couple were intrigued by the almost fully-reclining driving position of our F1 cars.

Innes in the British Racing Partnership Lotus-BRM managed fastest time during the first session and bad weather on the second practice day left him on top. I made one of my better starts and led the field away, staying in front for three glorious laps. Jimmy, in his usual irrepressible form, moved through to the lead, but I was pleased to follow him home in second place.

Innes, Graham, John and Jimmy had raced in close and hectic company during the opening laps, until Jimmy moved out ahead. Ireland was extracting everything the Lotus-BRM had to give in an effort to catch Surtees in the new Ferrari, but overdid things going into Woodcote and spun through a couple of tyre-smoking circles in front of the pit counter. Innes apparently worred the pit staff more than himself, as he carried on at unabated pace to finish fourth.

Hard on the heels of Silverstone came Monaco. Jimmy was fastest on the first day of practice, but the two works BRMs and Surtees' Ferrari were obviously going to provide strong opposition. I had been having trouble with fuel injection, but by the seven o'clock session the next morning the mechanics had cleared the throats of the V8 and I managed a more respectable time.

Patricia, who had made great progress, was out of plaster and enjoying the sunbathing, paddle-boating and parties on the beach. Monaco is one place where the size of one's yacht reflects income more than the size of one's car. The harbour is crowded with some of the finest luxury vessels in the world and we enjoyed ourselves on the yacht Ken Gregory had hired and moored near the chicane.

Graham took command of the race when the flag fell, but Jimmy wasn't long challenging him. Time and again the Lotus nosed alongside the BRM, but Graham wasn't being put down. Eventually Jimmy managed to nip into the lead and once in front he fairly flew.

Surtees, Ginther and I were racing in each others' pockets, but at half-distance, after eating a couple of slices of orange, I decided to move up. Apparently everyone else was thinking along the same lines. As I tried harder, Richie put his foot down further and in front of him Surtees was doing likewise. Graham was a few seconds ahead of John's Ferrari and Jimmy was romping away in front. Suddenly, with his gearbox jammed, Clark spun hard against the wall at the Gasometer Hairpin.

There was a yellow flag out, but we all slid around the outside, avoiding the now-defunct monocoque. The world champion was leading and the heat was on.

We were not far short of the record on every lap. Graham had a 10 sec lead on Surtees, with Richie just ahead of me, but soon we both headed the Ferrari. I thought John might be having the same trouble as I. My right foot was so sore from pushing on the brake pedal that I could hardly bear to stop for some of the tighter corners. This was probably a good thing . . . had I pressed harder, I would probably have worn the brake pads completely away.

With 10 laps to go I made an effort to catch Richie, but the thought of a BRM one-two spurred him on and I could make no impression. Then Surtees began to close up on me and in the closing laps we both pulled out all the stops. With four laps left Surtees broke Clark's lap record trying to catch me; on the following lap I equalled it staying in front. On the last lap John set a new lap record, but failed to catch me for third place by 1·3 sec. It had been another close Monaco finish for me.

The Belgian GP at Spa was as wet as Monaco had been hot. The fast Spa circuit requires full concentration on its high-speed sweeps when it is dry. In rain it is treacherous.

The rain teemed down and soon there was evidence on the track where several cars had spun. It was just a matter of plodding on and hoping the race would soon finish. Clark was flying out ahead as usual and lapped the entire field during the race. In the closing laps, my pit crew emerged from shelter and began to signal enthusiastically that I was catching the man in front. Ahead I could see two columns of spray. I knew one was Jimmy, who had just passed me, so presumed the other sheet of water hid second placeman Dan Gurney, in the Brabham. I pressed on as fast as I dared and overhauled both cars to move into second place. Dan was half blinded in the spray, with a broken lens in his goggles.

I was damply delighted with my last-minute placing, as it

meant I led the world championship by one point from Graham, Jimmy and Richie.

When I was dislodged from the top of the championship by Jimmy winning four Grandes Epreuves in a row, I seemed to keep falling. The McLaren jinx had arrived and was staying for the season.

I managed a front-row grid position at Zandvoort for the Dutch GP and for the first two laps was hard on the heels of the Clark Lotus. Then the Cooper jammed itself in fifth gear and I was on the sideline.

A change of cars didn't help. Innes and I were putting in a mighty effort at Le Mans with the DB4 GT Aston Martin, that I had tested earlier in the year, when the engine burst after four hours. I was roaring down the Mulsanne straight on full, glorious song with the big car, when a sudden loud clatter from the engine, accompanied by a tingling sensation at the top of my spine, told me my rear wheels were covered in oil and I was still doing the best part of 175 mph.

I managed to negotiate the fast kink in the straight and coasted to a stop on the grass before the hairpin. I turned off the master switch and walked dejectedly back to the signalling pits at Mulsanne corner. A quarter of a mile behind me, a large pall of smoke spelt accident; a car had slid on the oil I deposited on the fastest part of the circuit, crashed and caught fire. Back at the pits stories filtered through of the multiple pile-up, with a little French Alpine and another Aston Martin.

At Rheims for the French GP I worked my way through to second place behind the "Flying Scotsman" and was beginning to feel racing to be worthwhile again, when the V8 suddenly cut out and that was that. The transistor ignition "black box" had overheated. The bad luck surely couldn't last. But it did.

The British GP at Silverstone found the two Brabhams on the front row of the grid, and Australian hopes were high as they led the field in the opening laps. Jack's engine was first to go, but Dan lasted a little longer before his V8, too, expired in a billowing cloud of smoke. I knew just how they felt . . . my own race had finished after only six laps in a similar cloud of smoke.

Jimmy motored serenely on for his fourth consecutive win, but there was a sign of the times emerging for those who cared to take notice. John Surtees was at last making the Ferrari motor and for much of the race argued second place with Graham's BRM, until the BRM coughed and spluttered on the last lap with no fuel left. Graham coasted home a furious third. The Ferrari was starting to go quickly and in the German GP John showed the field a clean pair of Ferrari exhausts to win from Jimmy in a V7 Lotus. I wasn't around at the time . . . I was lying semi-conscious in a hospital bed not far from the circuit.

I had been a little sceptical when Stirling Moss woke from his Goodwood accident and said, "If you told me I'd been hit by a bus, old man, I'd have believed you." I thought he must have had some recollection of at least the initial stages of getting involved in the accident. Now I know just how blank that space can be.

I woke up in Adenau Hospital, not far from the Nürburgring, and only logic told me I must have gone off the track somewhere. How, when, or where, I had not the slightest idea and, apart from what people have told me since, I still do not recollect anything leading up to, or surrounding the accident. I must have banged my head somewhere, as I was out cold for about an hour. It seems that the mind conveniently whitewashes anything it would be better not to remember.

This can be upsetting, too. My legs were sore and I assumed I must have been ejected from the Cooper cockpit at some stage and scraped a bit of skin off here and there, but I was worried that others in the ward with me—one with a very black eye, one with a foot in plaster, and another who didn't look so good either—were something to do with my accident. It was with apprehension that I started questioning the steady stream of visitors who came to ask *me* what had happened.

I can clearly remember the race for the first two laps. I had passed Richie into fourth place, Graham's BRM had slowed with a broken gearbox and I was up to third half-way around the second lap. I remember seeing John and Jimmy tussling for the lead about a quarter of a mile ahead, then everything goes blank. Almost as though I had been making a film, the scene was cut and switched to the hospital in Adenau.

I stayed in hospital a couple of days before I was allowed out with my right leg in plaster, as a precaution against a possible cracked bone, and Eoin drove me back to England. Doctors at the Kingston hospital stripped off the plaster and X-rays showed nothing had been broken, but it was very sore and I hobbled round on sticks for more than a week. Fortunately the Tourist Trophy was a fortnight away and by then I was able to put enough weight on my legs to drive.

Innes and I were again in the works Aston Martins to do battle with the Ferraris, which were out in force, and the light-weight E-type Jaguars, now fitted with five-speed gearboxes. Our cars were handling far from well, as officials had decided almost at the last moment that the wide-rimmed wheels which the team had been using since the new Dunlop R6 tyre had been announced, were not as specified on the homologation sheet. The narrower rims were definitely not as good, so Innes and I had a fairly hectic time.

Innes was really motoring in the opening laps, mixing it with Parkes and Hill in the leading GTO Ferraris, until he spun in Woodcote on two successive laps and lost time in the pits having a tyre change. He had worn large flat spots on the tyres in his spins and these were affecting the handling. My car sounded decidedly poor and the oil pressure was playing odd tricks. I stopped for more oil, but soon afterwards the engine expired. Yet another non-finisher on my record.

After my crash on the Nürburgring I had thought hard about my future. I had once promised myself to give up racing after my first big shunt, but realize now that would have been the worst possible thing I could have done. It's essential to go straight out again and have a go, if you are ever going to look yourself in the eye again.

It is pretty obvious now, after close analysis of the wreckage, that the right rear wishbone broke. The rear wheel turned right and the Cooper turned suddenly left at 100 mph.

Before the accident I was on top form, confident and enjoying getting right on the limit, but my shunt made me think harder of things mechanical and the possibility of more breakages.

With this in mind, I wasn't very happy when a rear hub broke up on the banking, throwing the Cooper sideways at 140 mph, during practice for the Italian GP. The rough banking was worrying others, too, and the race was transferred to the road circuit only. The usual Monza slipstreaming dices told the tale of the race. Surtees had the beautifully-made monocoque Ferrari and set the practice pace. In the opening laps it seemed that he would call the race tune as well, but Italian hopes died when the V6 engine gave up after 17 laps. Jimmy won again, and this fifth title race victory gave him the championship for 1963 with an unsurpassable number of points. It was certainly a crushing success for both Jimmy Clark as driver and Colin Chapman as constructor.

It was my first time back in the Cooper seat since being so hurriedly evicted in Germany and I was pleasantly surprised to pass Innes, who was stopped on the back of the circuit with a seized engine, and move up to take his third place on the last lap.

It didn't mean an improvement in Cooper or McLaren fortunes, however. The Oulton Park Gold Cup race found Tony and me struggling home fifth and sixth. And at the Watkins Glen and Mexican championship races, engine breakages kept the pair of us on the retirement lists. It had been a disastrous year for me. Since that brief spell at the top of the championship ladder after Spa, I had finished in only two motor races!

For all its trials and tribulations, its triumphant high spots with a laurel wreath and the dismal feeling as you leave a broken car to trudge back to the pits, motor racing has become a way of life I wouldn't think of changing.

It has both narrowed and broadened my outlook, giving me fantastic opportunites to travel the world, meet people and make firm friends around the globe.

I haven't had any time for other organized sport, but am sure I could not have met truer sportsmen anywhere. True in the fullest meaning of the word. Sportsmen like Graham and Phil Hill, Dan Gurney, Richie Ginther, Innes Ireland and Stirling Moss. Or men with more drive and determination than Jack Brabham, John Surtees and Jimmy Clark.

After five years in motor racing and 50 Grands Prix behind me, I have profound respect for the sport and the men who take part in it . . . and I'll always be grateful to my parents, who stood so firmly behind me in the early days.

After a dismal season of racing in Europe, Bruce had been gaining some consolation and satisfaction by setting up a team of specially-built Coopers for he and Timmy Mayer to drive in New Zealand and Australia, and although he had finished the book before leaving for the "down under" races his win in the 1964 New Zealand Grand Prix made the following worth writing.

The idea of building two special cars for Australasia came to me as I trudged back to the pits at Rheims, having left the defunct Cooper at the edge of the track. The cars would be fitted with solid, reliable $2\frac{1}{2}$-litre Climax engines with no transistors to go phut, no fuel injection to start fluttering, and the five-speed Colotti gearbox was a no-nonsense unit that we knew all about.

I discussed the project with John and we decided to base the car on the current Formula One Cooper, using the F1 chassis jigs and wrapping the frame in a stressed-steel skin, something like a monocoque. So the first Formula Tasman Cooper started. It was understood that Wally was only on loan to the works team until the start of September, so he set straight to work on building my chassis.

Timmy Mayer, the young American who had been driving Formula Juniors for Ken Tyrrell, was keen to do the "down under" season, so we got together with the idea of running two of these special new Coopers as works entries. However, the race organizers weren't initially very happy about the arrangement as they felt that Timmy was too much an "unknown" to the Antipodean public, and Charles Cooper finally decided that unless our cars were really works entries he didn't want them running as such. I think he was worried that if he or John were not present and we ran someone over, the Cooper Car Company might be held responsible.

In one way the failure of the team to get off the ground as a factory effort was a personal blessing, as it had always been a great ambition of mine to run my own team of racing cars.

With this added personal incentive to succeed, Timmy and I got together with Teddy Mayer (Timmy's brother and manager) and my secretary, Eoin Young, and we decided to set ourselves up as a private team. Eoin immediately wrote off to his and my friends in New Zealand and Australia to see whether this would be acceptable from a promotional angle and, presuming that it would be, work was started on a second car for Timmy.

In the meantime I had doubled up on my orders for parts to build a special $2\frac{1}{2}$-litre engine. I had one $2 \cdot 7$-litre and two $2 \cdot 5$-litre engines left over from the previous season and Timmy was able to contribute two engines. My idea was to make a short-stroke $2 \cdot 5$-litre engine using the $2 \cdot 7$ bore with a new crankshaft. I approached Laystalls and Coventry-Climaxes, who were both most co-operative and enthusiastic, and went ahead with orders for suitable pistons and some of the lightweight valve gear I had used the previous season.

With two cars this was obviously going to be a bigger project than ever before, with more organization and more responsibilities, so it was definitely time to put things on a company basis and Bruce McLaren Motor Racing Ltd. was formed with Patricia, Eoin and myself as directors. Nothing was changed really, but it seemed a bit more for us to get our teeth into. Eoin was in his element handling the public relations side and gave the new team a good build-up in New Zealand.

New regulations limited engines to $2\frac{1}{2}$ litres unsupercharged in Australasian races and to try and forestall boring processions the races were reduced to 100 miles.

I was all in favour of the colourful "anything goes" formula libre which had covered racing in New Zealand and Australia since the sport began, but it was obvious that these new regulations opened the door to a special car. Shorter races meant less fuel, less fuel meant smaller tanks, and consequently a slimmer car.

As the Coopers progressed, we instituted several new features. The chassis was wrapped in the stiffening steel sheet which also doubled as the body sides. All the fuel was carried in a seat tank and a couple of smaller tanks on either side of the driver's knees. We decided to replace the top rear wishbone with a top link and a long radius arm, and this, together with a few different fittings, meant we were able to crop the back of the chassis and fit a neat tail with a small fin. Both cars were painted British racing green with a couple of silver stripes and a central stripe on the tail—the New Zealand motor racing colours. A well-known artist in the racing world, Michael Turner, had designed a neat team badge for us with a kiwi as the central feature on a chequered flag background and a racing car silhouette on the top of the shield. Sports editor Phillip Turner described it in *The Motor* as "a kiwi being run over by a Cooper!"

We found ourselves in a quandary when it came to recruiting mechanics for the tour. Wally, Harry Pearce and Timmy's American mechanic, Tyler Alexander, were to have made the trip, but after the cars were shipped we discovered that Harry wasn't able to go, and there was a strong possibility that Tyler would miss out as well as the US Army also wanted his services.

Eoin cabled Lenny Gilbert, one-time stunt-flier, motor racer, entertainer, dance band drummer, restaurant owner and water skier, asking if he would join the team for the eight races, and his immediate reply indicated that he was delighted.

As it turned out Tyler wasn't drafted and arrived in New Zealand which meant that we had three full-time mechanics, and Colin Beanland, who had accompanied me to Europe in 1958, was available for the Australian series. Our full complement was Patricia and me, Timmy and his wife, Garrill, Teddy Mayer, Eoin Young, Wally Willmott, Tyler Alexander, Lenny Gilbert and Colin Beanland—so our team was impressive if only from the size of the air tickets and the hotel bills.

I must admit that I was a little disappointed at the meagre size of the field recruited for the series, but when I saw the two Brabhams on the front row of the grid in the South African Grand Prix and remembered that Jack, New Zealander Denny Hulme, Australians Frank Matich and Bib Stillwell and Englishman Graham Hill would be pedalling Brabhams "down under" I stopped being disappointed and started hoping that our team would be a success.

It was going to be a full-scale Brabham v. McLaren battle with both Jack and me running two-car teams.

The first round went to the Brabham contingent. Jack was home in England for New Year, while Denny was having his first run with the $2\frac{1}{2}$-litre Brabham, and on the tight bumpy circuit he was quicker than we were and there wasn't anything we could do about it.

But with the Grand Prix at Pukekohe just a week away there

was plenty to do and the mechanics worked as hard as they knew how to ensure that both cars would be in peak condition. Jack had also realized that the new Tasman Formula left openings for a special car and had constructed a couple of slim-line lightweight Brabhams—one for himself and one for Frank Matich.

I'd been having a bit of drama with the compression ratio in my engine and a set of special pistons had been hurriedly flown out for the mechanics to fit after Levin. This meant running the engine in, and as the only circuit available in Auckland at the time was a banked quarter-mile cycle track I made myself dizzy blatting around the oval once every 20 sec for an hour and a half.

After the practice sessions we knew that all our work had been worthwhile. With the improved valve gear we were able to rev to 7300 rpm, a distinct advantage over the old limit of 6800 rpm—and the engines were really singing.

I managed fastest lap in practice, but Jack and Denny weren't too far behind and it was obvious that Matich was also going to be a man to watch.

Jack and I both won our race heats and as we lined up on the grid for the Grand Prix I was very conscious of the fact that it was my best-ever chance to win.

When the flag dropped I was caught with tyres smoking from too much wheelspin and it was Timmy who took the lead having made a jet start from the second row. Jack was quickly on his tail and I was close behind. As we braked at the end of the Pukekohe straight Jack nipped past Timmy and for a full lap Jack, Timmy, Frank, Denny and myself were racing wheel to wheel. After a few laps Jack and I managed to draw away from the battling ruck slightly and on the eighth lap I used a slight advantage on top speed to sneak by Jack as we entered the braking area.

With the field behind me I was concentrating on keeping it there, but Matich was making it hot for the others. In fact he put in a lap faster than my best before his engine blew asunder, laying a film of oil that spun Timmy down to fourth place behind Jack and Denny. The pace was really on and I couldn't afford to relax for a minute. By half distance I had only been able to open a four-second gap on Jack, but he was fully extended and wasn't letting the distance between us increase further than he could help.

We were lapping the mid-field men when disaster struck Jack. I had passed Tony Shelly going by the pits into the tight left-handed "Elbow" but Jack was committed either to pass Tony in the narrow braking area or lose a few fractions to me while he followed the Shelly Lotus through the corner.

Jack decided to bank on the fact that Tony would know he was there, and attempted to overtake almost right on the corner. The unfortunate result saw Brabham hurtle up over the rear wheel of the Lotus and slew off to the side of the track with a rear wheel almost torn off.

I was unaware of all the drama behind me and I'd been trying so hard to beat Jack for the New Zealand Grand Prix for so many years that at first I couldn't believe it when I saw Wally holding a signal saying "JACK OUT".

From then on I concentrated on finishing the race at all costs and eased up as much as I could without letting Denny and Timmy, who were running second and third, close on me too quickly. When Jack crashed I was left with a lead of nearly half a minute, but Denny was only 4·5 sec behind at the finish. I'd really been pussy-footing it to make sure of the race that I'd been trying to win for eight years. With Timmy following home in third place we were delighted at our team success and there was plenty of champagne flowing that night.

Wigram was another fast circuit and once again the Cooper showed up to advantage, but a bout of throttle sticking was puzzling us. Both Timmy and I had been caught with an over-load of revs when we most certainly didn't require them during practice, but we thought we had cured the trouble on race day.

Timmy wasn't so sure after his throttle stuck open yet again and spun him off while he was leading his heat, and when I realized that my throttle was jammed on the third lap of the Trophy race as we barrelled into the tight new loop, I wasn't really impressed either.

I was running third on the heels of Jack and Denny, and with the option of risking a stall by spinning and punching my way slowly through the bales, I chose the latter course. The impact was only slight and it must have looked a good deal more spectacular than it was, but it seemed an age before I found a gap in the field to nip back into the race. By this time I was in eighth place and a full 20 sec behind the Brabhams, thundering along in triumphant team formation up front.

I was furious at myself for getting into such a situation when my car was capable of winning the race, and it was probably this that spurred me through the field at such a rate that I was soon tailing the two Brabhams who were doing everything to try and shake me off.

A few laps later and I had nipped past Denny, but taking Jack was obviously going to be a lot more difficult. The most logical place to pass was at the end of the 150 mph straight, under braking for the hairpin bend, but Jack was braking very late and very hard right in the middle of the road—just as I would have done in the circumstances.

With only a few laps left we came up on a back marker just entering the loop. Jack elected to take him on the outside while I took a chance on the inside running. Fortunately (for me) the driver of the slower car saw the Cooper nose first and swung over to let me through, unwittingly committing Jack to a spin or a shunt with the hay bales.

Once again I wasn't aware of all the excitement surrounding Jack's little escapade, but I knew that I was in front and I stayed there until the chequer flashed out a few laps later.

The last race in the New Zealand series at Teretonga Park was a fantastic result for our team. Timmy and I crossed the line side by side in the main event, and again in the eighth-lap "Flying Farewell" placing first and second both times. Added to that we each won our race heats.

But we didn't have things all our own way by any means for Denny Hulme was using a wide set of Goodyear stock car tyres which by virtue of superior traction and braking made the Brabham nearly 1·5 sec a lap faster than our Coopers. A scorching sun had made the track like a honey pot, and although Denny romped away in the opening laps he suddenly found the limit of the Goodyears and spun backwards into a post, leaving Timmy and me to dictate the rest of the race as we pleased.

Postscript

THE AUSTRALIAN series wasn't as kind to our team. In the Grand Prix at Melbourne's Sandown Park, my precious specially-tweaked short-stroke 2½-litre Climax engine blew apart while I was running a close second to Brabham, and later in the race fuel starvation robbed Timmy of a sure second place.

Ford's had lent us a pair of station wagons and a truck, so transport wasn't a problem, but winning races seemed to be. We had been mentally reserving the Warwick Farm race for Frank Matich with his lightweight Brabham, and he backed this up by setting the fastest practice lap. However, he was a little too eager in the race, and after snatching the lead from Jack in the early laps went off the road. Jack and I spent more time on the grass verges than on the track in the closing stages, but he managed to stay ahead by a few inches to win, while Timmy was third not far behind me. At Lakeside a week later Matich roared off into the lead again, but he blew up, and Timmy had a brief spell in the lead before his short-stroker blew up too. I had a bit of drama with John Youl and Denny Hulme and eventually finished third.

The Longford race in Tasmania was the saddest of the series. Although on points I had already won the Tasman Championship from Jack despite the fact that he had won at Sandown Park, Warwick Farm, and Lakeside, we had to wait until Longford for the official presentation. During practice and while having a real tilt at the fastest lap, Timmy's Cooper became airborne over a tricky hump before the pub corner, smashed sideways into a tree, and Timmy broke his neck when he was hurled out.

The news that he had died instantly was a terrible shock to all of us, but who is to say that he had not seen more, done more and learned more in his twenty-six years than many people do in a lifetime? To do something well is so worthwhile that to die trying to do it better cannot be foolhardy. It would be a waste of life to do nothing with one's ability, for I feel that life is measured in achievement, not in years alone.

Index

As the Author raced at all the circuits, and in all the competitions mentioned in the index separate entries have not been made under his name.